D0915649

WITHDRAWN

Europe in the Making

Europe in the Making

WALTER HALLSTEIN

Translated by Charles Roetter

with an Introduction by George W. Ball

W · W · NORTON & COMPANY · INC ·
NEW YORK

The author wishes to express his warmest thanks to Hans Herbert Götz and Karl-Heinz Narjes for their assistance in preparing the German edition and Richard Mayne for his help with the English edition.

This translation Copyright © 1972 by George Allen & Unwin Ltd.
Originally published in German under the title
Der unvollendete Bundesstaat
© Econ Verlag, Düsseldorf and Vienna 1969
First American edition 1973
Library of Congress Catalog Card No. 74-163368
    Library of Congress Cataloging in Publication Data
    Hallstein, Walter, 1901–
      Europe in the making.

      Translation of Der unvollendete Bundesstaat.
      1. European federation. 2. Europe—Economic integration. I. Title.
    D1060.H3213 1973 382'.9142 74-163368
    ISBN 0-393-05246-X
Published simultaneously in Canada
by George J. McLeod Limited, Toronto
PRINTED IN THE UNITED STATES OF AMERICA

1   2   3   4   5   6   7   8   9   0

Contents

CONTENTS

Foreword

'Theory', 'doctrine', 'Utopia' (in its modern realistic meaning), 'forecasts', 'planning', 'futurology', 'vision' – the reader will no doubt find traces of all these in this book. Its aim is to be systematic, clear, and vivid; to open new prospects, and to challenge the imagination.

The object of the book is two-fold: on the one hand, to present what is real, and, on the other, to explain the need from which this reality arose. The reality is the Communities, or the 'Community', as it is referred to here, since the merger of the Executives has in practice, if not yet formally, merged the Common Market, Euratom, and the ECSC. The need is for political unity in Europe.

This then is a book that deals with practical, technical matters, not with personal experience. Its purpose is to set out soberly and exactly what is at stake in the task begun in 1950 – of unifying Europe: what we have achieved and what we still have to achieve; what the strong points of our enterprise are, and where its weaknesses lie; the opportunities that beckon and the dangers that threaten; what it represents both in its present stage and in its dynamic potential.

At the same time, this is a political book. But since politics is in essence a struggle between human beings, the author has not sought to hide his own view on the questions under examination. I believe that all the essential decisions and actions undertaken in pursuit of our European policy are correct, and I expect ultimate and complete success – on condition that this policy is unswervingly pursued. The fact that it was the right policy in the past does not make it the wrong policy today. There will be much to develop but little new to invent. All that is essential in our enterprise has already been begun. All that remains is to act upon it.

That is the cause for which this book pleads.

WALTER HALLSTEIN

Preface to the English Language Edition

This is the third version of the present work. The first – the German edition – was completed in the autumn of 1969. The second was completed in the autumn of 1970, and was published in French, Italian, Spanish, and Swedish.

The changes in the text – most of which are additions – reflect the dynamic process of European integration, its progress and its setbacks, its ups and downs. The Summit Conference of the Six held in The Hague in December 1969 formed a fitting conclusion to the European Community's transition period, and marked the beginning of a new balance of interests on the part of its member states: it confirmed their financial solidarity in the agricultural field, it decided to consolidate the Community by means of economic and monetary union, and it opened the way to entry of the United Kingdom, Ireland, Denmark, and Norway. The years 1970 and 1971 were taken up with the effort to fulfil this programme. The Community set out to overcome the issues involved in the 1965 crisis – the Community's own financial resources and the budgetary powers of the European Parliament; it drew up a stage-by-stage plan for economic and monetary union; it completed the regulations for the common market in agricultural products and took a first step towards agricultural reform; it extended the scope of the European Social Fund; it renewed its association with the African states and offered generalized tariff preferences to all the less developed countries; and it carried through to success the negotiations for the entry of new member states.

But already, by May 1971, new storms had blown up. A new international monetary crisis called in question the plan for economic and monetary union, and endangered the common market for agriculture. Relations with the United States threatened to develop into a general crisis of confidence. At the same time, the outlines of a long-prepared Soviet attack on the Community's foundations began to emerge more clearly.

In this situation, solidarity was essential; and it was enhanced by the concentration of energy on the Community's enlargement, and by the success of this great endeavour. A further promising sign is the lively discussion now developing in Europe about the tasks for the future. These include, in particular, economic and monetary union, the efficiency and democratic legitimation of the Community's institutions, and a constructive relationship with non-member countries, especially in Europe and the Mediterranean, with America and with the states of Eastern Europe. It is no less encouraging that this discussion already involves both Government and public opinion in the countries that are now in the process of joining the European Community.

WALTER HALLSTEIN

March, 1972

Introduction

I first met Professor Walter Hallstein in Paris early in June, 1950, when, as the West German Secretary of State for Foreign Affairs, he led his country's delegation to the Conference that gave shape and substance to the European Coal and Steel Community. At that time, I was occupying a tiny office under the stairs in a four-story gray building on the Rue Martignac which served as the headquarters of the French Planning Organization. The founder and chairman of the French Plan—that remarkable European, Jean Monnet—had summoned me from my law practice in Washington when the concept of the Schuman Proposal was first being hammered out.

Since it was curious indeed for an American to be even marginally involved in such a uniquely European affair, I sought, so far as I could, to stay out of sight. Nevertheless, I knew all—or most—of what was going on, shared a common exuberance at the extraordinarily constructive spirit of the proceedings, and was aware, in particular, of the exceptional leadership Professor Hallstein was contributing. As head of the German delegation, his role was anything but easy, since the Federal Republic was then but one year old and it was only five years since the Third Reich had collapsed into putrescent rubble. Yet, in spite of the fact that the Bonn Government was still an unproven experiment, Walter Hallstein quickly gained the respect of the other delegates, bringing rare insight to constitution-making, while never for a moment losing sight of the larger purpose of the exercise.

What that purpose was he had no doubt, for he fully shared Monnet's conviction that, though the mandate of the conference was limited to coal and steel, it was to be no sterile essay in economic bargaining. Instead, it was a venture into hitherto unexplored territory, the attempt at a deep breakthrough along a narrow economic and political front in contrast with earlier efforts at international cooperation that—too broadly focused—had yielded more rhetoric than achievement. Monnet, Hallstein and the other perceptive statesmen meeting in Paris held no illusions about the forces they were setting in motion. They knew very well that a common market limited to coal and steel was not a logical concept but an economic monstrosity that—once created—

3

would produce such strains and pressures as to compel progress on a broader front. Thus, they made the calculated gamble that an effort restricted to two basic commodities would lead by its own contradictions to something like the Treaty of Rome and the European Common Market.

That their unspoken prophecy fulfilled itself in less than a decade is now history. Yet success was not foreordained. Had final ratification of the Common Market Treaty—the Treaty of Rome—been delayed until after the thirteenth of May, 1958, when General DeGaulle came to the leadership of France, the treaty might well have been aborted. As it was, the successful conclusion of the Rome Treaty is very likely the single act for which the French Fourth Republic will be longest remembered.

But if it was a matter of luck that General DeGaulle, on coming to power, found himself confronted with a binding treaty he felt obliged to honor rather than an unratified proposal he might well have rejected, it was equally fortunate that the first President of the European Economic Commission should have been Professor Hallstein. A weaker and less astute man would not have been equal to the challenge; he could never have guided the Community through the dark period of obstructionism that began early in the 1960s when the General finally put behind him the agonizing problem of Algeria and turned his hand to Europe. It is to Walter Hallstein's eternal credit that, by the strength of his will, the firmness of his belief in the European destiny, the clarity of his thought and leadership, and the force of his personality, he held the Community on course in defiance of the thunderbolts that issued from Mount Élysée, encouraging the governments of the other five member states to fight back with such effect that the opposition was repeatedly forced to give ground. Meanwhile, even under siege conditions, there were substantial accomplishments. The customs union (which was the first task of the Community) was established and progress was made in many other areas.

It is little wonder then that Professor Hallstein's chronicle of these critical years reminds one both of Thucydides and the authors of the *Federalist Papers*; for, while the book describes the tensions and frustrations of the conflict that marred the period, it at the same time dissects with insight and dispassion the fundamental constitutional issues presented during the drafting and actual operation of the treaty.

As Professor Hallstein realized better than anyone, the principal cost of Gaullist obscurantism was the loss both of time and momentum. Yet, though the General's *non* became as much a Pavlovian reflex as the Kremlin's *nyet*, such constant frustration did not lead Walter

4

Hallstein to despair but to a deeper resolution. If anything, it only reinforced his conviction that, if the objectives of the Treaty were to be fully achieved, the member nations would have to sublimate their purely national interests in a broader European purpose—which meant in practice that no nation could constantly have its own way.

That, of course, was precisely what President DeGaulle intended that France should have. The thrust of his policy was rigorously to deny the institutions of the Community any independent power or initiative in the hope of reducing them to loose arrangements for consultation. Not that Professor Hallstein was surprised by the vehemence of the French position; on the contrary, he clearly perceived that the central factor which made the General's reactions predictable was his incapacity to understand the meaning of federalism. There were historical—one might even say environmental—reasons for this; federalism lay outside the General's conditioning and experience. Though, in his aspirations for France, he often appeared to identify himself with Louis XIV, he still thought of *la grande nation* in terms of the unitary state created by Napoleon, with every administrative and executive decision centralized in Paris. Thus, the whole concept of federation was alien to him, just as it was familiar to Hallstein, who had lived his whole life under a federal system and had played an active role in giving operational effect to the constitution of the Federal Republic of Germany.

The point is an important one: General DeGaulle could never understand that there need be no contradiction between national loyalty and the commitment to a federal government because he failed to comprehend the conception of diversity in unity—or, in other words, the fact that a state could still maintain its cultural and even political integrity while forming part of a larger union. It is a point Americans tend to take for granted; in Texas particularly it is a central article of faith.

Beyond that, Professor Hallstein also notes how French opposition to the political evolution of the Community clearly fitted General DeGaulle's desire to achieve some form of Franco-Soviet *entente*, refusing to recognize that, though the Kremlin would respect a Western Europe organized to speak with a single voice, it had little interest in playing bilateral politics with a middle-sized West European nation.

It was this element of self-deception that led to the final failure of the General's grand design. Yet it is a poignant conjecture that, had he been willing to concentrate his extraordinary ability on the construction of a strong and balanced political entity in Western Europe, he could have played a commanding role on the world stage. Suspicious of

5

Great Britain, and particularly of Britain's relations with America, he tried to maintain the Community as a continental club in which France would continue as top dog.

What this ignored, of course, was that Western Germany, even in rump form, was the most populous and industrially the most powerful state of the Six, and that, once France recovered from her atavistic preoccupation with *la gloire*, the potential dominance of an increasingly self-confident and assertive Germany would become apparent.

Only the addition of Britain could assure a solid foundation for a European structure that could never be more than precariously balanced on the twin pillars of a Franco-German *entente*. But, beyond that, British participation in the work of the Community was essential for the further reason that it could contribute a leavening pragmatism to the French obsession with theory and codification. Throughout history Britain has shown a remarkable genius for creating stable, yet flexible, institutions almost without realizing it, adapting old forms and practices to changing requirements through a subtle employment of fictions and interpretations so that few contemporaries could discern the evolution taking place before their eyes. As Hallstein saw it, this was precisely what Europe needed—a large dose of pragmatism that would make the obsession with such abstractions as sovereignty irrelevant.

Thus, Britain's entry into the Community at the beginning of 1973 promises to add two long-needed elements to the European mix: first, an effective counterweight to the potential strength of Germany that can bring a reassuring solidity to the total structure, submerging ancient rivalries and antipathies in a more spacious conception, and—second, but equally important—a practicality uncluttered by theory as a needed offset to French Cartesianism.

Today the enlargement of the Community holds the promise of a new era of progress. That the structure of the Community needs further evolution is persuasively demonstrated in the pages that follow. To be sure, Professor Hallstein does not put forward novel ideas, but he powerfully presents the principles that he and the other founders of the Community have had clearly in mind ever since the Schuman Plan became something more than a gleam in Jean Monnet's eye.

The strategically important step—the action that would produce the most effective breakthrough toward a politically effective structure—would be to delegate to the Assembly some effective legislative powers while, at the same time, providing for the direct election of its members by the peoples of the constituent states. That step has, of course, been contemplated from the beginning; in fact, the Treaty of Rome expressly authorized the Assembly to "draw up proposals for elections by direct universal suffrage in accordance with a uniform procedure in all member states," but up to now this project has been on the back burner.

"What is lacking under the present system," Professor Hallstein wisely notes, "is an election campaign about European issues." Only such a process "would give the candidates who emerge victorious from such a campaign a truly European mandate from their electorate; and it would encourage the emergence of truly European political parties."

As matters stand now, the Assembly is composed of delegates appointed by the parliaments of the member countries from among their members. To Americans, such a method of selection should not be unfamiliar since it resembles the manner in which individual state legislatures selected the United States Senate prior to the adoption in 1913 of the Seventeenth Amendment of the Constitution. But the United States Senate is a second chamber designed to represent the interests not of the people at large but of the individual states, while the Assembly of the Community, if it is to become an effective legislative body, must constitute the instrument by which the peoples of Europe express their collective will, leaving it for the Council of Ministers to evolve into an upper house through which the interests of the member states are expressed.

Essential to the integrity of the Community is the decision to invest the Assembly with the power to raise money and supervise its expenditure. In fact, a key chapter of the struggle Professor Hallstein recounts is the effort of the Commission to gain control over the Community's own finances. Yet, success in that endeavor would likely be only the beginning of a process. Once a directly-elected Assembly were to come into being, it could probably be counted on to enlarge its own mandate. Not merely the experience of Britain, but also of the United States has made clear that when a legislative body feels that it directly reflects the interests and desires of the people, it will play a more and more assertive role. One need only recall Mirabeau's famous rebuke to the Marquis de Dreux-Brézè, who echoed the king's command for the States-General to disperse: "Go, Monsieur, tell those who send you that we are here by the will of the people, and that nothing but the force of bayonets shall send us hence." Such daring assertion was possible only for an Assembly confident of the validity of its mandate.

The creation of a directly-elected Assembly would automatically transform the public's attitude toward the Community, providing an irrefutable answer to the nationalistic politicians who have, up to now, scornfully dismissed the Commission in Brussels as a "technocracy." For the unstated gravamen of this charge has not been that the members of the Commission were too narrowly trained or are too specialized in their roles, but that, as the Treaty now stands, their authority cannot be justified under any broadly acceptable principle of political legitimacy. To be sure, even today the entire Commission can be required to resign on the Assembly's vote of "no confidence," but since the Assembly is not yet directly elected and has no legislative power or machinery for the serious scrutiny of the Commission's activities, the Commission cannot be said, in any satisfying juridical sense, to be "responsible" to the Assembly. Instead, as matters now stand, most of its decisions are subject to reversal or amendment by the Council of Ministers—which means that, if it should fall under weak leadership, the Commission could easily lose its power of initiative, thus degenerating into little more than an instrument for governmental cooperation.

For the Council to take decision by something less than a unanimous vote requires no Treaty amendment but merely an act of will, since the Treaty empowers the Council to take a progressively increasing number of decisions by the vote of a qualified majority. Unhappily, however, the French Government in January, 1966, was able, by threatening the life of the Community, to blackball the members into a tacit understanding that the *liberum veto* would be preserved and that the Council would not overrule dissenting members, and there the matter has rested.

Such a state of affairs is, of course, wholly unsatisfactory. If the Community is to progress at a pace—and in a direction—consistent with the expanding scale and scope of world requirements, the individual member states must be prepared to accommodate to the will of at least a qualified majority. It is a proposition so elementary as to leave little room for argument except in terms of unreconstructed nationalism—or, in the American vernacular, unreconstructed states' rights.

During the early years of the Community, Americans watched with fascination and applause the emerging political architecture of a new Europe, and it was widely acknowledged that the United States had a vital stake in encouraging Europe's determined march toward unity. Today that view is no longer accepted without cavil, for reasons that should be carefully examined.

The first is simply a loss of conviction that Europe is really moving toward unity—or, in other words, is likely to build anything more than a defensive commercial bloc antipathetic to United States interests.

We Americans are an impatient lot, and during the long discouraging period when French nationalism seemed an insurmountable obstacle to progress many quickly made the easy transit from hope to cynicism. Viewed from this side of the Atlantic, Europe appeared on dead center with little prospect of moving off it, while America, preoccupied with its own problems, grew alarmed at Europe's commercial success as the United States' balance of payments slipped further into deficit.

How long America's disenchantment—or at least loss of interest in Europe—may continue will depend not only on Europe's actions but also on the character and direction of American foreign policy.

At the moment, the American people see America's role largely as a choice between two variants of isolationism. Those who favor a return to traditional policies contend that America should withdraw from major world responsibilities, since, they assert, the two great Communist powers have renounced their expansionist ambitions and—in any event—most of the other nations of the world, particularly those of Western Europe, now have the resources to look after themselves. This is the classic form of isolationism, but there is also an active variety toward which, without explicitly admitting it, the American Government seems to be tending. This line of policy—exemplified by the President's Peking and Moscow trips in 1972—rests on the thesis that only the United States can deal effectively with the two major Communist powers and that America should, therefore, play a free hand in seeking a power balance, leaving its allies—Western Europe and Japan—to join the strategic game as independent balancing powers at a lower level of effectiveness.

Whichever line of policy America pursues over the next few years, Europeans can no longer count on America's uncritical support for Europe's efforts to pull itself together. To be sure, if Europe makes rapid and visible progress toward political unity, a favorable American response will almost certainly be forthcoming. But, if the imminent expansion of the Community does not quickly disclose a renewed will toward unity, America may be expected to pursue an increasingly niggling and querulous line toward the Community's activities.

Today, preoccupied with domestic disarray and our mindless but endless Indo-Chinese imbroglio, America has become introspective and self-centered. Unwilling to face the fact that the weakening of our competitive position is largely our own fault and not to be blamed on the unfairness of foreigners, some Americans take refuge in a squalid and unworthy self-pity. At a time when scapegoats are in great demand it is easy to blame our trouble on the European Common Market, and particularly on the Community's Common Agricultural Policy.

9

Unfortunately there are few Americans, either in or out of the government or the universities, who fully appreciate how foreign policy and international economics intertwine. No one at the very highest levels of American foreign policy since the days of Dean Acheson has been prepared to focus on the inextricable relation of economic and political policy—and today that is more than ever true.

The result has been to leave the public discussion of Europe's efforts toward unity largely in the hands of professional economists, businessmen and lobbyists for labor and agricultural interests, who, concentrating on narrow commercial, economic or academic interests, are occupationally disabled from understanding the broader implications of what has happened—and is happening—in Europe.

Given these circumstances, it is extremely fortunate that Professor Hallstein's book is now being published in America. Not only should this book help put the progress of Europe in focus for the American reader, but it should also tend to temper American impatience by making clear the vast difference between the creation of unity in Europe today and the welding together of a handful of American colonies on the eastern littoral of North America two centuries ago. It is a point that needs elucidation if Americans are not to draw some misleading parallels.

The difference is not merely that—unlike the nations of Europe today—the thirteen colonies had had no experience as independent political entities but on the contrary had shared allegiance to a common sovereign within a common colonial system. Nor is it merely that—unlike Europe—the American colonists spoke the same language and derived their institutions from a common tradition. These, of course, are obvious points of distinction but there is another, fully as important. What complicates the building of Europe today is that, particularly within the last century, the governments of all major industrial states have assumed social and economic responsibility of a pervasive kind—responsibility for the public welfare and public health, an obligation to maintain the economy at a stable level, avoiding booms and panics, a commitment to maintain substantially full employment, and so on. What creates the greatest impediment to integration—and ultimately to political unity—is that each government has sought to achieve these ends through systems and programs of its own design, tailored to meet special national requirements without much regard to the impact on neighboring states.

To harmonize these elaborate and confusing systems—which requires, among other things, the development of a common monetary policy and even a common currency—is a monumental task, as Professor Hallstein makes crystal clear. It is a task that was unthinkable in those simple pastoral days when a group of American colonies bound themselves together to form what was to become a great nation.

This is the point we Americans must bear in mind as we watch the continuing struggle of Europe to modernize its economic and political structure. The critical problems arise because governments have undertaken to deflect and manipulate market forces, not because Europe is industrialized while the American colonies had agrarian economies. In fact, it has been the persistence of an agrarian sector in Europe that has posed the most nettlesome problems for the unifiers.

That the Common Agricultural Policy of the Community cuts across the most cherished principles of intelligent commercial and economic policy is scarcely surprising. Fragmented as it is and subject to uncontrollable vicissitudes of wind and water, the farm community poses a claim for special protection and assistance that has been recognized all over the Western world. In the United States, our constantly changing farm policy has become a *potpourri* of bits and pieces of special legislation each designed to benefit a particular narrow farming interest —often at the expense of foreign producers and invariably at the expense of the American consumer. Yet America's farm policy is no more complex or haphazard than that of most other Western countries. No modern nation today has developed a rational farm policy nor is it likely to do so. As Chancellor Erhard used to say to me, "In agriculture we are all sinners."

Consider then the problem facing the politicians of Western Europe charged with melding five quite distinct national farm policies into a common policy for the whole Community. To reach any agreement at all was an extraordinary *tour de force*. Without question the result is an atrocity; yet for that very reason the policy in its present form seems unlikely to have a long life expectancy.

Perhaps the greatest benefit thoughtful Americans may derive from Professor Hallstein's book is a feeling of urgency—an anxiety that Europe promptly get on with the business of unity, since, in a very real political sense time is of the essence.

Positioned as it is between two powerful centers of power, Western Europe is today subject to strong conflicting pressures. America encourages unity but with diminishing conviction; the Soviets strive more than ever to strengthen latent tendencies toward fragmentation. The Kremlin of Brezhnev and Kosygin pursues two principal objectives: one is to stimulate the withdrawal of the American presence and influence from Europe; the other to encourage those nationalist rivalries that inhibit the union of the West European peoples—a union that would frustrate Soviet ambitions for political dominance on the European land mass.

Though these objectives are by no means new, Soviet tactics have undergone radical change. Instead of seeking to achieve its ends by tension and the threat of force, the Russians are pursuing a soft line in an effort to gain what they could not achieve by a hard one. It is this that probably explains the Soviet's interest in negotiating special bilateral treaties with individual Western European states, such as the treaty concluded as a part of Chancellor Brandt's *Ostpolitik*; if other European states could be tempted, one by one, to make their own deals with Moscow, the fabric of unity would be torn apart.

Quite likely this also explains the frantic Soviet pressure for a European Security Conference, by which the Kremlin presumably hopes to create a sense of well-being approaching euphoria in Western Europe, thus weakening the pressures for collective action and subtly encouraging the United States to withdraw its presence.

Up to this point, these policies have, to a limited extent, been successful. In fact, were it not for the imminent entry of Great Britain into the Community, one might fear the possible relapse of Europe into a continent of rival states, each unwilling to make even the smallest concession to a nostalgic sovereignty that is every day more illusory.

Thus what we are witnessing is a race against time—a contest that pits the forces of cohesion against counter-forces that would tear Europe apart—a contest with high stakes since the cost of defeat might well be nothing less than Soviet political dominance of the old continent.

What then are the prospects?

Pessimists will contend that the drive for a united Europe will probably continue as an essay in frustration and compromise, since British entry is not likely to provide the stimulus needed to move the great enterprise off dead center. In that event, one could expect an accelerating tendency for America to turn away from Europe.

It is my view, however—which I am certain Professor Hallstein shares—that British accession will provide the essential new element needed to overcome the present inertia; that it is, in fact, likely to ignite explosive forces propelling the peoples of Western Europe down the course Professor Hallstein has so brilliantly laid out. To be sure that course will not be easy but we will, I feel sure, see significant progress in the months ahead, and, as Europe gains increasing self-reliance, one can expect trans-Atlantic relations to enter a new and more constructive phase.

I hope, therefore, that Professor Hallstein's book will be widely read in America as an antedote to the pessimism and cynicism with which my countrymen have been accustomed to view Europe, particularly in the past three or four years. It is time, at long last, that we stop discussing the European question purely in tradesman's argot and began to focus on the political realities that are likely to unfold in the months ahead.

As a stimulant to thoughtful reassessment of the meaning of Europe, one could ask for nothing better than Professor Hallstein's comprehensive work, for it is at the same time both thoughtful and prophetic—the definitive book that no one else could have written.

GEORGE W. BALL

New York City
August, 1972

Chapter One

The Foundations of a United Europe

The present drive towards European unity draws its strength in equal measure from two sources: a romantic vision and hard-headed commonsense – the centuries-old dream of a united Europe, and the needs of the age of space.

Europe is no new creation. It is a rediscovery. The main difference between the formation of the United States of Europe and that of the United States of America is not that America did not have to merge a number of firmly established nation-states, but that for more than a thousand years the idea of a unified Europe was never quite forgotten.

It is sometimes said, especially in France, that in our time the nation-state is the only valid and acceptable expression of political unity and organization. That is not so either in theory or in practice. Of course many European nation-states on the Continent, particularly during the nineteenth century, were strongly influenced by the French Revolution, but it does not follow that this type of nation-state, highly centralized, non-federal, and neglectful of regional interests, is the highest and only form of political organization known to man. History has always known other types of states and presumably always will. Not every nation is gathered together in one state. Sometimes a state embraces only a part of a nation. At other times a state consists of a number of nations. In short, the different types of states that exist are endless.

Such French objections are understandable. Their history has given Frenchmen no experience of how a federal system works, and some of them tend to overlook the fact that what Europe is striving for is a federation, and not a unitary, centralized state like their own. The point is important because in a federation the member-states continue to exist, and not merely on paper. They are not eliminated by the larger federal unity. Germans on the whole are

15

far less concerned about this, largely because their history is a history of federations and confederations, and also because they live in a federal republic and in their dealings with officialdom are daily brought face to face with the difference between authorities at the state level and authorities at the federal level.

The time has come for a stand to be made against a narrow and dogmatic view of national loyalty. The adherents of European federation are not, as they are sometimes called, 'stateless functionaries'. They are patriots who have a wider loyalty – to Europe. They know that the two are not in conflict, and that their country's fate and that of Europe are inextricably intertwined and will become more so in the future. Above all, they know that Europe shares a sense of values: of what is good and bad; of what a man's rights should be and what his duties; of how society should be ordered; of what is happiness and what disaster. Europe shares many things: its memories that we call history; achievements it can take pride in and events that are shameful; its joys and its sufferings; and not least its tomorrows.

This is not to deny the existence of national differences or to denigrate their value. On the contrary, our aim is not that Europe should become a melting-pot. Europe is variety, and we want to safeguard the riches of its national differences in character, temperament, talent, taste, beliefs, and customs. What we want to remove are the facets that divide, the wasteful use of resources in fighting one another – above all, the elements that can spell death and destruction when strongly individualistic and different entities exist side by side.

Language is no barrier in this respect. We have to look only to Switzerland, the classical proof that a multiplicity of languages does not stunt society but enriches it. The day, we hope, is not too distant when we shall be able to cite the experience of our Belgian friends. Language, in other words, need not be an obstacle; it can serve as an incentive – a truth soon discovered by our European officials in Brussels and in the research centres of Euratom. For further proof we have only to turn to the Dutch, many of whom are fluent in a number of languages; and the European schools we have set up are a model of how such results can be attained.

Is our aim, then, one European Federal nation? I repeat: not necessarily – but it is not necessarily to be excluded. National sentiment and national selfhood are not immutable, and need not remain what European history has sometimes made them out to be. The nation-state will not always be accepted as the ultimate form of political organization, as a kind of political absolute: men will no longer worship it as an idol, as they sometimes have in the past. It will cease to be monolithic. At the same time mankind is reaching the end of that chapter in its history when a nation's importance and glory were measured by its victories and the extent of its power, and particularly so in the very fields of political and economic activity in which we are striving for European unity. The use of modern weapons would mean suicide. Interdependence is no longer a slogan but a reality; and as if by instinct politicians today tend increasingly to consider the effect of their actions on many if not all aspects of world politics.

Recent German history strikingly reflects this trend. In Germany, national sentiment and national pride were monstrously misused and led to unparalleled disaster. Inevitably German glory was tarnished and there were some Germans who tried to bring their confused fellow-citizens to see that nowadays every citizen must share in his country's responsibility towards the rest of the world. This was right and proper; but it was an intellectual answer and therefore not enough. National self-awareness and national sentiment are the means not only to certain goals, but also and above all a sense of belonging to one's people. It is not something that can be expressed only through symbols; it is something one's senses must be able to feel, almost to touch. The Germans speak of 'the Fatherland' but it is hard to extend that concept to the whole world. In any case, are we certain that man's age-old dream of 'One World' will ever become reality? Are we certain that every frontier in the world will ever come down? We are not even certain whether they should. Perhaps it is in the nature of things that competition even between larger entities should be a driving force of history. It is neither wicked nor stupid to point out that we are closer to some people than to others, and any future world order will have to recognize that fact.

Who, after all, would wish to deny the cultural unity of the Continent? Western civilization, which today covers the whole vast Atlantic area, has its roots in Europe. It has been shaped by Greek philosophy and Christianity. Even at the peak of the nationalistic

17

phase of European history, art, literature and science never developed exclusively within national confines. The flow and exchange of ideas across frontiers never ceased. It was naturally in art and literature that European influence asserted itself most strongly. That influence was less marked in other spheres of human activity, like politics, whose history became little more than the sum total of a number of individual national histories; or in the law, which in each country tended to reflect the different choices made by the national sovereign power.

In conclusion, let us remember that states are man's creation. Their purpose is to serve man, and it would be wrong as well as foolish to make them into idols, sacrosanct and immune to change. Where change is seen to be necessary to order society better and thereby improve the quality of life, changes ought to be welcomed and encouraged.

And that is the case in Europe. The aim of unifying Europe is not – as its enemies assert – to form a new arbitrary power bloc. It is not to establish an *ad hoc* – and perhaps short-lived – combination of forces for use in some sinister balance-of-power game; and the so-called 'Europeans' are not motivated by opportunism or hopes of winning a quick advantage or profit. Nor is their work part of some vast aggressive venture. The unification of Europe is truly an organic process, with long-lived cultural, economic, and political roots. That process now has a concrete shape and structure, which in essence are political. That is why the Community organization of Europe could be a model for the world.

II. THE SHOCK OF TWO WORLD WARS

Such are the bases of European unity. On the face of it they appear to be geographical, ethnic, psychological, linguistic, and cultural. But appearances are deceptive. It took the boundless excesses of nationalistic policy in the Second World War, and the equally total disaster they caused, to make obvious that in politics, and in economics also, the countries of Europe must sink or swim together. The holocaust left no doubt about the need for unity.

It was a shock to discover how far Europe's relative share of world production had shrunk, particularly when compared to the

United States of America. In 1913 the countries of Western Europe had produced roughly half of the world's industrial goods. By the 1950s West Europe's share had dropped to little more than a quarter. And, while in 1959 69·4 million workers in America succeeded in turning out a gross national product of 483·4 thousand million dollars, a labour force of 72·4 million in the countries of the European Community attained a combined gross product of only 162·9 thousand million. In other words, accepting the official rates of exchange as a basis of measurement, every West European produced goods and services to only a third of the value of those produced by his American counterpart.

There were political arguments, too.

European civilization was threatened from the East by political forces. They were strong and growing stronger; they had vast resources; they were expansionist; they were sustained by a pseudo-religious fervour and an almost missionary zeal. Defence against them required a close-knit military alliance, firm political conviction, and the greatest possible economic strength.

Even *vis-à-vis* her friends, Europe faced an economic and political challenge. In five years Europe had received some 14·7 million dollars in aid; but the post-war phase, in which charity had played a key role, was coming to an end, and charity was being replaced by competition, the highest civilized form of economic relations between free and equal partners. No single state, not even a community of states, could hope to cope alone with the massive problems that presented themselves: the defence against Communism, the fight against poverty, aid to the less-developed countries, the difficulties created by agricultural surpluses, the stabilization of the economy, and the safeguarding of currencies. These problems could be tackled only by a Europe organized to work together. For at that stage three parts of the non-Communist world seemed to stand out: the United States, Great Britain and her Commonwealth, and Continental Europe.

The strongest spur to action, to building a united Europe, was a clear political need: to bring to an end the demoralizing situation in which Europe was at the mercy of political decisions taken by others outside Europe, and instead to enable it once more to share in the shaping of events. The aim was by no means to turn Europe into a 'Third Force'. Far from it. For the Europe that was about to

19

unite belonged fully to the non-Communist world. The aim in seeking unity was rather to become a strong, respected partner within it. The later formation of OECD, with the United States and Canada as full members, was the first institutional expression of this new transatlantic relationship.

Within Europe, too, the drive towards unification was largely political. It was plain after the First World War that the so-called 'European system' had lost its force. But it was not until after the Second World War that the outline of a different kind of system began to emerge. The old 'European system' can best be described as a multiplicity of strictly independent sovereign states. They did not always act in isolation. They formed alliances; but these were never permanent. They constantly dissolved and re-formed according to the dictates of national self-interest at any given moment. A guiding and relatively stabilizing element in this system was provided by the so-called 'Concert' of the then Great Powers, and by British diplomacy, which supported first one power and then another in order to prevent any one country from dominating the Continent. There was in fact a delicate balance of power which, as experience was to show, depended largely on the state of Franco-German relations. It was an ailing survivor from the nineteenth century.

This system failed; it failed the only test that would have justified its continuance into our century: it failed to preserve peace. The 'Concert' of the Great Powers became cacophony. The time had come to give Europe a new look. The credit for launching this great historic venture belongs first and foremost to the men who guided the affairs of France and Germany, and particularly to Jean Monnet, Robert Schuman, and Konrad Adenauer. Credit is also due to the wisdom and determination of those responsible in Italy, in particular Alcide de Gasperi, with his clear sense of purpose and deeply-held convictions, and to the leaders of the Benelux countries, to men like Spaak and Beyen. All in turn took decisive steps to bring union to birth. Dutch diplomacy, in particular, was crucial in the transition from the Coal and Steel Community to the Common Market, the European Economic Community. The nineteenth-century balance-of-power system was over, in form as in fact.

Common interests were to be resolutely served by joint efforts to create a stable, balanced structure. That, in a nutshell, was the 'European' idea.

It was not automatic. It was a conscious choice by those responsible. This can best be seen in the example of Germany, whose leaders deliberately avoided a foreign policy directed towards the East with the reunification of Germany as its aim; nor did they choose to seek special and exclusive links with the United States. Viewed objectively, these were real possible alternatives, which in the conscious and subconscious minds of others gave rise to the so-called *incertitudes allemandes*. It was not long before Federal Germany's deliberate policy decision of 'opting for Europe' brought its first rich harvest: such seemingly intractable problems as the Ruhr, the re-arming of Germany, and the future of the Saar were all rapidly resolved; above all, Franco-German relations were rebuilt on a positive, constructive basis, with immeasurable benefit to the future of Europe as a whole. Finally, right from the very beginning Europe's efforts to integrate enjoyed the splendid support of the United States. Without this support, which was given in the expectation that Europe would eventually federate and create – to quote Churchill's famous words – 'a kind of United States of Europe', little progress would have been possible. Its moral value was in no way diminished by the fact that it also served a practical purpose in the context of America's world-wide defence system: it helped to secure the European front, the European frontier. Quite the reverse: European integration was not only sought, welcomed, and encouraged. It was also jointly defended.

All this may explain the strength of the new movement. By contrast, the forces that sought to preserve the past were weak. At the same time, two psychological factors worked in favour of change, and gave deep roots to Europe's willingness to found a new system going beyond the nation-state.

First, the 'atomic age' had brought about a new sense of proportion. Science and technology had almost immeasurably widened the area that man could control either alone or collectively, and this at an ever faster pace. The world's most influential political and economic entities were now the size of continents. The various national territories in Europe which were now seeking common cause could each be crossed in less than a day. In Europe, and indeed in the world, men had become neighbours, and were ever more aware of the fact. This change of dimension was not of man's choosing: it was imposed on us by the march of events.

Secondly, national sovereignty in Europe was constantly being narrowed and devalued.

Narrowed, because the sovereign nation-state lost its greatest attribute, military power. The technology of war – like all technology – had escaped from the European politicians; and nationally they were never to recapture it. Military uniforms today are harder to tell apart than diplomatic uniforms.

Devalued, because the unprecedented abuse of national power and nationalistic ideology had caused a holocaust of destruction in Europe on a scale without parallel in history, and thereby drastically weakened the credit of the nation-state. Many European post-war constitutions contain provisions for the transfer of powers, previously exercised by the sovereign nation-state, to supranational common institutions. It is no coincidence that the combined territories of the six founder-members of the European Community cover virtually that part of free Europe which the nationalistic excesses of the Second World War had brought to the brink of complete destruction.

This brief review of the basic motives for uniting Europe shows very clearly that, although the process of integration may be termed 'economic', it is in fact essentially political. It is part of the whole movement that sought, right from the beginning, to pool all the appropriate functions of the individual member-states. In the past this movement had led to the plan for a 'European Defence Community' which unfortunately failed to materialize, and linked to the Defence Community were plans for a 'Political Community'. Moreover, it is worth recalling the provisions for the establishment of a 'European University' in the Euratom Treaty. Even today public pressure for 'political union' is very noticeable and shows that 'economic integration' is part of a wider process. It is not, in intention or reality, an end in itself.

But it is not only the motives and aims of European unification that are political. It is also its means and methods.

These first developed in the European Coal and Steel Community for the heavy industry of the member-states, which from the beginning was treated as an experiment and model for future integration in wider fields. A 'Common Market' was established in coal and steel – in other words, similar national market conditions throughout the whole Community area. All customs, tariffs and quotas were abolished and artificial distortions of competition, including those in the private sector like cartels, were forbidden. Key economic policy-making for coal and steel was transferred from the individual member-countries to the Community. The Community itself was organized along lines which were plainly federal: an executive was set up, a 'High Authority' which was independent of the member-states, their governments and parliaments; there was a federal body, the Council of Ministers, in which the governments of the member-states worked together; a Parliament which was entrusted with a number of elementary parliamentary functions, such as consultation in certain fields of legislation affecting the whole Community, and supervision of the executive; and finally a Supreme Court of Justice.

This was the model which in the European Economic Community was later extended into a general Common Market to cover goods, capital, and labour of all kinds (free movement of workpeople, liberalization of services, and the right of establishment for firms). The centrepiece is a customs union. But this is surrounded by a substantial body of common law and common economic policies.

Why is a customs union alone not enough? The answer was given with classical simplicity in one of the last pamphlets to be published by the former League of Nations. It dealt with the subject of customs unions, and was re-issued by the United Nations in 1947.

For a customs union to exist, it is necessary to allow free movement of goods within the union. For a customs union to be a reality, it is necessary to allow free movement of persons. For a customs union to be stable, it is necessary to maintain free exchangeability of currency and stable exchange rates within the union. This implies, *inter alia*, free movement of capital within the union. When there is free movement of goods, persons and capital in any area, diverse economic policies concerned with maintaining economic activity cannot be pursued.

23

III. THE LOGIC OF INTEGRATION

Here we touch upon what may be described as the final factor in the unification of Europe. It is an anonymous force, but it only works through human will. It might be called material logic. Economics is not unlike the alphabet: it forms a coherent whole, it possesses an inner logic, which is stronger than the capricious dictates of politics. Without this inner logic, there would be no economic science; and one of its results is that action in one field of economic policy has repercussions in all the rest.

That is why the Treaty of Rome, in seeking to set up a Common Market, does not deal only with the abolition of customs barriers between the member states but also with hundreds of different forms of action which in their entirety constitute a coherent economic and social policy. A common customs tariff for the whole Community inevitably leads to a common trade policy, for a common tariff can only be administered jointly. Further, it becomes necessary to ensure that the attempt to create conditions of free competition between the member-states by removing one set of obstacles – that is to say, internal customs barriers between the member-states – is not nullified by other sets of obstacles, such as preferential or discriminatory transport rates, exchange manipulations, or cartels. Consequently the Community has to exert a measure of discipline, a pressure to joint action, in all fields where the barriers between its members might otherwise be rebuilt. In certain cases, moreover, the so-called 'natural' free flow of economic resources within the Community cannot be brought about simply by removing a few obstacles like internal tariffs. The removal of tariffs by itself has that effect only where free market conditions prevail. Where that is not the case, where economic *dirigisme* is the order of the day, there a Community which aims at creating an internal market among all its member-states has no choice but to adopt the discipline of a common policy, for instance in agriculture and transport.

Let me take a central element of our Community, the free movement of goods, to show how the interrelationship of all aspects of economic policy acts as part of the dynamic of integration.

The removal of customs barriers, some people still argue, is sufficient to achieve the free exchange of goods, at least as far as

24

industrial products are concerned. Of course the Treaty of Rome laid down a fixed time-table for the gradual removal of customs barriers. In fact, it was possible to shorten this time-table; the last customs barriers within the Community disappeared and the common external tariff was finally completed on 1 July 1968, eighteen months ahead of schedule.

The removal of internal tariffs presented few basic problems. But it soon confirmed our view that trade depends not only on tariffs but also on a whole series of other things.

There are administrative barriers. There are also tax barriers. Trade cannot be free so long as within the member-states there exist different turnover taxes linked to different systems of tax rebates, and different arrangements for sharing the tax burden between varying types of manufacturers, importers, and exporters. The different turnover taxes must first be harmonized; then the rates at which they are levied.

And that is not the end of the matter. Every tax system is an integrated whole. Changes in turnover tax, which is so important an element of indirect taxation, must lead to other changes, in direct taxation too. What is more, by losing national control of turnover taxes, the member-states lose financial flexibility – which has an important effect on budget policy. In short, the truly free movement of goods within a Community means that the member-states must accept not only a good deal of interference in their administrative processes but also even a restructuring of their taxation and budget policies.

What is more, the free movement of goods in this instance concerns only industrial goods. Agricultural products are another matter altogether.

When the Rome Treaty came into force, each of the member-states operated a vast complex of differing systems for protecting its domestic agriculture. There were quotas, long-term contracts, and the like. It would have been impossible simply to sweep these restrictions aside from one day to the next. Guaranteed fixed prices for certain products, for example, would have become unworkable if huge quantities of these products had been allowed to pour in from abroad. To make possible a free flow of agricultural products within the Community, it was necessary to establish something as challenging, not to say revolutionary, as a common

25

European agricultural policy. This was a task which EFTA, for example, did not even attempt.

The first step in this direction was to establish a common system of marketing; the second was to fix common prices for basic agricultural products which applied throughout the whole Community, from Schleswig-Holstein to Sicily, from Passau to Le Havre. The hard bargaining over common cereal prices in December 1964 showed just how difficult this task was, not least in its political implications. But without achieving these two preconditions – a common marketing system which involved integrating the different agricultural policies of the member-states, and the fixing of common prices – it would have been quite impossible to introduce the free movement of agricultural products.

Even these preconditions, however, were only the beginning of the matter. The common prices for agricultural products are naturally quoted in practice in each national currency. But what happens if one member-state devalues? Either it raises its cereal, sugar, and milk prices by the amount it has devalued in order to keep in line with the common agricultural price structure of the rest of the Community, although that may cause internal inflation and so rob it of much of the benefit it may have expected from devaluation; or it leaves its agricultural prices at the level they were before devaluation, with the result that its agricultural prices fall below the level in the other member-states, and its agricultural products are dumped on the rest of the Community on a massive scale, while the other member-states find it virtually impossible to sell their products in the state that has devalued.

This second eventuality had above all to be prevented, because it would have contravened one of the central aims of the Community, the free movement of goods. So when the Community faced this question for the first time towards the end of 1964, in fixing common prices for cereals, the Council of Ministers solved the problem by deciding to express the common price in 'units of account'. By this means it was hoped to protect the common price-structure for agricultural products from fluctuations caused as a result of devaluations or revaluations of currencies within the Community. Naturally this solution is only temporary; it will cease to be necessary once there is a monetary union within the Community. Inevitably the temporary solution, agreed in 1964, lost much of its effectiveness when, in 1969, the French franc was devalued and the German mark was revalued, but fortunately this event strengthened the heads of government of the Six, at their summit meeting in The Hague towards the end of 1969, in their resolve to press ahead with the creation of a monetary union as speedily as possible.

A change in the exchange rate has up to now been the ultimate weapon in the economic armoury of a country if there is too great a long-term imbalance between its internal and external economic development. The future removal of that weapon is a further argument for aligning the economic policies of the member-states. The opening of the frontiers presses us in that direction, for a single market demands a single system for conjunctural (i.e. short-term economic) policy. Unfortunately – and this must cause concern – the development of means for evolving and implementing a common economic policy has lagged behind the gradual removal of obstacles to the free flow of trade. Without a common economic policy, a balanced development between agricultural and other areas of economic activity becomes impossible. As long as industrial prices are determined by the law of supply and demand and by national economic policies, while the level of agricultural prices is decided by the Community on a common basis, agriculture will always be in danger of running into difficulties.

In short: it amounts to an over-simplification as well as a refusal to face reality to maintain that all one needs to do in order to ensure the free flow of both industrial and agricultural products is to throw open the frontiers. What is needed is something much more ambitious: common Community bodies with wide powers over substantial areas, affecting the shaping of taxation, budget, economic, and monetary policies.

This argument makes economic sense. It makes even greater sense from the practical point of view of the individual businessman. The more closely knit the Community becomes, the more competition will cease to exist between national economic systems, and grow instead between different enterprises. Such a development is acceptable to the business world only if the conditions of competition are the same throughout the Community. In other words, the national economic systems of the member-states have to

27

be integrated. That means that the subsidy policies of the member-states must become a matter for the Community; that there must be a common transport policy; that energy prices must be brought into line, and this in turn implies a common energy policy. It also means that large areas of national legislation which affect competitive conditions are themselves affected by integration: cartel legislation, company law, patent law, laws and regulations dealing with debts, commercial law, enforcement, etc. Finally, it means that no member will eventually be able to pursue its own separate economic or trade policies with reference to non-member-states. For the establishment of a Community like the EEC involves not merely the joint administration of a common external tariff, and the disposal of the dues thus collected; it means that the Community must act as one *vis-à-vis* the rest of the world.

Thus it is that the psychological chain reaction set off by integration does not stop at the frontiers of social policy. Even such matters as foreign and defence policy, which are not covered by any Community treaty, more and more demand a common European discipline. Politics is indivisible; and necessity is the spur.

IV. NOT BUSINESS BUT POLITICS

The political nature of 'economic integration' is therefore plain. Integration in the economic field is not merely a step on the way to political integration: it is already political itself. For what is being integrated is not 'economics', or production, or trade, or consumption: it is not the work of employers, or workers, or salesmen, or consumers. The EEC is not setting up cartels or trade unions or consumers' associations. What the Community is integrating is the role of the state in establishing the framework within which economic activity take place. This role has increased enormously in the present century, not least as a result of two 'total' World Wars, but also because of the political urge to greater social solidarity, and the growing knowledge of the science of economics, which has encouraged us to try to control events like the recurring cycle of boom and depression, which were previously accepted fatalistically as phenomena of nature.

This far-reaching influence of the public authorization on the conditions in which economic activity takes place was not the product of the European Community: it existed already. There are those who object to state interference in economic affairs; but they are wrong to blame European integration for such interference and to assert that it smacks of economic *dirigisme*. All the European Community is doing is to co-ordinate and integrate the powers it found its member-states exercising in running their separate national economies, and any complaint that there is too much state interference should be directed rather to the states concerned. The Community, moreover, is not attempting to co-ordinate every single strand of power a member-state may possess for regulating its economy; the Community is federal, not unitary, and shares its responsibilities with the member-states. At the same time, integration inevitably affects the member-states' policies, and on the whole in a liberal direction. The basic law of the European Economic Community, its whole philosophy, is liberal. Its guiding principle is to establish undistorted competition in an undivided market. Where rules are necessary to achieve this, they are rules to make freedom possible. For – to adapt a quotation from Kant – even freedom is 'not the natural condition of man'. Consequently, such compulsion as may be necessary is directed first and foremost against those powers possessed by member-states which restrict the freedom of competition, and not against the citizens of Europe for whom this new freedom and the benefits that will flow from it are to be secured.

Let me summarize my argument by quoting from my introduction to the Commission's memorandum of 24 October 1962 on 'The Action Programme for the second stage in the development of the Community':

> The so-called economic integration of Europe is essentially a political phenomenon. The European Economic Community, together with the European Coal and Steel Community and the European Atomic Energy Community, is a 'European political union in the economic and social field'.

Chapter Two

Law in Place of Force

I. THE RULES OF THE GAME

The European Economic Community is a remarkable legal phenomenon. It is a creation of the law; it is a source of law; and it is a legal system.

First, the Community is a creation of the law. This is the decisive new element in Europe's history. Previous attempts to unify Europe depended on force or conquest. Now unity is to be achieved not by might but by an intellectual, a cultural force: law. The majesty of the law is to achieve what centuries of 'blood and iron' could not. Only unity by consent has a chance of surviving. That means not only equality before the law for all belonging to the Community but also a common legal system. For without a common legal system there can be no equality before the law. The Treaty of Rome recognizes this truth and is thus an organization for peace.

The Treaty of Rome and the other Community treaties are by their nature acts of creation. They have created new legal entities, the European Communities, with a new legal system. They differ in their essential character from traditional international treaties. For they are concerned not with the international law of contract between sovereign states – that is to say, with a bundle of rights and obligations by which the signatories to a particular treaty agree to abide – but with the public international law of association.

This in itself implies the second point: the Community is a source of law. Plainly it would not have been enough for the Treaty merely to set up an association of states; the association had to be supplied with a motor to enable it to develop into its declared goal, the economic and social union of Europe. To that end the Treaty broadly confined itself only to setting out the aims of the Community, establishing the institutions that were to initiate the necessary action, and laying down a time-table. The institutions had the task of filling in the framework provided by the Treaty and they were given legislative and administrative powers for that purpose. Although the Community is not a state, it has a state's power to legislate, to hand down legal decisions, and to have them carried out.

The Community's powers of legislation vary according to the nature of the subject-matter with which it is dealing. Where one of the Treaty's aims can be realized only by laying down uniform rules and regulations, no matter how detailed, throughout the whole Community, there the Community is endowed with the exclusive right of legislating directly. Where there is no such compelling need for uniformity within the Community and unity *vis-à-vis* the rest of the world, there the Community organs restrict themselves to working indirectly through the legal systems of the member-states.

Finally, there are tasks outside the central field of integration which under the Treaty are to be settled by agreement between the member-states.

The Community's laws are called 'regulations'. They differ from legal regulations or ordinances issued by individual states in two important respects: they are 'Community' regulations in the sense that their effectiveness does not stop at national frontiers and that they apply uniformly and completely throughout the Community; and they directly affect everyone within the Community, be he an individual or a legal entity like a company, and do *not* have to be ratified by or embodied into a national legal system before they come into force.

The Community's legislative power rests jointly with the Council of Ministers and the Commission.

In most cases it is the Council of Ministers which has the power to issue regulations, but occasionally that power is exercised by the Commission. The decision-making process takes the form of a dialogue between the Council and the Commission. Under the Treaty it is almost always the Commission that has the duty of proposing and drafting regulations for submission to and approval by the Council. The Council can alter such a proposal only by a unanimous vote. There follows a period of discussion in which the Commission takes part, before the Council proceeds to a decision. The Commission therefore fulfils two functions:

31

since it has the exclusive right in most cases to take the initiative, it acts as a motor in the Community law-making process; it also acts as an 'honest broker' during the discussions in the Council, seeking to reconcile divergent national or Community interests.

There is a second way by which the Community is building up a body of law of its own, and that is by means of 'directives'. A 'directive' can be addressed to all member-states or to only one or two. It lays down the Community purpose that is to be realized, and it binds the state to which it is addressed to carry out the instructions it contains, but it is left to the member-state to implement these instructions in its own way. Unlike a 'regulation', a 'directive', therefore, does not create new Community law. It does not interfere with the various national legal systems. On the contrary, it works through these systems. The method of the 'directive' thus embodies one of the key principles which the founders of the Community had in mind: how to combine the necessary unity with the safeguard of individual national diversity.

There is a third form of Community legal act known as 'decisions'. Basically, a 'decision' is meant to settle a specific, particular case.

Finally, the Community may issue 'recommendations' and 'opinions', on matters of either general or particular concern. Such 'recommendations' or 'opinions' do not have the force of law but their practical importance can be very great.

Thirdly, the Community is a legal system. It is a coherent system based partly on the Treaty itself and partly on the acts of the Community institutions, and in particular the regulations issued by the Council of Ministers. It is not limited to rules for the smooth functioning of the Common Market; like any true legal system it seeks to guarantee that the Community institutions act in accordance with the law, and to afford appropriate legal protection to those affected by them.

On the one hand, the member-states have bound themselves under the Treaty to work together to unify Europe. They have undertaken faithfully to carry out all obligations arising from the Treaty or the acts of the Community institutions. They are pledged to smooth the work of the Community and to avoid anything that might threaten the goals of the Treaty. But the strictness of these obligations is modified by a number of protective clauses – 'emergency brakes' made necessary by the scope and the risks of the whole enterprise. Yet the use of these 'emergency brakes' has been kept well within reasonable bounds. In the majority of the difficult cases that have arisen, the Commission, working together with the member-state concerned, has been able to find a solution within the framework of the Treaty.

The member-states, however, are not the only bodies responsible for the Community. On the other hand, there is the individual, the ordinary man in the street. He, too, bears his share of responsibility. He, too, is affected by the legal system of the Community. Indeed, he is affected by it more strongly and more directly with every day that passes. The Community's legal system confers on him both rights and duties. As a result he is subject in varying degrees to two legal systems – as a citizen of one of the Community's member-states to his national legal system, and as a member of the Community to the Community's legal system. Of course, this is not a new experience for citizens of countries with federal constitutions.

It is far from easy exactly to define the place of Community law, with its many novel features, within the general structure of jurisprudence and to draw accurate lines of demarcation between the Community and other legal systems. Inevitably these matters have been and are the subject of lively controversy.

The Community's body of laws is neither a mere bundle of agreements between a number of sovereign states nor is it something that somehow has been tacked on to existing national legal systems. What the member-states have done by founding the Community is to surrender a part of their separate national sovereignty, and to create an entirely new and independent legal system to which both they as states and their citizens are subject.

What then is the relationship of the Community's legal system to that of a member-state? The answer is simple, at least in theory: they both interlock at many points; they must both frequently be referred to in legal matters; and consequently the authorities, particularly the Courts of Law, and the citizens of the member states must apply both bodies of law where they are relevant.

The existence of two closely-linked legal systems is not without precedent. One has only to look at the various kinds of federal association all over the world. Conflict between the two systems

33

is usually avoided by setting down clearly the areas in which the state and those in which the federation is competent; in border-line cases where there is a dispute over who is competent, the rule generally applies that federal law takes precedence and blocks the implementation of state law.

According to the desire of its founders, the European Economic Community is part of a structure aimed at federation. The constitutional structure they created was clearly federal in intent and design. The law of the Community, therefore, should take precedence over the law of the individual member-countries.

This thesis of the superiority of the law of the Community over national law is not accepted by everyone. Those who argue against it point to the fact that the Treaty of Rome had to be ratified by each of the national parliaments of the member-states in accordance with their constitutions before it could come into force. Consequently, they maintain that the legal powers with which the Treaty invests the Community are equal to each state's right to legislate, and subject to each state's constitutional law. If one followed this argument to its logical conclusion, then each member-state could in the last resort alter any part of the Community's laws and regulations as it pleased. The Community's sovereign rights in both the legal and administrative sense would soon be different in the various member-states – which would call in question the Community's ability to carry out its functions effectively.

For this reason, the European Court of Justice has confirmed that Community law takes precedence, and in this connection the Court handed down two important declarations:

Firstly: the member-states have completely and conclusively handed over a part of their sovereignty to the Community system they themselves created. This surrender of sovereignty cannot subsequently be reversed by any measures, taken by a member-state on its own, which are in conflict with the Community concept.

Secondly: It is a basic principle of the Treaty that the unique character of the Community's legal system, which is enshrined in the principle that it applies uniformly and in its entirety throughout the length and breadth of the Community, must in no way be tampered with by any member-state.

The upshot is that Community legislation which is within the competence of the Community takes precedence over the national law of any member-state with which it may be in conflict. Furthermore, Community legislation not only takes precedence over previous national law; it is actually a bar to the implementation of any incompatible national law enacted thereafter.

In setting up a European Court of Justice, our aim was very ambitious: to crown the constitutional structure of the Community with a Supreme Court which was a truly constitutional body. This European Court was to be like the Supreme Court of the United States in the days of its greatest glory under Chief Justice John Marshall. It was under his guidance that the broad outlines of the American Constitution were given content, form, and body by the US Supreme Court.

We were not disappointed. The European Court of Justice, because of its independence, settled what was in dispute, defined what was vague, and clarified what was in need of clarification. Without its guiding hand, the Community could not hope to develop as it has developed and as it will develop. The decisions of the Court, to which I have just referred, are the apex of its achievements so far.

Law is not only for use, but also for change, completion, and progress. It is the business of the Community institutions, within the limits of their mandate. But it is also the business of the member-states which have to apply the Community's rules. In this respect the national courts have an important responsibility – to ensure that national jurisprudence develops in accordance with the growing corpus of Community law. Moreover, there are tasks which are entrusted to national Ministers of Justice – in particular in private law and its procedures, a matter of particular concern as regards company law. It is therefore both practically and symbolically important that the Ministers of Justice of the Community's founder-members, on the initiative and under the presidency of the French Minister of Justice, René Pleven, met as the Council of Ministers of the Community for the first time on 3 June 1971. The main object of the meeting was to sign a Protocol entrusting to the European Court of Justice the final interpretation of two agreements between the member-states: on the recognition of companies and legal entities, and on the legal responsibility for and the execution of court divisions in civil and trade matters. In addition, the Ministers agreed on a regulation

35

governing time limits in Community law. They also agreed in principle on consultations between the Community member-states in other international legal bodies: the first practical case was in the UN discussions on universal purchasing norms. The other subjects considered showed special concern for institutional and procedural progress; one example is the work on a European company. It is also encouraging that the President of this meeting envisaged further sessions of a similar kind.

In conclusion, let me point out that it is not only national law and the national right to legislate that cannot override Community law, but even fundamental national constitutional decisions. This is giving rise to a great deal of concern. Some people argue that the basic constitutional provisions of the member-states must be brought into line, that there must be an element of constitutional conformity among the members. Otherwise, they fear that the fundamental rights of the individual, the division of powers within a state, so essential to the preservation of the democratic process and indeed of democracy itself, would be threatened. What they overlook is that the states which founded the Community inserted legal provisions into the Treaty to prevent this from happening. These provisions are different in kind from those found in national constitutions, but they are effective all the same. While the power of the state, for example, is held in check by the fundamental rights enumerated in its constitution, the power of the Community is limited to the areas in which it has been given specific competence, and such competence is strictly defined. Moreover, the Community institutions derive their authority from 'the source' of the Treaty, and the Treaty imposes clear limits to the authority it transfers. Again, most states seek to prevent their government from becoming too powerful by the classical constitutional device known as the division of powers. The Community has a different system of checks, balances and controls which involves its four main institutions – the Council of Ministers, the Commission, the European Parliament, and the Court of Justice – and their relationship one to another. From the point of view of democratic practice and control, it is worth noting that the Commission is responsible to the European Parliament, which can force it to resign, and also that the Ministers belonging to the Council are each responsible for their actions to their respective national parliaments. Furthermore, there are provisions for most extensive and detailed consultation with all parties affected by the economic activities of the Community, particularly with enterprises or associations of enterprises, before any Community institution reaches a decision. Finally, let us remember that the constitution of the Community – like the Community itself – is in a state of evolution, a process which is bound to give the European Parliament greater strength and importance.

The features and trends outlined above justify the claim that the Community's legal system conforms to the fundamental principles essential to a free democratic constitution. Naturally it does not reflect all the basic provisions of the six separate national constitutions. How could it? After all, the Six comprise constitutional monarchies as well as states with a presidential system of government. The demand for a common constitutional structure within the Community and its member-states was expressed in its most extreme, not to say absurd, form by a British author: 'Purely on grounds of constitutional necessity', he explained, he could not imagine Europe other than under the House of Windsor! To view the position in its true perspective, the Community must be seen not as a sovereign power made up of six parts delegated to it by six separate sovereign states, but as a Community venture equipped with a legal system of its own which its member-states have created in accordance and conformity with their national constitutions.

II. THE CONSTITUTION OF EUROPE

1. *The Federal Solution*
The conception sketched here is enough to leave many lawyers breathless. We have tried to rise above the legal forms and traditions of the past. Many would no doubt call our attempt 'revolutionary', and it may well be that future generations will come to regard the philosophical and legal concept underlying Europe's constitution as the most creative achievement in the evolution of jurisprudence in our age, and perhaps even as the most original feature in our effort to integrate Europe. While the Germans have welcomed this concept and influenced its application and evolution, because their history has made them familiar over the cen-

EUROPE IN THE MAKING

turies with a wide variety of federations and confederations, our French friends have had the greatest difficulties in coming to terms with it, because their historical experience is dominated by the concept of the highly-centralized state.

The French Revolution has taught them: '*Il n'y a que l'individu et l'Etat*'. There is only the individual and the state – nothing above, below, or between. If some Frenchmen claim that a 'supranational' Europe means the end of the existing nation-states, then one cannot accuse them of unfairness – only of being wrong, illogical, and unrealistic. Many of the world's great states are federations. The citizens of such states are subject to two public authorities – that of the member-state and that of the federation. Admittedly, integrated Europe is not yet a federation, or a state; but it shares one important characteristic with a federation proper: an element of sovereignty of its own, conferred upon it by and derived from its member-states. How can it best perhaps be expressed? Alexis de Tocqueville, describing the United States, foresaw the semantic dilemma:

> The human understanding more easily invents new things than new words, and we are thence constrained to employ a multitude of improper and inadequate expressions. . . . A form of government has been found out which is neither exactly national nor Federal; but no further progress has been made and the new word which will one day designate this novel invention does not yet exist.

We have, in the meantime, found a word. At the suggestion of Carl Friedrich Ophuels, we chose the word 'Community'. It expresses what we are about.

The problem we faced at this point was: what form should the union of Europe take? We had three choices open to us: unitary, international, and supranational or 'Community'.

If we had adopted the first solution, we should have had to accept the unitary structure upon which the French state is built. Member-states would have given way to a central European authority.

If we had adopted the international solution, member-states would have been virtually left as before. We would have created a partnership of states, bound by a series of international agreements

38

to achieve certain clearly-defined aims and purposes, with clearly-defined rights and duties on the part of all concerned. The fundamental sovereignty of the contracting states would not in any way have been affected: the body with the ultimate power of decision, the Council of Ministers, would no doubt have had to abide by the rule that it can act only unanimously. Such a solution is far from unsuitable when a large group of nations decides to work together to pursue only limited objectives – in other words, where there is a relatively low denominator of common interest. It is a solution that has been adopted in organizations embracing a wide range of European powers, like the Council of Europe in Strasbourg. It is also the solution adopted by the OEEC/OECD which grew out of the Marshall Plan, and to which the USA, Canada, Australia, and Japan now belong; and nobody would deny this body's considerable achievements in stimulating the flow of trade and money in Europe.

The third solution takes us somewhat further. It has been called 'supranational' but if we stick to the language of the Treaty of Rome and describe it as the 'Community' solution, we are probably nearer the mark of what we are actually trying to do, because the use of the word 'supranational' appears to some to imply that we are bent upon destroying national identities. The 'Community' concept, by contrast, implies – and rightly – that states renounce merely a part of their sovereignty, or rather that they put parts of their national sovereignty into a common pool which is controlled by 'Community' institutions whose decisions are in fact their own. One could call this solution 'federal', but we must remember that some people object to the use of the word 'federal' because to them it carries the implication that the Community arrogates to itself the right of being a state. That is certainly not our aim. A state is competent in all matters touching public policy but, unlike a state, our Community is competent only in certain limited spheres which are clearly laid down in the Treaty. The Community resembles a federation only in so far as its member-states transfer part of their national sovereign powers to a union to which they all belong but which has its own identity, different from that of any of its individual members. In this one respect the Community is not dissimilar from a federation. It also serves the purpose for which it was set up, namely, to achieve a balance between a central

European authority, deriving its power from the parts of the national sovereignties transferred to it, and the separate national authorities of the member-states. A Community of such a kind on the one hand acts as a guardian of the individuality and diversity of its nation-states, and on the other provides the basis for the vast continental-sized organization which our global age demands.

Some people may still want to ask whether the Community is a 'federation' or a 'confederation' in the contrasting terminology of nineteenth-century constitutional theory. In my view, the alternatives are false. For the Community is neither. It is not a federation because it is not a state. And it is not a confederation because it is endowed with the power of exercising authority directly over every citizen in each of its member-states.

The Community, like every association – be it of individuals or private or public bodies – has a constitution. A constitution is essential to define the aims and purposes of an association; the terms of membership; and last but not least the ways in which its business is to be conducted.

The constitution of the Community is that of a union of states, entrusted with certain objectives for the common good. It is therefore not unlike the constitution of a state; and like a state, it has not only 'institutional' but 'constitutional' problems. It is a living thing. Its essential character cannot be discovered only by studying the text of documents. Much of it is 'unwritten'. Of course, its chief source is the Treaty which founded the Community, but from that source have flowed regulations, directives, and opinions, not to mention ways of transacting affairs which have grown up over the years but which for all concerned are as binding as any formal legal decision. In this respect the European Court of Justice is performing a truly constructive, not to say creative, task of law-giving interpretation and guidance.

Two main principles have influenced all who have been concerned with giving form and content to the Community: the rule of law and democracy. Everything it does must be founded on this double basis: it is the fountain-head of the Community's creation, its evolution, its relationship to its member states and to individual citizens, and of the way it works from day to day. As a parliamentary democracy, the Community is still imperfect, however, because the European Parliament has not yet acquired its full role.

These two principles underlie the Community's structure, its basic values, and its institutions.

2. *An Incomplete Community*

The European Community has been called a 'small European' union, and hitherto it has consisted of only six states: Belgium, France, Germany, Italy, Luxembourg, and the Netherlands. This was an accident of history. Of course, it would have been preferable to combine the whole of Europe in one large union. The advantages of such a larger entity hardly need elaborating. The use of resources could have been better marshalled and rationalized; production, industry and the economy in general could have been more effectively stimulated; and a union embracing the whole of Europe would plainly have carried greater weight in world affairs. In fact, our ancient continent would have won back and been accorded the place to which its contributions in the past and in the present entitle it.

But such a union was impossible. In the first place, Europe was divided into East and West, into Communist Europe and non-Communist Europe. In the second place, where union was feasible, that is in Western Europe, unification could proceed only on the basis of free choice. One cannot force people to accept what may be best for them. Great Britain in particular was invited to participate both before the Coal and Steel Community was founded and before the negotiations began which led to the Treaty of Rome, but in both cases she preferred to remain outside. The link with the Commonwealth was still very much a reality, not to mention the fact that the whole concept of integration, untried as it was at the time, seemed fanciful in pragmatic British eyes. Nor was Britain the only country to hold back. Some felt that their economies were not yet advanced enough to allow them to take the risks which joining the Common Market might have involved. Others felt inhibited by their traditional policy of strict neutrality. Others still were anxious not to incur the displeasure of a powerful and possibly dangerous neighbour. But it would have been stupid of us – in the light of the reservations of others – to say: 'All or none.' Nothing would have been less constructive in the name of

41

allegedly trying to be perfectionist. We have been called pragmatists. In reality to 'seek the attainable' is not to lose sight of the goal.

The European Community is incomplete not only in the geographical sense, but also in terms of the powers and functions with which it has been entrusted. When the Coal and Steel Community was set up as the first step in European integration, the argument was frequently advanced that what we were seeking was only a 'partial' integration. 'Partial' then was used in a pejorative sense, carrying the implication that such integration as there was had deliberately been taken out of the context of European politics; that it represented a half-hearted effort and was never intended to mean more. One does not hear much of this kind of criticism nowadays, not least because we are now agreed that our first task must be to co-ordinate and integrate economic and social policies, policies which have after all up to now been the prerogative of every separate nation-state acting on its own. Technically, it might be objected that any union based on the federal concept is always bound to leave areas of policy and action where there will be no attempt at integration, because otherwise the member-states will cease to be separate states. In practical terms, however, all agree that a great deal more remains to be done; that, for example, integration in the field of economic and social policy should eventually be extended to foreign and defence policy. And all agree that integration should proceed step by step within the realm of what is possible. Our motto is not: 'Let us have everything or nothing.' And our ambition is not to set up a complete and perfect 'federation' in the true meaning of that term at one single stroke, for the very practical reason that we would be trying to set up a kind of 'never-never-land'.

3. Basic Values

The Community seeks within the framework of its structure to implement and pursue certain accepted basic values: peace, unity, equality, freedom, solidarity, prosperity, dynamism, and certainty. These represent (not necessarily in order of preference), to use a phrase fashionable in Germany today, the 'socio-political' criteria of the Community's policy of integration.

The longing for *peace* is undoubtedly the strongest motive for unifying Europe. In the present century Europe has seen two world wars in which the founder-members of the Community took part. One of the purposes of establishing the Community – expressly stated at the time of the foundation of the Coal and Steel Community and also implicit in its successors – was to deprive the member-states of individual national control over their economic war-potential. It would be a mistake to ignore the fact that pressure to integrate member-states' defence policies is largely motivated by the same reason. None of us needs convincing that it is not enough in these days to forbid war. It is far more effective to make it impossible. I believe that it has already been proved – if proof were needed – that one of the best ways of achieving this is to bind together potential enemies in a community, and I venture to suggest that although the European integration does not yet cover defence, war between member-states of the European Community has become quite unthinkable. This represents a gain of incalculable value. Our efforts at integration can claim to have established for its members the first true system for the maintenance of peace in Europe's history.

Unity is the watchword. For unity means size and space. It means that problems of production, labour, capital, and the location of industry can be tackled on a larger, more comprehensive scale than before. It means greater sources of revenue, a larger market, the concentration and more rational use of resources, and higher productivity. It means that frictions – even when they cannot be eliminated – can at least be identified, contained and so tamed, not to say 'domesticated'. And because it reduces or even eliminates friction, unity means peace. Many of the political questions between the member-states that might lead to differences cease being problems of foreign policy and become instead matters of internal Community policy. Finally, unity means greater influence in world affairs. A united Europe will once again make its voice heard in international politics. United, the nations of Europe will win back the right to determine their own fate. At the moment that is still in the hands of the super-powers. In world terms, the individual nations of Europe are still more like pawns than partners who share in the great policy decisions that affect their lives.

Unity also means *equality*. We have already seen that unification has led to 'new forms' of equality. No citizen of the Community must on account of his nationality be worse off than any other Community citizen. He must not be discriminated against. 'All Europeans are equal before the law' is our guiding principle. This insistence on equality is one of the strongest forces in the social life and structure of the Community. Its effects make themselves felt in all branches of politics. The farmers may have been the last to discover it, but they are certainly aware of it today. Their demands for incomes equal to those earned in other sections of the economy have become a formidable weapon in the pursuit of their farm policy.

The principle of equality also applies as between member-states. No state takes precedence over another; there is no such thing as hegemony. History teaches us that the domination of one power over others does not work. When it was attempted, it seldom lasted long, and the attempt, as well as the subsequent failure, has always caused conflict and periods of uncertainty. Furthermore, there is no power within the Community today that would qualify for dominance by reason either of its material potential or of its psychological or moral authority. Naturally, the fact that the member-states vary considerably in size presents problems, but these the principle of equality helps to resolve. One problem is how to determine the proportion of each member-state's contribution, particularly in manpower, to the institutions of the Community. As in federal structures which are conceived on democratic lines, this raises the question whether the composition of the Community's institutions (the Court of Justice, the Parliament, the Council of Ministers, and the Commission) should depend on the number of states or the number of citizens in each of the member-states. Which of these two yardsticks would be fairer, 'more equal' in its effect? The answer that was accepted is a mixture of the two possible alternatives. For the smaller states would have done very badly if the number of their citizens had been adopted as the determining factor: if all states had been treated as equals, regardless of size or population, they would have done unreasonably well. The mixture that was adopted is basically not unlike that which prevails in the German Federal Republic.

Peace, unity and equality all serve the cause of *freedom*. To begin with, there is the freedom of movement beyond national frontiers throughout the Community – the free movement of goods and four 'special' freedoms: the European right of establishment (by which nationals of any of the member-states – whether individuals or companies – are freed from all restrictions on residing in another member-state); free movement of services; free movement of capital; free movement of work-people who, whatever their nationality, are entitled to seek work anywhere within the Community. These freedoms apart, the whole economic and social system of the Community is liberally orientated. It is basically a market economy; the businessman, the *entrepreneur* is free to make his own decisions; employees are free to choose where they work; the consumer is free to choose what he buys. It is not for officials to lay down what or how much is produced, let alone where, when, or for how long. Enterprises are guided by the conditions of the market, by the law of supply and demand. Free enterprise opens an infinitely greater market for their goods than they enjoyed previously. Employees choose the place where they want to work and they are free to seek another anywhere in the Community. The consumer, for his part, is not allocated certain goods of a predetermined quality at a fixed price; he chooses what appeals to him, what suits him as being the cheapest and best, and the choice he has is wider than ever before as a result of the enlarged market and the greater competition it stimulates.

The concept of solidarity complements the freedoms mentioned above and reduces the dangers which the ruthless use of free enterprise might cause. The Community, like the Federal German Republic, practises a market economy, tempered with a sense of social responsibility. A market economy is not postulated as a kind of immutable dogma; it is merely the best economic system man has so far devised and tested. It is part and parcel, as well as the tool, of a healthy, stable society which seeks to provide conditions in which all its members can lead satisfactory lives. Since the free-enterprise system is by its very nature in a state of constant movement – much more so than any other economic system – it is naturally essential to guard against the danger of one section of society, or even specific individuals, being unfairly affected by the changes, variations and necessary adjustments resulting from the interplay of market forces. Not only economic but also social

45

policies are being integrated within the Community area. Anyone who examines the facts will find that the so-called 'Economic Community' is a social Community as well.

It is not materialistic to include *prosperity* as one of the Community's basic values. Solidarity naturally implies that prosperity is meant 'for everyone' and not just for the few. Prosperity also contributes to the realization of the other values which inspire the work of the Community. It is easier to keep the peace – both internal peace and peace with the outside world – where there is no desperate case of need; people who are content and satisfied are usually also people who are peaceable. Civilization thrives and flowers where there is prosperity, and social advance becomes easier. Prosperity tends to spread its benefits: people can afford to be more generous to those less fortunately placed; aid to under-developed countries is not immediately regarded as a 'sacrifice'.

All my remarks so far on the values animating the Community are simple truths which may well have become accepted as commonplace. But to my mind there is no element in the work of the Community that is as inspiring, as spectacular as the urge to move forward, to advance – in one word, *dynamism*. By this I mean the driving forces that are essential to continue the process of European integration. Integration does not proceed on its own as though propelled by some law of nature; it is a guiding principle that had to be built into the Community. Integration is not a product, but a process. It is a *création continue*. Every fresh step we take creates new situations, new problems, new needs which in turn demand yet another step, another solution to be worked out on a European basis. There is nothing automatic in this process. Nothing in politics is automatic: everything is a matter of human will. Naturally there is a certain flow in the way events move: situations and problems come up in a steady stream, and if we are sensible, we try to tackle them on a broad European basis. The European 'challenge' never stops. Of all the many practical and technical, as well as idealistic and moral, elements that are part of the fabric of the Europe we are building, this 'challenge' is the most constant, the most permanent.

Still, all the Community's basic values which I have enumerated would be worth little if one other essential element were missing:

the element of *certainty*. We live in an age of change, of movement, of uncertainty about the future. At such times man stands in particular need of assurance about what is likely to happen. He searches science for evidence with which to calculate the probable course of future events. In the society in which he lives he looks for laws, rules, regulations, guidelines, to give him some fairly clear idea of the conditions upon which his life and his work depend in the months and years ahead. It is not enough for the Common Market merely to be there; the Common Market must be a firmly-established, secure institution with an assured future. Otherwise no businessman can plan ahead or make long-term investments. There must also be social security. Economic policy must be such as to ensure a stable rate of economic growth. Money, too, must be stable, that is to say 'secure'. These are just a few examples of the important part played by the element of certainty, and it is by means of the Community's legal system and its policies, applied throughout the whole of the Community area, that it is hoped to bring about and strengthen this essential feeling of confidence.

4. *The Rule of Law*

The question then arises: can the Community's basic values be given legal form, or, more important, if they can be given legal form, can these values be enforced by individual citizens of the Community's member-states in courts of law? And secondly, are there basic rights belonging to a citizen of the Community which can be compared to the basic rights of the citizen in a state with a constitution?

The answer to the first question is: no. The general nature of the basic values I have enumerated makes it impossible to translate them into 'legal rights' which the individual citizen can enforce in the courts. They find expression in certain directives contained in the Treaty, and in the rules and regulations issued by the Community. The protection they afford the individual is indirect in its effect: they constitute guidelines, albeit important guidelines, for the decisions and actions of the Community's institutions.

The procedures adopted by the European Court of Justice, however, as well as the writings of eminent jurists like Hans von der Groeben, have recognized that at least some of the principles enshrined in the treaties establishing the Community come very close to providing the individual with the kind of protection which the basic laws of his national constitution afford him. This is true particularly of the clauses providing for equality between individuals and companies within the Community (the insistence on non-discrimination) and for such freedoms as the free movement of persons, goods, services, and capital. Apart from this, the European Court of Justice has in its deliberations been influenced occasionally by the fact that in certain cases before it the principles underlying the legal systems of the six member-states were similar; such an approach could eventually lead to the growth of a body of case-law, embodying what could virtually be described as a Community bill of rights.

Both these tentative developments are noteworthy, because the only legally binding rule which commits both the member-states and the Community – as well as its institutions – to respect human rights, is, apart from the appropriate provisions of the Community treaties, Article 3 of the Statute of the Council of Europe. That article reads:

> Every member-state of the Council of Europe recognizes and accepts the principle of the rule of law and the principle that everyone who comes under its legal and sovereign authority is entitled to the basic human freedoms, and to human rights . . .

Article 3 must not be confused with the 'European Human Rights Convention'. For the 'European Human Rights Convention' is not legally binding for the whole of the European Community since one member-state of the Community, France, has not ratified it.

It would be a mistake to underestimate the importance of establishing a Community law which embodied the basic rights of its citizens. Admittedly, the absence of such a law has not so far raised any practical difficulties. But the recognition of and respect for human rights in all the member-states is surely of the essence of the spirit that animates the Community, a Community that is built upon law and has its own legal system. It is unthinkable even to imagine that a state which did not respect human rights would ever be allowed to join the Community. These rights are an expression of all that is civilized in the constitution of the states, of all that is democratic; they are essential, irrevocable conditions for membership of the Community.

For these reasons the suggestion that the Community as a whole should legally and formally bind itself to adhere to the 'European Human Rights Convention' deserves serious consideration. It is unlikely that a list of basic human rights, drawn up for inclusion in some future federal European constitution, would look very different from the list contained in the Convention.

5. *The Purse-strings*

The arrangements for financing the Community – a subject vital to the work of all public bodies – could for more than a decade hardly be described as perfect. Only the Coal and Steel Community enjoyed an income of its own, derived from contributions from the industries concerned. The European Economic Community and Euratom, on the other hand, were – to quote Bismarck – 'pensioners of the states'. Once every year the Council of Ministers held a budget debate. It was never a very inspiring occasion, because the national financial officials who did the preparatory work for their masters in the sub-committees of the Council of Ministers, and who had only limited authority to commit their countries, were guided by one overriding consideration: fiscal economy. Unfortunately, public opinion at the time was not nearly enough aware of how much the work the Commission had in hand suffered as a result, time and time again. There is no lack of proof of the damage this parsimony caused by delaying many of the Community's operations.

That this happened was not the fault of the Treaty. The Treaty lays down the way in which the 'Financial Contributions of the Member-states' are to be raised according to a carefully-calculated scale of contributions, and goes on to say that this measure is merely a transitional and initial step. Article 201 of the Treaty states explicitly:

The Commission shall study the conditions under which the financial contributions of Member-States provided for in Article 200 may be replaced by other resources available to the Community itself, in particular by revenue accruing from the common customs tariff when finally introduced.

The Commission shall for this purpose submit proposals to the Council.

49

The Council may, after consulting the Assembly as to these proposals, unanimously determine the provisions which it shall recommend the member-states to adopt in accordance with their respective constitutional requirements.

The language of the article is clear and incisive. The matter to be examined is not 'whether' the financial contributions of the member-states are to be replaced by a Community income but 'under what conditions' this is to take place. Again, another question for discussion is not the replacement of members' financial contributions 'only' by the revenue accruing from the common customs barrier but by such revenue 'in particular', thus leaving open for consideration the exploration of other sources of Community revenue.

Of course, some may say that Article 201 states only the obvious. Once internal customs barriers within the Community are abolished, and common customs tariffs established, it becomes plainly impossible to credit the member-state across whose borders goods from outside the Community happen to be imported into the Community with the duty collected on such imports – or, for that matter, to credit any other member-state with the amount. There is simply no control within the Community area of where and in which country such imports eventually end up. Nor should there be such control.

The Council of Ministers therefore acted according to the letter and spirit of the Treaty when it decreed, as far back as January 1962 in Regulation No. 25, that once the common market in agriculture came into force, the revenue derived from the levies imposed on agricultural products imported from non-member countries – these levies are a species of variable duties – should go to the Community, and that this revenue should be used for common Community expenditure.

The Commission also acted equally within the framework of the Treaty and its constitutional position, when, having been asked by the Council of Ministers to submit specific proposals for the financing of the common agricultural policy, it raised, in April 1965, the wider, more comprehensive problem of the financing of the Community in its entirety.

The Commission at that time proposed a two-stage solution for

50

the implementation of a common agricultural policy. As a first stage, the Commission proposed dealing with the contribution of the member-states to the section of the Agricultural Fund which was to meet the cost of export restitutions and of market intervention. This contribution was to rise year by year. As a second stage, the Commission proposed that all revenue from the levies on agricultural imports from non-member countries should go to the Community (as the Council of Ministers had already decreed in Regulation No. 25). The same was to happen with revenue from the tariff on industrial imports from non-member countries (as provided in Article 201 of the Treaty). This was to be brought about gradually, on a scale increasing year by year over a period of five years, so that the full amount of the revenue raised in this way would not have gone to the Community until 1972. Member-states were to be asked to contribute to the Community budget only to the extent that the revenue derived from agricultural and industrial imports fell short of the Community's financial needs.

The Commission combined its financial proposals with a request to involve the European Parliament more deeply in all matters affecting the settlement of and control over the Community budget. It did so in the hope that any move in that direction would eventually promote direct contacts, discussions, and debates with a politically responsible body on matters of substance affecting the whole Community. To this end it suggested a new procedure for passing the Community's budget and for controlling it. Particularly as regards the role of the European Parliament, the Commission proceeded with the greatest caution and circumspection. Its reasons were tactical, for in this sphere it expected to run into strong opposition. It was not mistaken.

Its proposals came to nothing. The French reacted vehemently against them; the reaction of the others was initially lukewarm. French diplomacy chose this particular moment to launch an attack on two basic principles governing the conduct of the Community's business: the majority voting system in the Council of Ministers, and the position of the Commission. For months France absented herself from meetings of the Council of Ministers. This crisis in the history of the Community did not end until January 1966. The French diplomatic offensive failed, thanks largely to the

51

firmness of the other member-states and to their devotion to the letter and spirit of the Treaty.

The point at issue, however, the financing of the Community, one of the most important constitutional questions facing the Six, remained open and undecided. It was one of the greatest achievements of the Hague Summit, the meeting of the Heads of Governments of the Six held in the Dutch capital on 1 and 2 December 1969, to agree among themselves that an answer to this question must be found. In their communiqué (Communiqué No. 5) the Heads of State or Government 'reaffirmed the will of their Governments to pass from the transitional period to the final state of the European Community and accordingly to lay down a definite financial arrangement for the Common Agricultural Policy by the end of 1969'; they also agreed 'progressively to replace . . . the the contributions of member-countries by the Community's own resources' and 'to strengthen the budgetary powers of the European Parliament' (*sic*).

Sixteen Ministers and six State Secretaries (State Secretaries on the Continent are very senior officials ranking immediately below Cabinet Ministers, but unlike Secretaries of State in Britain, the US and the Commonwealth, they are not of Cabinet rank), subsequently spent three days and two nights in almost continuous session – it was in fact the longest session in the history of the Community – to hammer out the details of the agreement reached at The Hague Summit. At four o'clock on Monday, 22 December 1969, they announced the conclusions of their deliberations. The Community was to have its own direct revenues. This income was to come from all customs duties and agricultural levies, and from a small portion (1 per cent, to be exact) of the revenue from the as yet not completely harmonized value-added tax; the member-states were to be allowed an administrative rebate of 10 per cent for collecting and transmitting these various revenues to the Community. With the exception of the Community's administrative budget, the way in which these revenues are spent is determined by the provisions in the Treaty specifically dealing with this aspect, and by the appropriate body of regulations and rules of the Community. This means that the disposition of the Community funds remains in the hands of the Council of Ministers, whose decisions are generally based on proposals submitted by the Commission:

changes in the areas of authority within the Community were not under discussion.

The revenues so raised are to cover the whole of the Community budget which was estimated at well over 4,000 million dollars. These arrangements are to come into force from 1975 onwards (the beginning of the so-called 'normal' or final phase).

An interim arrangement was made for 1970, and there is to be a transitional period from the beginning of 1971 to the end of 1974. During this transitional period all receipts from levies on agricultural imports would go to the Community, as well as 50 per cent of the customs duties collected at the beginning of the transitional period, with the proportion to be handed over increasing by stages; at the same time, during the transitional period, the amount of the customs duties retained by any member-state must not be raised more than 1 per cent from one year to the next or lowered more than $1\frac{1}{2}$ per cent.

The shortfall in the Community's budget during the transitional period is to be met by financial contributions by the member-states. The proportion of each member-state's contribution has been worked out on the basis of a complex 'key' percentage system, taking into account a vast number of factors, and as a result of these calculations the Federal German Republic is to contribute 32·9 per cent to the shortfall in the Community's budget, France 32·6 per cent, Italy 20·2 per cent, the Netherlands 7·3 per cent, Belgium 6·8 per cent, and Luxembourg 0·2 per cent. Even after the beginning of the so-called 'normal' phase in 1975, certain safeguards have been built-in which set limits to the financial contributions of the member-states up to the end of 1977; these mean that national contributions are not to exceed or to fall below the contributions of the previous year by more than 2 per cent.

Next, the Ministers and the State Secretaries turned to the question of budgetary control by the European Parliament. Their discussions on this topic appear to have been no less difficult and no more congenial than on the previous topic.

What emerged eventually, was this: Once the so-called 'normal' phase is reached, that is from 1975 onwards, the European Parliament is to have the final say, subject to certain limitations. The budgetary procedure that is to come into force in 1975 will have four stages: to begin with, the Commission draws up a draft

53

budget for the Council of Ministers, who use the draft as the basis of the budget proposal they submit to the European Parliament; at this second stage the European Parliament can either approve the budget proposed by the Ministers – in which case that marks the end of the constitutional budgetary process in this particular instance – or it can, by a majority vote of its members, alter the proposed budget; if the budget proposal is altered in this way, the third possible stage is reached, and the budget goes back to the Council of Ministers, who can in turn alter Parliament's change by a system of weighted majority voting; should this happen, the possible fourth stage of the process comes into play; Parliament can again either accept the changes adopted by the Council of Ministers or it can reject them. A rejection, however, requires both a simple majority of members and a three-fifths majority of the votes cast.

For the transitional period up to 1975 the following new arrangements were agreed: The Council of Ministers is not to alter Parliament's own budget. As far as that part of the Community budget is concerned that does not deal with the implementation of regulations, rules and policies of the Community as a whole – in other words, primarily the administrative budget which includes press and information services – the Commission proposes an upper limit to any proposed increases in national contributions – and it does so in the light of the size of the Community product as a whole, of national budgets and of the cost of living. As far as that part of the Community budget is concerned that deals with the implementation of regulations, rules and policies of the Community as a whole, the European Parliament is for the first time to be accorded the right to suggest and propose changes. The burden of shaping the budget, then, will in future be shared not only by the Commission and the Council of Ministers but also by the European Parliament.

Looking back over the prolonged struggle to evolve sensible financial provisions in accordance with the constitutional requirements of the Treaty and the Community, one can hardly escape reaching the following conclusions:

1. Although the results that have emerged cannot be described as ideal, they are satisfactory at least in so far as they establish the beginnings of a budget policy which is the Community's own.

54

2. At least five and a half precious years, in which much progress could have been made, have been senselessly wasted.

3. The Community's anonymous non-Gaullist opponents – who are to be found in all countries, and like to pose as 'realists' and as such obstruct the Community and its work whenever they can – have proved too weak to deprive the Community of its financial autonomy.

4. Patience, determination and tenacity have been rewarded.

Chapter Three

The Community Institutions

'Who runs this country?' is the simple, direct question which American observers are apt to ask when they want to discover how a country conducts its affairs and who makes the relevant decisions. It is also a perfectly proper question when it comes to the Common Market, for the Community discharges many of the functions which usually fall within the competence of the separate nation-states. Consequently the third question we must seek to answer about our Community is the question of how it is organized.

Has it a government, a parliament, an administrative apparatus, and law courts? Where there are such institutions, what is their competence and their relationship one to another? Are there such individuals as 'European' civil servants? Since the Community is made up of a number of member-states, what role does traditional diplomacy play? How influential are the 'experts'? Are the so-called 'technocrats' all-powerful behind the scenes? What power do the individual member-states exert over the Community and its institutions? And what about the ordinary citizen, the man in the street? In most nation-states those who share similar interests and aims can band together in trade unions, employers' organizations, and trade bodies to put forward their views more effectively; is the same true within the Community? Is there room for public opinion in all its many facets to form and express itself and make its weight felt?

To find the answer to all these questions, we must turn to the Constitution of our Community or – more important still – to the way our Constitution functions in practice.

The institutions of the Community are the European Court of Justice, the European Parliament, the Council of Ministers and the Commission. I give the four main institutions of the Community in their formal order of precedence, following the custom prevailing in most democracies, which lays it down that the Chief Justice of the Supreme Court ranks immediately below the Head of State; but I should like to reverse the purely formal order of precedence and begin at the other end, with the institutions that initiate action.

Two of the institutions mentioned, the European Court of Justice and the European Parliament, have, from the beginning, served all three European Communities: the Economic Community, the Coal and Steel Community, and Euratom. On the other hand, the three Communities retained separate Councils of Ministers and separate 'executive' bodies until July 1967. It was only then that they were replaced by one Council of Ministers and one 'executive', the Commission, for all three Communities. That was the first step towards the creation of a single European Community. The next step is the formal fusion of the Treaties of Paris, which set up the Coal and Steel Community, and of Rome, which created the European Economic Community and Euratom, in one single agreement.

I. THE COMMISSION

Every action is initiated by the Commission as the executive organ of the Community. It is the most original part of the Community's machinery, with no precedent in tradition. It represents the interests of the Community as a whole, not only against the particular and perhaps occasionally conflicting national interests of its member-states but also *vis-a-vis* the outside world; for the Community must speak with one voice and not with six or ten. For that reason the Commission is entirely independent of the governments of the member-countries, who are not entitled to give it instructions. Admittedly, the nine Commissioners (their number was fourteen from 1967–1970 and may soon be fourteen again) who constitute the Commission are appointed for four years by unanimous agreement between the six governments, but they cannot be dismissed before their period of office is up, either by the six governments or by the Council of Ministers. That can be done only by the European Parliament's passing a vote of no confidence in the Commission; and in that case it would not be individual Commissioners who would have to resign, but the Commission as a whole.

The function of the Commission is threefold: to serve as motor of the Community, as guardian of the Treaty, and as 'honest broker'.

It has a responsibility to draft proposals and plans. This responsibility is not discretionary: it is obligatory, and it is obligatory in two ways. In the first place, the Commission is in duty bound to initiate action in all the many fields laid down in the Treaty of Rome, so that the Council of Ministers is in a position to take the appropriate decisions; in other words, the Commission is entrusted with what virtually amounts to a monopoly in taking the initiative in all matters affecting the Community. There are a few exceptions to this general rule, but these ought to be removed at the earliest opportunity. In the second place, the Commission is called on to initiate action when the interests of the Community as a whole, in the widest meaning of that phrase, so demand.

Furthermore, the Commission is 'the guardian of the Treaty of Rome'. It has to see to it that the Treaty's provisions are kept, and to intervene when its provisions are broken. If necessary, it has to report breaches of the Treaty to the European Court of Justice, a procedure it has adopted in a number of cases and with considerable success.

Finally, although the Commission takes part in the deliberations of the Council of Ministers as a matter of course, its function on these occasions is not merely to initiate and to submit plans, but to help the Council to reach decisions, to act as an 'honest broker' who stands outside national interests. But naturally the Commission must never abuse that function by lending its hand to a compromise which does not accord with the letter or spirit of the Treaty.

To some extent, the Treaty invests the Commission with its own power of decision; this applies in cases where the Commission gives effect to the 'European Laws' contained in the Treaty itself or adopted by the Council of Ministers, and where their implementation calls for a body with an unbiased, objective point of view – a body, moreover, which enjoys a certain amount of latitude of action.

Looking back over my own years as President of the Commission, I had this to say in my farewell address to the European Parliament on 21 June, 1967, on the way the Commission tackled its work:

> The members of the Commission had to constitute a unified, independent, integral body. The Commissioners had to be one, bound together by the principle and practice of collegiality. It is entirely right, in my view, that the Treaty gives the President neither the power to lay down guidelines on policy nor special voting rights when it comes to decisions. Admittedly, every Commissioner was given 'special responsibility' for a particular area of the Community's activities, but this extended only to the preparation leading up to and later to the execution of decisions; the decisions themselves were entirely and exclusively a matter for the Commission as a whole. And no Commissioner could regard himself as the guardian of the interests of his own country, although his colleagues on the Commission naturally looked to him as the most competent and best qualified interpreter of the situation and political circumstances prevailing in his country. This necessity to think and act as 'European' Commissioners undoubtedly makes the highest demands on the moral integrity of the members of the Commission. But it is on this point that the survival of a true European Community depends.

That, as I explained, is how things ought to be. But are they so in fact? Sceptics may well argue that if a Commissioner from one of the member-states is more intelligent, more experienced, more adroit and imaginative than a Commissioner from another member-country, then the first member-state is bound to gain. I think it is fair to pose this question, not least because, despite the fact that the period for which the Commissioners are appointed lasts only four years, there has in fact turned out to be on the whole a certain continuity in the composition of the membership of the Commission, whereas the composition of the Council of Ministers has varied continuously, owing to upsets in the national parliaments of the member-countries and to changes in government brought about by general elections. Probably the only exception in this continuous change in the composition of the Council of Ministers has been the Dutch Foreign Minister, Dr Luns.

On the face of it, then, the relative quality and qualifications of the various Commissioners may seem to matter. But on the basis of experience gained in the first decade of the first Commission of Nine of the European Economic Community, I deny most emphatically that the relative strengths or weaknesses of the individual Commissioners brought the slightest advantage or disadvantage to the member-countries whose nationals they were. Whatever strengths or weaknesses individual Commissioners may have had had a way of disappearing and of being balanced out in the joint deliberations of the Commission, and it is after all the whole Commission acting as a collegiate European body that makes the decisions. This is not to say that individual Commissioners did not put their personal stamp on the work they did and the results they achieved in the special areas of responsibility allotted to them.

So, are they 'technocrats' after all, these gentlemen in Brussels? Whenever this charge is made – for it is a charge which is not meant to be complimentary – the implication is that the Brussels 'technocrats' are in some way a separate and peculiar breed, different in kind from politicians. Yet is not the work done by the Commission the same as the work done by the Ministers? The Commission submits to the Council of Ministers its carefully prepared plans and projects for approval or rejection. If that is not dealing with politics, then one can only conclude that trade and social questions fall outside politics. What is more, the Ministers, too, might well be dubbed 'technocrats' – only, unlike the Commissioners, national 'technocrats' sustained and supported by a national bureaucratic apparatus of tens of thousands of civil servants. At the same time, political requirements should be involved in the appointment of members of the Commission. But perhaps it would be best if we abandoned mistaken and somewhat condescending attempts to distinguish between politicians and 'technocrats'. The truth surely is that politics, the art of governing, has subtly changed in recent times, that it has become more rational, more detailed, more 'technical' – in short, more exact and professional. I think that is the reason why the late President Kennedy introduced entirely new methods of collaboration with the so-called expert 'technicians' into the governmental structure of the United States.

The Commission is served by a Secretariat-General. Originally this Secretariat was meant to be little more than a technical body to assist the Commission as and when required; but under its outstanding French Secretary-General, Emile Noël, it soon acquired a more important role and, though hardly ever noticed by the general public, became an essential part of the Commission's machinery.

The Commission is also served by a staff which performs the expert detailed work required. Although this staff has grown out of the fusion of the three separate staffs which had previously served the EEC, the Coal and Steel Community, and Euratom, it numbers no more than about 5,500 civil servants, a figure that includes the top brass, the Directors-General, as well as the most junior chauffeur. In law their status is that of European public servants.

Broadly speaking, the Administration is organized along the lines of Ministries in national governments. There are a number of Departments, each with a Director-General at its head and responsible for a certain sphere of activity. Each Director-General controls a number of Directors whose Directorates in turn are sub-divided into Divisions. I have never shared the view that in selecting its civil servants the Commission could loftily dismiss the question of the nationality of the candidates, by simply saying: 'We recognize only Europeans.' Such an attitude appears to me not only to be naïve and dogmatic but also to ignore political reality. It is only natural that the nations making up the Community want to see their membership reflected in the composition of the Community's Civil Service. Consequently the Commission follows a rough and ready rule of thumb in filling posts in its Civil Service: a quarter should to to the French, a quarter to the Italians, a quarter to the Germans and a quarter to nationals of the Benelux countries. Incidentally, under this scheme the Benelux countries tend to come off slightly better than the other three.

The terminological question of whether the Commission can rightly be called an 'Executive' may seem pointless, in view of all that has been said. But susceptibilities are such that it has some psychological and political importance. The Commission is not an executive body in the sense that it directly introduces and itself enforces the Community's decision on the member-states. That happens only in a few special cases, for example, in questions relating to cartels. Normally, the Commission informs the member-governments of the directives and regulations issued by the Community, and it is left to the national governments to carry them out. It is a method that has proved itself in Germany, where federal laws are enforced by the *Länder*, the States. In the United States a different constitutional principle prevails: there federal laws are enforced by the federal authorities, and State Laws by the State authorities. The method adopted by the Community has one overwhelming advantage, particularly at this stage when the concept and the reality of common European policies are still a new and strange phenomenon to many ordinary citizens: the decisions of the Community reach them through authorities and civil servants they know, and, more important still, in a language with which they are familiar.

Experience, however, has shown that much still remains to be done to make co-operation between the institutions of the Community and those of the member-governments more effective. The problem often is to find the right institution for the job in hand. For example, practice has revealed that the Council of Ministers by its very nature is not the best instrument for dealing with matters of administration affecting all the member-countries, and many of its functions in this sphere have already been transferred to the Commission.

This trend will have to continue. As I see it, the Commission should eventually be empowered to take all measures necessary for the implementation of the Treaty on its own authority, without having to rely on special and specific approval by the Council of Ministers. Such reserve powers of the Council of Ministers as may be required during a period of transition should be gradually reduced, and the executive authority and competence of the Commission should be limited only where the Council of Ministers and the European Parliament jointly so decree.

Furthermore, as the big and small policy decisions that come before the Commission multiply, the collegiate principle, by which the Commission, and the Commission alone, must at present exercise its executive authority, will in some way have to be relaxed. This could be done by giving the different departments of the Commission under their Directors-General greater responsibility, or by setting up separate agencies. The departments or the agencies would of course continue to act under the general supervision of the Commission, but they would enjoy a measure of limited executive authority in specific fields without having to run to the Commission for approval in every case.

II. THE COUNCIL OF MINISTERS

The Council of Ministers is by its nature the federal institution of the Community. It consists of members of the national governments of the member-states, and they are sent at the discretion and on the instructions of their respective governments. What ministers are sent to particular sessions depends on the subject under discussion: they may be ministers of foreign affairs, economics, finance, justice, labour, agriculture, transport, science; or they may hold some other portfolio. Usually more than one minister is present on behalf of each country, because the Council's deliberations as a rule touch on a number of subjects. Naturally the respective foreign ministries play a leading role and are represented regularly: the depth of their involvement in the Council's work depends partly on tradition, partly on personal interest, partly even on individual temperament.

It is the Council that harmonizes and reconciles the interests of the separate member-states and those of the Community as a whole. It acts not as a mere international conference of ministers from different countries, but as a Community institution. It must take decisions where the Treaty so requires, and its decisions must be reached in pursuit of the aims laid down in the Treaty. The members of the Council must keep the objectives and requirements of the Community firmly in view, even though they view them through 'national' eyes. Their object is to find not the lowest common denominator between the member-states but the highest common ground between the member-states and the Community as a whole.

The Council takes all major policy decisions. It issues the laws, the 'regulations' of the Community.

It is here that the 'dialogue' between the Council and the Commission takes place, and it is this 'dialogue' which forms the core of the Community's organization and its policy-making process. In this sphere, more than in any other, the Commission exerts a stimulating as well as a harmonizing influence. It was of course always meant to play this role in the Community structure, and it does so not only at the sessions of the Council of Ministers, but also at the sittings of numerous special committees – in fact in virtually every activity in which either the Treaty or the Community's laws and regulations demand common action.

To breathe life into the Treaty is a continuous, unceasing process which demands action in a hundred different fields of activity. But it is of course an inexorable rule of politics and of what I might call long-term 'strategic' economics that one cannot pursue a hundred different objectives with equal force and energy at one and the same time. One can do only so much at any given moment, and so one's actions fall into a pattern, a cadence, a certain time sequence. This sequence reveals more clearly than anything else that the pursuit of our ultimate aim imposes its own logic on what we do.

It also reveals something else. It reveals that there are two elements at work as we strive to integrate Europe. One is coldly factual, almost scientific. It deals with the laws of economics. It shows what repercussions a decision in one field of economic policy is bound to have in other fields and what further action may therefore be required. It provides the answer to the question: what is it that has to be done?

The second element, by contrast, is arbitrary, almost opportunistic. It is the sum total of the conditions, the influences which eventually determine whether or not the members of the Community can agree jointly among themselves to do what ought to be done. In other words, it provides the answer to the question: what can be done? Here we see a true example of politics as 'the art of the possible'. After all, an election campaign in his own country can well cause a member of the Council of Ministers to refuse, or at least to delay, agreement to a measure that is generally recognized as necessary.

Integration, then, demands knowledge of the facts and circumstances of the case on the one hand and, on the other, political instinct. The former determines whether action should be taken and what action would be most suitable; the second, the extent and the timing of the action. Not that this distinction has been 'institutionalized' – that is to say, that one Community institution has been entrusted with playing the former and another the latter role. Of course the European executive, the Commission, is particularly concerned with gathering together all available expert knowledge on every case. The success of its work depends on that; for in the last resort, the authority and respect which the Commission commands rest on the soundness of the proposals it lays before the Council of Ministers. Perhaps it is this aspect of the Commission's work that leads some people wrongly to dismiss its members as mere 'technocrats'. If so, a tiny grain of truth, albeit misunderstood, has been magnified to stir up controversy and convey an entirely false impression.

In commenting further on the distinction between the strictly factual and the political aspects of integration, it is only right to point out that the Council of Ministers has increasingly tended to lay down its own time-table for taking decisions, by adopting the method of setting dead-lines by which specified parts of its work must be completed. But it always does this with the agreement of the Commission. In any case, it would be quite untrue to suggest that the Commission's task is non-political. As we have already seen, the Commission has the sole and exclusive right of initiating action in all matters affecting the Community as a whole. It must use its own judgement when it comes to determining what is important and what is not, what needs immediate attention and what can wait a little. It must on some occasions proceed with moderation; on others it must be demanding and forceful. Above all, it must have the determination to see a thing through to the end. Where it is not itself invested with the power of making a decision, its job is to choose a time at its discretion to lay a proposal on the matter before the Council. The proposal must be so formulated that the Council can legalize it and make it Community law by a simple 'Yes'. From time to time, the Commission suggests to the Council that it, the Commission, be invited by the Council to take initiative in certain matters and to submit appropriate proposals to the Council by a fixed date. This may sound very involved and paradoxical but it has the advantage that, if the Council accepts the suggestion and extends the invitation, it is bound to give positive consideration to any proposal the Commission may make.

Discussions about the agenda at meetings of the Council of Ministers are, however, concerned not only with what subject should be dealt with first and what second or third; frequently

65

they are also about what subjects should be taken and decided on together. There were occasions when a member-state was prepared to see action taken in one sphere only if action was agreed and decided on in another at the same time. The reason for this manoeuvre is always the same; the member-state concerned wants to balance the sacrifice it feels it is being asked to make in one sphere against a definite advantage it hopes to gain from action in another. Such linking of subjects (sometimes politely but shamefacedly called 'synchronization') raises difficulties both in practice and in theory. The Treaty recognizes only a general over-all balance within the Community as a whole; the sum total of all the sacrifices each member-state is asked to bear is compensated by the sum total of all the advantages it gains. Consequently, any individual measure that comes up for consideration can, as a matter of principle, be discussed only on its own merits. So-called 'package deals', therefore, present a very special kind of problem, and the Commission has always been extremely reluctant to get involved in such arrangements. We were afraid that attempts at 'linking' different issues and striking bargains, far from promoting progress, might prevent decisions being reached. This was not always the case, but it has happened frequently enough to justify our misgivings. To be sure, the method was mostly employed by member-states when it was a question not of carrying out a specific provision of the Treaty but of filling in gaps and omissions in the Treaty. The Rome Treaty is basically only a 'framework' Treaty, a pre-treaty, a *pactum de contrahendo*, a pact which binds the parties to it to negotiate and conclude further contracts. It sets out a series of objectives in broad outline, leaving the details to be filled in later. The common agricultural policy is a typical example. So were the provisions for accelerating the establishment of the customs union. As a result these and similar cases in fact involved what one might call resumed treaty negotiations, even though the agreements reached were formally unanimous decisions by a constitutional body established under the Treaty, the Council of Ministers. It is a development that is interesting in theory as well as in practice.

As a matter of fundamental principle the Council takes its decisions by majority vote. In questions which are not of great importance, a simple majority is sufficient, and in such cases each member-state has one vote. Most questions, however, require to be decided by a 'qualified majority', the votes of the original six member-states being weighted as follows: France, Germany, and Italy, four each; Belgium and the Netherlands two each; and Luxembourg, one. In questions of extreme importance – as when a Commission proposal has to be decided on, particularly a proposal that may lead to a Community regulation – the required qualified majority must consist of twelve votes. In the enlarged Community of ten, Britain, France, Germany, and Italy are to have ten votes each; Belgium and the Netherlands five each; Denmark, Ireland, and Norway three each; and Luxembourg two. Where the Council decision follows a proposal from the Commission, the required qualified majority must consist of at least forty-three. This means, in the light of the Community's constitution:

Each member-state has at least one vote in the Council.

The qualified majority corresponds to about two-thirds of the weighted votes.

Even though proposals of the Commission require only a qualified majority to be accepted, they can be altered by the Council solely by a unanimous vote, that is to say that each member-state can prevent a Commission proposal being changed in the Council to its disadvantage.

In the Community of Six, the votes of the member-states with large populations are deemed to constitute the required qualified majority only in cases where the resolution before the Council is interpreted as being a Commission proposal in accordance with the Treaty, i.e. only if the Commission approves the resolution. In the Community of Ten, the four largest member-states cannot command a majority alone, and the votes of at least six states are required when the Commission has not made the proposal on which the vote takes place.

In the Community of Six, the group of member-states with comparatively small populations, even when in a minority, can block resolutions which have not come about as a result of a Commission proposal according to the terms of the Treaty. In the Community of Ten, all the smaller states together can block a decision.

The Council can pass resolutions even against the vote of one of the member-states with a large population.

The principle of majority voting is basic to the constitution of the Community. It indicates the lines along which the Council of Ministers may eventually evolve into a Chamber of States, an Upper House. The requirement of unanimity or the right of veto by one state – which amounts to the same thing – is the exception, not the rule. There is one other exception but, if I may, I should like to call it 'half' an exception. It is to be found in the provision which lays it down that the admission of new members requires a unanimous vote. This requirement was included in the Treaty not at the behest of any single state, but by spontaneous and general agreement among all the founder-members. And understandably so. For the admission of new members falls within the competence of the Community only in a procedural sense; in fact, it goes right down to the foundations on which the Treaty is built; it touches the areas of sovereignty which the member-states have not surrendered to the Community but have retained in their own hands; it involves virtually the conclusion of a new treaty with different members, and consequently it must be treated as such.

During the crisis of 1965, French diplomacy tried to do away with majority voting on all issues which, in the judgement of a government of a member-state, affected that state's vital national interests – although a Commission proposal that was materially justified and yet harmed a vital national interest would be a contradiction in terms. There was a divergence on this issue between France and the other member-states. An effort was made to resolve this conflict in Luxembourg in January 1966, but all that emerged was 'an agreement not to agree', an arrangement which hardly deserves to be called even a 'compromise', and which has no legal force. Certainly the Council has shown a marked reluctance since then to reach decisions by a majority vote in cases where there was a possibility that unanimity might be insisted on. Such habits become accepted all too easily, and the Commission must be on its guard that they do not eventually result in the tacit abandonment of the principle of majority voting. If need be, the Commission must turn to the European Court of Justice for help on this issue. For it is on this issue that the Constitution of the Community is at present most seriously threatened and that the Commission is in duty bound to act as its guardians.

Looking ahead, the Community should consider ways and

means of strengthening the principle of majority voting. It could do it by adding appropriate provisions to the Treaty, and these provisions could affect various sectors of the Community's work. They could extend majority voting to areas where unanimity is at present essential, like, for example, the harmonization of laws and legal systems. They could restrict or make more difficult the use of the veto where it still remains to invoke it. One way of doing this would be to tie the use of the veto to a weighted minority voting system, so that the member who wanted to use the veto would have to be joined by one or more states. Another way would be to empower the European Parliament to nullify a veto – naturally only by a special majority. To return to a point I raised a little earlier, it might also be advisable to make specific provision for arresting and indeed reversing the trend of avoiding decisions in the Council of Ministers when majority voting might be challenged. For example, the European Parliament might be declared competent to deal with a Commission proposal which would require only a qualified majority in the Council of Ministers to be accepted, should the Council fail to reach a decision within a set time limit.

The Council's achievements are impressive. This is shown by the Official Gazette of the Community – the publication in which its laws and regulations are issued. Up to 2,700 Regulations are published every year. Undoubtedly the Council is heavily over-worked. It holds between thirty and forty sessions a year – which involves a great deal of time and effort on the part of ministers whose main duties and responsibilities lie in their own countries. Various methods have been tried to ease their burden, such as appointing deputies, and delegating work to committees subject to the authority of the Council, but these methods have not been exploited as they can be. There appears to be only one way still open that offers some prospect of relief: a better and more effective division of the work-load within the member governments. (This is true even of the Federal German Government.) Admittedly, its special committee of 'State Secretaries for Europe' is doing excellent work, but its effectiveness is sometimes blunted by the somewhat diffuse division of responsibilities between different departments.

Like the Commission, the Council is supported in its work by a substructure, consisting of two main pillars: its Secretariat-General and the Committee of Permanent Representatives.

The Secretariat-General of the Council is concerned primarily with providing the Council with the general, non-specialized services it requires for the smooth discharge of its functions, such as the preparation of its sessions, the drafting of minutes, the issuing of statements, publications, contact with other institutions of the Community, and similar matters.

The Council's main support, as far as the substance and subject-matter of its work is concerned, comes from the Committee of Permanent Representatives. These are national civil servants whose position is not unlike that of the representatives of the *Länder* in the Federal German capital, Bonn. They hold the rank and title of ambassadors. Naturally it is part of their duties to see that the institutions of the Community, particularly the Commission, are made aware of their countries' respective national interests, but that is by no means the most important aspect of their work. Their main work is done when they meet as a body in committee. Their meetings, however, are not meetings of the Council of Ministers at a lower level – though one or two ambassadors very understandably would like to think of them as such. The point is that the Council operates at only one level, that of the ministers, and that the Committee of Permanent Representatives is there to assist the Council in the preparation and subsequently in the execution of its resolutions. Inevitably, this can bring the Representatives into conflict with the staff of the Commission or even with the Commission itself. (Such conflicts are not unfamiliar in Bonn between the officials of the *Länder* attached to the *Land* – representatives in the Bundesrat, the Upper House of the German Parliament, and the Federal Ministries.) Unfortunately, the problem involves a little more than a clash between different bureaucracies and perhaps personalities. It is not merely what one might call a psychological problem, which can be resolved with a little tact all round. It goes deeper than that. There is the far more serious aspect that the Permanent Representatives tend to seek unanimity among themselves in everything they do. As a result they are constantly searching for the lowest common denominator on which general agreement can be reached, instead of aiming higher at more positive, more constructive solutions

70

which the method of majority voting alone can produce. Moreover, their approach strengthens the Council itself in its already far too pronounced reluctance to decide matters by a majority vote, a reluctance which has proved extremely detrimental to progress. The European Parliament, therefore, is more than justified in keeping a sharp eye on how the Community's institutions and the bodies set up to assist them to divide the work and functions allotted to them, and on what influence they exert on one another.

But apart from constitutional issues, the work of the Committee of Permanent Representatives is of the greatest value to the development of the Community. They all belong to the *élite* of the national civil services from which they come. The Council of Ministers could not function without the preparatory work done by the Committee; for the body of Community laws and regulations is so technical, detailed and complex that the Council would have to meet every day if it tried to deal on its own with all the questions before it. Of course, every member of the Committee of Permanent Representatives can call on his own Civil Service at home for assistance whenever he wants to; this places him on occasion in a somewhat more fortunate position than the staff of the Commission, which has to rely on its own resources entirely. This disadvantage becomes particularly apparent when once a year the Commission's staff faces the long, painfully laborious job of going over increases in its personal establishment and the budgetary consequences thereof with experts from the various national finance ministries, sent to attend the Council for the purpose. There has not been one occasion when these discussions have not ended in deep disappointment.

The various channels of communication between the Committee of Permanent Representatives and the staff of the Commission on the whole work well. Indeed, these constant contacts at different levels help to create an intellectual and psychological climate in which co-operation comes easily and naturally. People become involved and work together to find solutions to the Community's problems in accordance with the Treaty. This spirit of co-operation survives even differences and upsets in the Council of Ministers. In fact, occasionally it helps to smooth them over. Consequently, to dismiss the Committee of Permanent Representatives as merely another international conference of diplomats would be a very superficial and unfair estimate of the quality of its contribution.

III. THE EUROPEAN PARLIAMENT

In a democracy the system of government rests entirely on the authority of its people, its citizens: 'The power of the state is derived from the people.' And the channel for this in the European Community is the Parliament, which represents the people.

The Parliament formed a part of all three European Communities right from the beginning, but the way in which the now-merged European Community is at present organized leaves quite a lot to be desired from the parliamentary point of view. In fact, the Community can best be described as an 'underdeveloped' democracy. Even if we examine merely the legal status of the European Parliament, we find that it has little, if anything, in common with that of national parliaments in the democracies. In a parliamentary democracy, parliament elects the government, makes the laws and controls the budget. Admittedly, there is a European Parliament, but it does not elect a government because there is no government, in the accepted sense of that term. What we do find laid down in the Treaty are a number of functions not unlike those of an ordinary government, and these are exercised either separately by the Council of Ministers and by the Commission in accordance with the division set out in the Treaty, or jointly by the two bodies acting together.

The European Parliament does control the Commission; for the Commission is the embodiment of Europe's common interests. This control is effectively the same as that exercised on governments in nation-states: the committees of the European Parliament are entitled to interrogate the Commission on its work; the Commission is obliged to submit an annual report and to explain and expound its position in plenary debates; finally, it can be forced to resign as a body by a parliamentary vote of no confidence. But the European Parliament does not control the budget and it has no legislative powers. The power to make Community laws rests with the Council of Ministers; and, while the European Parliament has the right to be consulted by the Council, such consultations can in practice be effective only in so far as the Commission supports Parliament's point of view and succeeds in persuading the Council to follow it.

The European Parliament does not control the Council of Ministers as a body. Each minister is subject merely to the control of his national parliament, and naturally such national parliamentary control means that he is answerable only for his own conduct and action at the sessions of the Council. He cannot be made answerable for the action of the Council as a whole, not least because the Council may have taken a decision by a majority and he may have been outvoted.

In view of this state of affairs, the European Parliament has striven hard to find some means of evolving a system of parliamentary supervision over the work of the Council of Ministers. It has succeeded in establishing yearly *colloquia* with the Council of Ministers. Moreover, members of the European Parliament can now submit written or oral questions to the Council. This is a useful beginning. It may not as yet have much direct influence on the decisions of the Council, but it is significant because it does influence public opinion, for the exchanges of view between Council and Parliament take place in public and attract a great deal of attention.

There is nothing technically 'illegal' about the Community's departures from normal democratic practice: they stem from the Rome Treaty, which was ratified by the parliaments of all the member-states in accordance with their respective constitutions. Nevertheless, these inadequacies are acceptable only as a temporary measure. Certainly almost all public opinion in the Community regards them merely as a provisional solution – a point of departure, no more.

Equally provisional is the method by which members of the European Parliament are at present chosen. The objection to it that one hears most frequently is that the European Parliament is 'not elected directly'. This formulation is not strictly accurate. After all, every member of the European Parliament is also a member of his national parliament – a circumstance which is of no small importance in helping to spread the concept of European unity in the national parliaments – and being a member of a national parliament, he is therefore directly elected. The trouble is that this election does not entitle him to admission to the European Parliament. To join that requires a further selection by his national parliament. In other words, the curious aspect of this procedure is not that the member has not been elected directly. It is that he has been elected directly, not to the European Parliament but to his national parliament to which he continues to belong even after he has joined the European Parliament. This fact that he has been elected only in a national election campaign is crucial to the whole issue. National election campaigns are as a rule mainly about national issues. A candidate's views on European questions arise only incidentally, if at all. What is lacking under the present system is an election campaign about European issues. Such a campaign would force those entitled to vote to look at and examine the questions and the various options on which the European Parliament would have to decide in the months and years ahead. It would give the candidates who emerged victorious from such a campaign a truly European mandate from their electors; and it would encourage the emergence of truly European political parties. The members of the European Parliament cannot at present be said to have a mandate of this kind, although they have in a sense been elected directly.

The problem is not, therefore, that Parliament exercises no control over the European institutions. Indeed it is doubtful whether, if the European Parliament had wider powers, the Community's laws and regulations (except on budgetary matters) would turn out to be very different. The real problem is that the absence of wider powers and the lack of a 'direct' European mandate from the electors undermine Parliament's ability to dramatize and popularize the great European questions and problems as fully as it could. This may not endanger the development of the Community, but it threatens to make the Community something that will become increasingly remote and incomprehensible.

It is only fair to add that the European Parliament does its best within the limits imposed on its activity. Its committees do excellent work, and as a forum of public political discussion it directs attention time and again to the essential criteria for building a united Europe. Hence, despite the inadequacies that have been mentioned, its influence on the development of the Community is considerable; it is an influence that extends over virtually the whole area of the Commission's work.

The need to reform the parliamentary system of the Community is recognized in the Treaty. Article 138, paragraph 3, of the Treaty lays down:

'The Assembly shall draw up proposals for elections by direct universal suffrage in accordance with a uniform procedure in all member-states.

'The Council shall unanimously decide on the provisions which it shall recommend to member-states for adoption in accordance with their respective constitutional rules.'

Of the two institutions mentioned, the European Parliament has been the only one to take action. Without delay, it drew up proposals for elections by direct universal suffrage in accordance with a uniform procedure in all member-states and submitted them to the Council of Ministers. These proposals lay in the files of the Council for more than nine years, from May 1960 onwards; no effort was made to deal with them. Plainly, the Council failed in its duty, a duty expressly imposed on it by the Treaty of Rome, in a matter of considerable importance to the Community. It was only in the middle of 1969 that the matter was once again placed on the agenda of the Committee of Permanent Representatives and of the Council. Later in the same year, the communiqué issued after the Hague Summit Conference of the Six devoted one sentence to the matter: 'The question of elections by direct universal suffrage is to be studied further [sic] by the Council of Ministers'.

Obviously the Treaty was designed to encourage the removal of the inadequacies in the Community's parliamentary system at the earliest possible moment, by the introduction of direct elections to the European Parliament. Under the Parliament's own proposals, this was to be done in two phases. In the first phase, elections to the European Parliament were to be linked with elections to the national parliaments of the member-states, and candidates were to have the opportunity of being elected both to the European and to their own national Parliament in the same election. In the second phase all seats in the European Parliament were to be contested in an election, entirely independent of national elections.

A directly elected European Parliament would be truly representative of all the peoples of Europe and their interests, and it would provide the motor for Europe's combined strength. If this is to come about, it would of course be necessary to move step by step towards a uniform system of electing members. For example, there might be a case for aiming at having one representative for 750,000 people. To ensure that even the smallest countries were adequately represented, every country would have to be allowed to elect at least, say, three members.

The powers of the European Parliament would also need to be extended by stages in a number of ways: Parliament should be given greater responsibility in determining the relations between the institutions of the Community; it should play a part in the appointment of the President and the other members of the Commission either by making the appointments itself or by being given the right of nominating or of objecting to candidates.

In the legislative field it must be given real powers as well as the right, like the Commission, to initiate proposals for Community laws. Again, this would have to be done in stages. As long as the Council remains the ultimate legislative authority, Parliament should be accorded the right of blocking legislation in certain special circumstances. But once Parliament is elected directly, it must be given an increasing share of the Council's lawmaking powers. In this way Council and Parliament would develop into a kind of two-chamber legislative body, and Europe's Parliament would be assured of effective influence over the Council's work.

Furthermore, the European Parliament would eventually have to be given full control over the Community's budget. The Hague Summit Conference of the Six indicated where a start should be made along this road.

Finally, the European Parliament could be empowered to refer to the European Court of Justice cases where the Treaty had been infringed. At present only the Commission has the right to do so.

The European Parliament at present consists of 142 members; in an enlarged Community of ten, it would have 208. Of their own accord, its members sit not as national delegations but as thirty-seven European political groups: in 1971 there were fifty-one Christian Democrats, thirty-seven Socialists, twenty-three Liberals (including those who regard themselves as close to the Liberals), eighteen members of the European Democratic Union, and nine members who are not formally associated with any of the above groupings. The nine include the Italian Communist deputies who have sat in the European Parliament since March 1969 – which means that the Communists, too, are now for the first time represented there.

IV. THE COURT OF JUSTICE

Since the member-states are as a matter of principle responsible for giving effect to and carrying out the Community laws, their enforcement in case of disputes is in the first instance left to the national courts. If the national courts, however, were the guardians of the Community laws, anomalies would soon arise in the administration of justice. In the first place, since national courts are by their nature concerned only with disputes in their own countries, there would have been no court of law which was competent to deal with disputes between member-states or between member-states and institutions of the Community, between different Community institutions (the first such case to be dealt with, in March 1971, was between the Commission and the Council); or between the Community and its staff or third parties. Secondly, the national courts – as past experience in similar circumstances suggests – would almost inevitably have interpreted the Community laws in different ways and hence undermined the uniform application of the Community laws.

The European Court of Justice was set up to avoid these two anomalies. It has the very special responsibility of seeing that the Community laws are interpreted on a uniform basis throughout the Six.

The Court is composed of seven judges who are supported by two advocates-general. It has, since its creation, met in formal session more than 1,500 times to deal with nearly 720 cases. In about 520 of these cases it has so far handed down a decision. Member-states have asked the Court for rulings on the interpretation of the Community laws 107 times in the first thirteen years since the Treaty came into force. Fifty-two such requests have come from Germany, twenty-four from the Netherlands, fourteen from Belgium, nine from France, five from Italy, and three from Luxembourg.

In its proceedings the Court has dealt with Community questions of every sort – questions involving heavy industry, agriculture, social policy, customs, taxation, rules of competition, patent law and, last but not least, questions involving individuals. It has been asked to give judgement in sixteen cases where member-states had infringed Community law, and in every instance its judgement has been respected and carried out.

The judgements the Court hands down breathe life into the body of Community law, and the reasoning that underlies these judgements demonstrates the soundness of the Community's rules. In fact, if it were not for the Court, Community law would not enjoy the respect and authority which governments, parliaments and ordinary citizens accord it today.

There is no doubt about the absolute primacy of the Community laws over national law, and there have been instances in which the European Court of Justice has overruled the decisions of national courts. Such cases are likely to increase in future, and when that happens it will become necessary to extend the powers and functions of the Court and make it easier for litigants to have access to it.

V. OTHER BODIES

Apart from its four main constitutional institutions – the Court, the European Parliament, the Council of Ministers and the Commission – the Community is also served by a number of ancillary bodies. The most important of these is the Economic and Social Committee which acts as a kind of 'Federal Economic Council' to the Community. Consisting of 101 members (to be increased to 153 in the enlarged Community), appointed by the Council of Ministers for a period of four years, it includes representatives of employers' organizations and trade unions, and thus reflects and helps to harmonize and integrate the vast variety of economic and social interests within the Community. It advises the Council of Ministers and the Commission on all important matters of economic and social policy. On some questions it has the right to be heard, but even where that is not the case its advice is usually treated with respect. The Committee has formed a number of specialist groups and sub-committees, and its expert advice is extremely valuable in formulating Community policies. But the contribution it makes goes beyond the purely practical. The mere fact that it brings together men and women from different walks of life to work as a team on European problems, makes it a powerful contribution to the growth of a European spirit.

Another important body is the European Investment Bank. Set up by the Treaty for the purpose of helping to finance 'smooth and balanced' development within the Community, it enjoys separate legal status.

Its main tasks are to encourage investment in the economically less-developed areas of the Community; to assist in creating more jobs; and to help finance modernization and re-equipment schemes and new projects of general Community interest, involving several member-states. In pursuing these tasks, it is to use its own resources and to avail itself of the facilities of the capital markets.

The Bank soon won the respect of the world of international finance and business and has shown all the virtues of a prudent yet imaginative banker. It has been extremely active – and effectively so – in all the tasks it was set. About half of its development loans have gone to Italy (which incidentally has supplied more funds in this field than any other country). The Bank has also helped to finance development projects in countries having association agreements with the Community, for example in Greece, Turkey, and some African states. It has assisted regions whose economic structure was unbalanced. It has raised money to develop the infrastructure of the economy, like long-distance transport, and more recently the industries of the future. At the same time, it has shown particular interest in the chemical industry, in coal and steel, and in the machine-tool industry. Those last-mentioned branches have received about two-thirds of its loans for industrial development.

Since its foundation the Bank has made loans totalling the equivalent of 1,813 million dollars. It has availed itself of the EEC's capital markets to a larger extent than was originally anticipated. In these markets it has raised no less than the equivalent of about 1,000 million dollars. It has also tapped the reservoir of European savings through the Eurodollar market to the extent, up to the end of 1968, of nearly 300 million dollars, all raised by international syndicates composed of European and American finance houses. This certainly marks a new form of co-operation between American and European investment banks.

VI. ORGANIC GROWTH

The Community cannot be understood merely by reference to the powers and actions of its institutions. Other factors, which escape juridical definition, play their part. They are often intangible, but they help to form the climate of opinion in which the Community does its work, and to sustain the principles on which it is based.

The most important factor is the attitude of the member-states and their governments. If one asks how far the Community has become a reality, one is in fact asking how loyal the member-governments have shown themselves to the letter and spirit of the Treaty. And with one or two spectacular exceptions, the general answer is positive. This is truly impressive in view of the self-denying ordinance that the Treaty imposes on the member-states.

The attitude of the member-states is important because it is the states that enforce and carry out the Community laws. The Community itself has no machinery for doing so, although its institutions have the right to supervise the way in which the member-states perform their duties. The Treaty contains detailed provisions as to supervision and examination.

But it is by no means the case that national civil servants come into contact with the Community only when they have to enforce the laws. Far from it. Of course they are involved at the sessions of the Council of Ministers, but more important still is the fact that they are brought in at the very early stages of decision- and law-making. They help to shape regulations as they are being drafted and formulated. It is impossible to exaggerate the significance of their participation in this process. After all, national civil servants are, by the very nature of their jobs, the last persons one would expect to yield even a fraction of national sovereignty, let alone to encourage actively the transfer of national powers and functions to Brussels. Here their participation in the law-making process works its own special magic. It brings them into continuous personal contact with officials of the Community who, by the nature of their jobs, must view every problem 'in the round', not from a particular national viewpoint but with a view to the benefits for the Community as a whole. There is a steady stream of civil servants from all branches of the administrations of the member-states passing through Brussels for conferences and consultations. There are experts on agriculture, taxation and the law; specialists on the intricacies of GATT; customs officials; dedicated guardians of national currencies; and a host of economic sages. Most of them, when they first arrive, are determined to protect their national interests as they see them. But contact with officials who have to take a wider view gradually changes their approach. They become involved, and sooner or later their attitude to the problems before them becomes more European.

In 1968, for example, the Commission held no less than 1,450 meetings with civil servants and experts from the member-states, involving more than 16,000 national officials. The way in which the Commission's Quarterly Economic Report is prepared illustrates how these contacts work in practice: the Commission's Directorate-General for Economic and Financial Policy prepares a draft; a European official of the Commission then checks the details with national ministries, the central banks, the economic institutes, etc. of each member-country; next, the report is carefully examined by the committee of economic experts (composed of national civil servants and independent economists) with the assistance of the Commission's Economic Committee and its relevant sub-committees. Similar procedure is followed in matters affecting agricultural policy.

Doing things in this way has one other advantage. It frequently makes it possible to reach agreement at the lower civil-servant level without taking matters to the Council of Ministers. Certainly it considerably reduces the length of the deliberations in the Council. But in taking full advantage of this process, two rules must be carefully observed; in the first place, the Council and the Commission must remain equal in status; the Council must not be placed in a position where it merely rubber-stamps matters put before it and so might be considered to have become subordinate to the Commission. And in the second place, it must always be crystal clear which institution is responsible for what; there must be no blurring of the respective areas of competence of the two institutions.

The European Parliament watches carefully that these two rules are strictly observed. And understandably so; for if they were to be broken, Parliament would have difficulty in exercising its function of controlling the Commission.

Another important factor in the evolution of the Community, particularly in the application of its economic and social policies, has been the attitude of the industrialists, bankers, farmers, trade unionists, businessmen, traders and workers within the Six. Right from the beginning they have assumed, with a degree of certainty which one can only describe as audacious, that the aims of the Treaty would be realized, and they have acted accordingly. Their attitude is reflected in all sorts of ways. There are new investment projects within the Community; new enterprises have been launched; new links have been forged between enterprises in different member-states (though the fusion of enterprises has so far been comparatively rare); trade and marketing patterns, both within the Community and with the world outside, have changed; and there have been considerable movements of workers. If all this were not happening, we would not be on the point of beginning to forge a single European economic entity.

The professional economic associations exert a steadily increasing influence on the process. Most of them have come together and organized themselves on a Community-wide basis. There is a European Association for Private Banks, a European Committee of Commercial Associations, a European Union of Industries, a European Committee of Farmers' Organizations, and a European Committee of Consumers' Councils. The sum total of such organizations in industry and agriculture already exceeds 250. It is a development which the Commission welcomes, because these combinations help to eliminate national differences of approach to and action on economic problems, and ease the Commission's work by providing a European framework for economic thinking and planning.

Workpeople, organized in trade unions, play an important part in this process. The trade unions were among the first and the firmest supporters of the idea of European integration, and their national associations sent representatives to each of the three Communities as soon as these were founded. In the spring of 1967 the national associations joined together to form a European Federation of Trade Unions. The first European trade union (the 'European Metalworkers' Union') was founded in Brussels in June 1971; with 3.2 million members, it represents 80 per cent of all organized labour in that branch of industry. With all these organizations the Commission has established a basis for close and fruitful co-operation.

No list of the factors which have a bearing on the future of Europe would be complete without mentioning the many private associations, big and small, which were formed to promote the idea and the ideal of a united Europe. They serve to remind us of the high objectives we have set ourselves. They generate enthusiasm for our cause, and they are a constant source of encouragement.

There is one last factor which must be taken into account – the publicity given to the Community's work by the press, radio and television. The news media are like a mirror which reflects everything the Community does in all its details, for the whole world to see and judge. There are now nearly 100 correspondents from Europe and the rest of the world accredited to the European institutions in Brussels. Among them are some of the men and women best informed about our work, which benefits from their reports, their comments and their criticism.

Chapter Four

Forces for and Against

I. VESTED INTERESTS

We have examined the structure of the Community, its institutions, and the powers and functions of the men who belong to those institutions. But what are the factors which determine how they exercise their powers and functions, how they formulate their policies and carry them out?

Both the supporters and the opponents of European unity frequently tend to answer these questions in a way that can be misleading.

The latter portray those who seek to make a united Europe a reality as idealists, given to wishful thinking and with their heads in the clouds.

The former take delight in pointing out that what matters is the 'political will'. What they mean by that is usually left somewhat vague. Surely they cannot merely mean that those who are trying to unite Europe are acting as they wish, and since what they wish to do is political, it therefore requires a 'political will'. That would be a circular argument. It is much more likely that what is meant is a firm belief in, a passionate commitment to, the ideal of a united Europe. There are many to whom it is virtually an article of faith that the world will become a better place and all mankind richer if only those who lived in Europe became more 'European'. Let no one underrate the force of such idealism. It drives us forward, and without it Europe would never become truly integrated. But it is not the only driving force, essential though it is. There are others, and just because they are more down-to-earth, this is no reason for ignoring their importance. Admittedly, 'man does not live by bread alone', but he does need bread in order to live. We must therefore look at the practical advantages which the European Economic Community is bringing about, the more so since an economic and social venture such as ours is concerned with material interests and benefits.

84

In short, the ideal of political union by itself is not enough. Economic good sense and social progress are equally important, and it is the combination of these three elements which provides the key to the successes we have achieved in the past and will achieve in the future. No one therefore need be ashamed if he pursues practical, materialistic interests in the Community. To do so is not an 'un-European activity', a sin against the ideal of European unity. On the contrary, it deserves and receives support. Naturally the touchstone of such support must be the extent to which it promotes the integration of Europe and the development of common interests. Certainly employers and workers both have an enormous stake in the Community because it provides them with a Continental-sized market and a vastly enlarged economy. But what of the consumer? What is his stake? This is a question we cannot avoid. The consumer is supposed to be king in a market-orientated economy whose aim is 'prosperity for all'. His position, however, cannot be assessed by simply finding out whether prices have gone up or down or remained the same. What matters is whether the Common Market has brought him advantages or disadvantages, or made no difference at all. What has happened is this:

(i) The abolition of customs barriers between the Six means that goods produced and circulating within the Community are cheaper. In some instances the reduction in price may be only relative, in the sense that the impact of rising costs is matched by the removal of customs duty. In any case, the national exchequers of the Six forgo substantial sums, and, as far as the ordinary consumer is concerned, these represent direct or indirect savings.

(ii) Increased competition within the enlarged economic framework of the European Common Market provides greater opportunities for producing a wider range of goods more cheaply.

(iii) An enlarged and correspondingly more competitive European market compels producers to rationalize and specialize. Again, the consumer benefits.

(iv) The Common Market provides the consumer with a wider choice of goods. He is able to pick and choose to a greater extent than before the Common Market was set up.

(v) When inflationary pressure inside one of the member-states

85

builds up to the danger level, the absence of internal customs barriers within the Community acts as a kind of automatic safety-valve, because goods and services at reasonable prices can flow freely across the frontiers of the Six. In other words, economic stability can, so to speak, be 'imported' from the other member-states.

(vi) The Community stimulates economic growth and consequently leads to a greater rise in national income than would have been possible otherwise. As a result, all wage and salary earners are in a position to consume more if they want to. For example, in Germany in the last twelve years the price of consumer goods has risen by only 35 per cent while wages have gone up by some 130 per cent.

(vii) The Community, as constituted by the Treaty of Rome and developed subsequently, encourages the free interplay of market forces. It is not some group of officials that determines in its wisdom what people need or should have; it is the consumer who decides what is produced and put on the market.

Apart from employers, employees, and consumers, the member-states, too, have a stake in the successful development of the Community. Their varying national self-interest is a strong incentive for working together at the integration of Europe.

The Federal German Republic About 19 per cent of Germany's gross national product is exported in the form of goods – which means that economic expansion and full employment in Germany depend on the success or failure of her export trade. In 1958 over a quarter of her exports, representing more than 4 per cent of her gross national product, went to the other five member-states. Consequently, the establishment of the Community, which allowed the free flow of goods across frontiers, secures for Germany a more assured market than she had previously for this important part of her export trade, and so leaves her less at the mercy of fluctuations in world trade as a whole. Moreover, while trade between Germany and the other five members represented 27 per cent of Germany's total export trade before the Common Market was set up, it has since risen to 40 per cent of the total. In other words, the German economy, which depends so heavily on

86

exports, is assured of greater stability and is less exposed to dangers.

At the same time trade with other regions or groupings such as EFTA has not suffered as a result of this trend. On the contrary, Germany's imports from the EFTA countries rose by over 150 per cent between 1958 and 1969, and her exports to the EFTA countries by about 150 per cent. Those in Germany who allege that German trade with the EFTA countries may have been adversely affected – it is impossible to measure this with complete accuracy – ought to remember that what the German economy may possibly lose in trade with the EFTA countries is made up by increased German trade within the Community, because any disadvantage that German exports may suffer in the EFTA countries, as a result of the preferential treatment the EFTA members accord one another, is balanced by the advantage which German products enjoy within the Common Market over products imported into the Common Market from the EFTA countries – the more so, since the European Community's common external tariff is, generally speaking, higher than those of some of the EFTA countries. Naturally, the trading pattern between EFTA and the Common Market has brought about some regional changes in the economic structure within the Federal German Republic, and we must keep an eye on the effects these changes may have.

There is a further element that is likely to benefit the Federal German Republic as well as the other five member-states of the Community. If the letter and the spirit of the Treaty of Rome are to be carried to their logical conclusion, then the Community must eventually pursue a common conjunctural policy. Once this comes about, the conditions which have a bearing on the economy of the whole world will have been altered dramatically. The European Community is already one of the world's most powerful industrial complexes, together with the United States, the Soviet Union and, more recently, Japan. The Community is also the greatest single trading entity in the world. As it continues the process of stabilizing its own economy, so it introduces an ever-greater degree of stability into world trade and the economy of our globe as a whole. A by-product of this development is that Germany's export trade with countries outside the Community, which continues to depend on the world economic climate, is bound to be able to operate under more favourable conditions than before.

It is sometimes suggested that the economic integration of Europe is helping Germany to become the dominant economic force in the Community, if not in Europe. Certainly Germany was the biggest member-state when the Community was set up, and she remains its biggest member to this day. But whatever start she may have had when the Community was founded has decreased and not increased since. Germany and France were and are, roughly speaking, economic equals. Both countries contribute about a third each of the gross Community product. The German share as a whole is slightly higher than the French, and the Germans produce a little more per head of population than the French since the revaluation of the mark and the devaluation of the franc; the increase in industrial production in both countries has, since 1958, been below the average Community rate of growth of the remaining third of the gross Community product; more than half is provided by Italy. This reflects her enormously high economic growth-rate since 1958. In that time Italy has increased by 170 per cent what she produces per head of population, and her industrial production had by 1969 increased by 141 per cent, as against the average Community increase of 100 per cent. To round off the picture, the rest of the gross Community product is contributed by the Benelux countries.

Germany is, as I have pointed out, more dependent, because of her economic structure, on her exports than are her Common Market partners, and this is still reflected in the relevant statistics. But, even so, Germany's trade within the Community has expanded less rapidly than that of France and Italy. By 1970 German trade inside the Common Market area had increased by just 500 per cent, as against the average Common Market increase of 630 per cent, while Italy's trade had risen by 933 per cent and France's by 763 per cent. On the other hand, Germany remains well ahead of both France and Italy as far as trade with countries outside the Common Market is concerned. Yet if one wants to get a true picture of the competitiveness of the French and Italian economies, one has only to note that both France and Italy increased their industrial exports to Germany by more than 870 per cent and 635 per cent respectively between 1958 and 1970 – eloquent proof, if proof is needed, of Germany's considerable importance to her partners in the Community, both as a customer and as a supplier.

A brief reference to the increase between 1958 and 1970 in the gross gold and convertible currency reserves of France, Italy, and Germany might not be out of place at this point: in France the reserves rose by 365 per cent to 4,900 million dollars; in Italy by 735 per cent to 5,000 million dollars; and in Germany by 160 per cent to 11,500 million dollars. The economic and social upsets which shook France in 1968 weakened her strong foreign-exchange position to some degree, but despite these quite abnormal events and the consequences they had, it would be absolutely wrong to claim that Germany was left in a dominant, not to say domineering, position within the Community.

France The traditionally protectionist outlook and direction of French economic policy at one time threatened the country with economic stagnation. In fact, so great was this threat that there was a serious danger that the twentieth century might pass France by altogether. The only way to avoid that danger was a challenge as formidable as joining the Common Market, which meant breaking with national protectionism and adapting to the conditions of an enlarged European internal market. Membership of the Common Market also offered the only means of effectively grappling with the serious social unrest and agitation – almost revolutionary in character – which had gripped France's agricultural population, at that time amounting to over a fifth of the country's total number of inhabitants. What the situation demanded was a wider outlet for French agricultural products, and an enlarged European market provided the only possible solution.

Belgium The Belgian economy has in the past rested on the twin pillars of heavy industry – coal and steel – and textiles. Unfortunately, both these industries are going through difficult times everywhere in the world, largely because the basic pattern of our modern economy is changing. Moreover, Belgian prosperity suffered as a result of the loss of its overseas possessions. The Belgians therefore had every incentive to look for new ways and means of stimulating and expanding their economy, and their geographical position provided them with the obvious key to their future. Lying within North-west Europe's 'industrial triangle', the heaviest concentration of industry in the whole Community area, they were ideally placed, but they could hope to exploit their

89

position only by integrating their economy with those of neighbouring France, Germany, and the Netherlands.

Italy For generations, Italy has suffered from the scourge of unemployment. Her great hope in joining the European Community, therefore, was that this scourge might at long last be removed. She has already made enormous efforts to step up production and exports and so exploit the new opportunities for expansion which a wider European market offers. Indeed, one can truly talk of an Italian 'export explosion'. Its effects have been felt mainly in France, but it has also made its impact in Germany. Another advantage which Italy hopes to derive from its membership of the Common Market is capital, which is sorely needed to develop the under-developed regions of the country. As a member of the Community she expects to find it easier to raise the required sums.

The Netherlands The Dutch economy has always to a large extent depended on its great ports. The creation of a Common Market without customs barriers or trade restrictions gave these ports a hinterland stretching deep into Central and Southern Europe and so offered the Netherlands new opportunities of expanding her industrial potential. Of course, it also offered her the chance of expanding her freight and long-distance haulage enterprises, a field of activity in which the Dutch had always played a leading role. Finally, Dutch, like French, agriculture needed more outlets for its agricultural products.

I have called this part of the book 'Vested Interests', but when the Treaty of Rome was concluded in 1957, they were no more than hopes and expectations. It is only since then that they have become 'vested interests', binding together the member-states more firmly with every day that passes and justifying their membership of the Community. Some people still tend to say in a rather melodramatic fashion that the economic integration of Europe demands 'sacrifices' on the part of all member-states, but I would suggest that it is not only a considerable achievement but also – to put it crudely but plainly – exceedingly good business. And it is good business for countries outside the Community.

Very well, the cynics may argue, it may be within the realms of possibility to harmonize some of the economic interests of the member-states and evolve a common Community policy. But what happens when the interests of the member-states conflict with one another or with the common Community interest? Is the gradual accumulation of these differences and conflicts not likely to bring the process of European integration to a full stop sooner or later?

The men who drew up the Treaty of Rome foresaw this danger and made provision for settling conflicting interests that might arise after the Treaty had come into force.

Such provision was entirely reasonable and justified. Of course, there are differences and conflicts between the interests of member-states, and they are neither few in number nor insignificant in substance. One member-state has special interests in Africa, a second in South America, and a third in Asia. One member-state favours keeping its foreign-exchange reserves in gold; another prefers convertible foreign currencies. There are significant differences in emphasis in agricultural policy; one member-state may encourage basic agricultural production; another may wish to stimulate dairy and meat production. In some countries agriculture may be regarded as a responsibility which the nation as a whole should shoulder irrespective of cost; in others the farmer may be treated like any other producer whose existence depends on his success or failure in the market-place. Again, in some member-countries, the government takes an active part in determining investments and shaping economic policy; in others, market forces are left free play.

There is no solution which can be applied universally in every case where it becomes necessary to strike a balance between conflicting interests and arrive at a common Community policy. Occasionally a solution is arrived at by what one might call 'arithmetic'. For example, when it is a question of fixing a common external Community customs tariff or quota with the outside world, the level may be decided by working out an arithmetical compromise between the various customs and quota levels which different member-states previously had with non-member countries. At other times, the solution adopted means that the Community will 'not only' do this, 'but also' do that. It will watch 'not only' over trade with Africa, 'but also' over trade with America; in international customs negotiations it will keep an eye over the Community's exports 'not only' of industrial 'but also' of agricultural products. In short, in finding acceptable compromises in order to reconcile conflicting interests, the Community must be prepared to show infinite resource and elasticity. For example, when common grain prices were first fixed for the Community as a whole, the level was below that prevailing in German agriculture, and it was decided to make up the difference to Germany out of Community funds; and when the revaluation of the mark created a new price differential, the Community agreed to further compensation payments.

It goes without saying that no community can exist without conflict. The partners in any joint enterprise are bound to be different, and that difference can be a source of strength. Indeed, tension can be creative and make for progress. Certainly in a European Community like ours there can be no advance, no development without opposition, and every time the common purpose triumphs over a particular and special interest our cause is strengthened.

II. OVERCOMING OPPOSITION

Any account which sets out to trace the development of the European Community cannot confine itself to the forces which are actively working for the unification of Europe. Nor can it deal only with the economic, social and political conditions prevailing on the Continent which argued for closer co-operation, nor solely with the various interest groups who wanted to see integration brought about, and were eagerly looking forward to exploiting the opportunities it promised to open up. Those of us who undertook to try to build a united Europe knew that our job would require hard work, patience and discipline; that it would be a long, uphill struggle. We also knew that it would mean argument, disagreement, conflict and crises. Such is the stuff of politics.

In the period between 1950 and 1957, when the basic principles upon which European unity was to be established were being settled, everybody was aware of the immense difficulties we faced. It is only the passage of time that somehow created the illusion in restrospect that everything was moving ahead smoothly in those years. Today it is easy to forget the formidable obstacles that had to be overcome in the 1950s. In West Germany, for example, the policy of reunifying Germany – a policy that was frequently misunderstood and misinterpreted – was given greater importance by many than the unification of Europe. In other countries there were people who were afraid of a unified Europe in which Germany would enjoy equality with and eventually become stronger and more powerful than her partners. Separate national military traditions formed another obstacle. And even then many sincere Europeans were arguing that to create a united Europe on the basis of the Six might preclude a larger, more comprehensive unification of Europe.

Once that period was over, one success followed another in rapid succession and apparently almost without effort. The right road, so it seemed, had been chosen, and there was no stopping the triumphant advance of the European Economic Community. The results we achieved in the early years – and many of them were indeed spectacular – appeared to confirm not only that Europe could in fact be unified but also that, in insisting on equality, the constitutional approach, and supranational law, we had picked the right methods to attain our goal. At that stage a superficial observer might easily have come to the conclusion that the forces opposed to unification had been routed once and for all and would cause no further concern.

Events, however, turned out somewhat differently. Not that the opposition made itself felt all at once and in full force. To begin with, the fundamental decisions that had been made on the way the Community should develop were not questioned. Such opposition as there was took place within the normal framework of discussion and in the ordinary course of exchanges of opinion. For example, there was some argument about whether German policy should be 'European' or 'Atlantic' and whether one excluded the other. There was also some concern that the unification of Western Europe might affect adversely the easing of tension between East and West.

The first serious danger sign came in 1963 with the crisis over British membership. It was not until just over two years later, in the middle of 1965, that battle was joined. Gaullist France turned from latent opposition to open attack on supranational Europe. But the attack failed. The firm front maintained by the other five member-states, including Germany whose attitude never wavered, eventually brought France back to the conference table at the meeting held in Luxembourg at the beginning of 1966. No less important, France did not formally 'withdraw' from the Community during the crisis. Of course it would have been a breach of the Treaty of Rome to do so, because there is no provision in the Treaty which allows any member to 'withdraw' and leave the Community, but that is probably not the only reason that restrained France. What is likely to have weighed far more heavily with the French government is the serious damage France would have suffered as a result of such a step. Integration had already gone too far, and French interests would have been grievously injured.

Although the direct French assault failed, the repercussions of the 1965 crisis continued to affect the work and progress of the Community in the years that followed. The French persisted in their open hostility to supranational integration. Old ideas of hegemony took on new life. It can therefore hardly have come as much of a surprise when France vetoed Britain's second attempt to join the Common Market. This veto was much resented by the other members of the Community. They left France in no doubt about their feelings, and their actions reflected their feelings. They hoped that by standing firm they would eventually wear down French opposition to the basic principles of the Community. But their hopes failed to be realized. In fact, the other members of the Community gradually became infected with some of France's nationalistic approach to Europe's problems, and there was a danger that what were thought to be important national aims would be given priority over common Community policies. Admittedly, the idea that a developing and more integrated Community was a matter of considerable self-interest to every member-state was never entirely lost sight of, but it was an idea that tended to be increasingly overlooked whenever a member thought an immediate national advantage could be gained. Moreover, integration was fast approaching the stage where economic and monetary policies, up till then the exclusive preserve of nation-states, had to be fused. In fact, we were coming close to tackling the core of the Community's concept and its practical implications. And these practical implications caused hesitation in many quarters. Were economic and monetary policies to be determined by the Community? If so, what remained of national sovereignty? There was a noticeable revival of nationalism, and national officials frequently tended to insist that theirs must be the dominant role in conducting the Community's business. Their arguments and those of their political masters were for the most part couched in modern, undogmatic terms, but they reflected an attitude, an approach, which we had hoped belonged to a bygone age. In this atmosphere even the Franco-German Friendship Treaty could not function as cordially and effectively as it was intended to.

The events of those years made two things plain.

In the first place, the establishment of the Community and its achievements to date cannot be taken for granted. The continued existence of the Community is not guaranteed by some law of nature. What has been won so far must be re-won every day – a fact which must be brought home particularly to those who expend their energies and their authority in constantly reminding the world how much still remains to be done in building a truly united Europe. Those of us who are working towards that objective are only too painfully aware of how much further we still have to travel! But it is only from the firm base of what we have achieved that we can move forward and seek to eliminate the remains of the old order in Europe. The Community is the lever by which the Europe of tomorrow can be created. For this reason, the maintenance of the European Community, its proper functioning and its creative forces are essential to the task of unifying and integrating Europe.

The second point which the events of the 1960s revealed was that the way in which member-states saw fit to conduct their foreign policy, constituted and caused the most threats to the advancement of the European cause.

Can the refusal of Gaullist diplomacy to accept the Community method be explained only on the ground of dogmatic obstinacy? – a refusal, incidentally, which never led France herself to break openly with the Community but which tried to push the other members to make this move out of sheer exasperation. It is difficult not to come to the conclusion that France's deliberate strategy of provoking crises in Western Europe was not unconnected with her attempts to evolve a new policy towards the East. Paris wanted to establish a special relationship with Moscow on European questions, in rivalry with the United States, but in Soviet eyes France had lost her freedom of action because she belonged to a supranational European organization. In those circumstances is it not reasonable to conclude that France felt it incumbent on herself to demonstrate her independence and freedom of action?

The other five member-states also tended not to adhere strictly to the Community method when it came to matters of foreign policy, and again this was most evident in their relations with the East, particularly their trade relations. As the end of the transition period drew near, foreign-trade policy was about to pass out of the hands of the individual member-states and, in accordance with the terms of the Rome Treaty, to be handed over to the Community. There was a marked reluctance, however, to prepare for this important change-over as far as relations with the East were concerned, and to negotiate and conclude Community trade pacts instead of separate national agreements. Germany seemed to be unable to absorb the lesson of past disappointments and time and again pinned wholly unrealistic hopes on advantages she expected to obtain by pursuing an independent national trade policy with the countries of Eastern Europe. As a result, she forfeited benefits which Community trade pacts might have brought; for example, such pacts would have included West Berlin without special provision having to be made. What is particularly irritating about the whole question of relations with the East is that there are no basic differences of approach between the member-states. Moreover, if one wants to argue that it is more difficult to work out a common foreign policy for the Community members than a common economic policy, then, in my view, one could hardly choose a weaker argument to support one's case than relations with the East. There are few realistic options open to Western Europe in its dealings with the East. They are certainly far fewer than in economic policy. And as regards defence policy against a possible threat from the East, there are no options at all. The position is crystal clear.

To round off this survey of the events of the 1960s, let us look briefly at the crisis about Britain's application for membership. This, too, is a tangled tale of confusion and error in the development of Europe. Undoubtedly the French veto was mainly responsible for the damage suffered by the European cause, and the factual arguments advanced by de Gaulle's government to justify the rejection of Britain's application could not obscure the real reason, namely France's wish to assert her pre-eminence in Europe. But the diplomatic response of the other Five and of Britain was also far from free of errors and mistakes.

But no matter how much serious attention all these elements deserve, there is one fact that stands out clearly from the events of the 1960s and outweighs everything else in importance: it is that the European structure has held together. And, more than that, it has not only held together, it has also not ceased to expand and develop. Admittedly, some of the events of the 1960s caused grave disappointment and deep concern. There was talk of 'stagnation', of 'paralysis', of 'decay', and often these dramatic words were used to mobilize the public's last emotional reserves in support of the cause of a united Europe. But we must not allow feelings of alarm and despondency to prevent us from making a cool and sober assessment of what was in fact achieved. The President of the European Commission, Jean Rey, was entirely justified in warning the Congress of Parliamentarians of the European Movement at The Hague in 1968 – it was this Congress that expressly and emphatically called for a 'summit' meeting of the Six – against pessimistic over-dramatization. After all, it was during this period, when the cause of European unity seemed to be losing ground, that quite a few important goals were attained: a common financial agricultural policy was agreed; the Kennedy Round was nego- tiated; at the peak of the third crisis within the Community in 1968, the customs union was completed; so was the common market for agriculture; the policy of enabling workers to move freely and take up jobs anywhere within the Community was implemented; and after lengthy and vain attempts to make some progress in evolving a common trade policy, we were able to make notable advances even in this field.

It would therefore be quite wrong to talk of European unification falling back. Our problem was not to reverse a backward trend but to speed up a rate of progress which had been slowed down. That was the task facing the 'summit' of the Heads of State and Govern- ment of the Six which met at The Hague on December 1st and 2nd on the initiative of President Pompidou, and the way the Summit

Conference tackled that task was a considerable achievement. It has been said that the work of the Summit Conference was not 'creative' in the true sense of that word. But how could a conference of six governments, with but a few hours at its disposal, breathe new life into every aspect of the Community's virtually limitless range of common activities, and find solutions to every issue? In any case, none of the issues was, generally speaking, new, and there was no shortage of ideas on how they might be resolved. After all, the inadequacies, which became apparent during the 1960s and affected our work, did not hit the whole organism of the Community in its entirety. It was the Council of Ministers that did not function properly – which admittedly was bad enough, considering the importance the Council occupies in the constitutional structure of the Community. But the other organs of the Community performed their work normally, at least in so far as the exercise of their functions did not depend on the Council: the European Court of Justice handed down decisions; the European Parliament gave its opinions, supervised, stimulated and served as a source of encouragement; and the Commission drew up proposals, acted as guardian of the Treaty and served as mediator and 'honest broker' between the member-states. All these organs – and their members – carried on with their work patiently, assiduously and tirelessly, regardless of any disappointment they felt about the state the Community found itself in.

What had happened was that the development of closer relations and understanding as between the member-states had become blocked. The first need was to unblock what had been blocked up, to renew the binding force of Europe's will to integrate, to unite the energies of the member-states and point them anew in the direction of the common goal which has always been the purpose of our Community. This was a task that could be tackled only by the heads of state and government of the Six. In view of all that had gone before, France's attitude was decisive in this matter. It was her decision that made the conference a success, because she decided in favour of normalizing the work of integration. This meant that she returned to the system established by the Treaties of Rome and Paris and accepted both the letter and the spirit of these documents. The Conference also marked a welcome change in Germany's attitude towards Europe. In the past German policy had shown a very understandable reluctance, a shyness almost, to do anything which could be interpreted as an attempt on her part to assume a leading role. At The Hague Summit Conference she emerged from this negative attitude, adopted a more positive stance, and launched a number of constructive initiatives. As a result of The Hague Conference, solidarity and confidence were restored once again, the essential pre-condition for solving any and all common problems among a vast variety of people.

It would be wrong, however, to see the result of The Hague Conference purely as a manifestation of goodwill. Admittedly, there were no detailed decisions on different topics – that was not the business of the Conference – but it reached a number of decisions on fundamental principles and issued instructions and invitations to the member-governments and the organs of the Community to pursue certain projects. It is this aspect of the Conference's work that makes The Hague 'Summit' such a significant event in the life of the European Communities.

Of course there are still painful gaps that need attention. Nevertheless the list of achievements is impressive, and what was done touches all the four main areas involved in the work of unifying Europe:

The Time Factor It was agreed to proceed with the final phase leading up to the completion of the Community – its coming of age – irrespective of the fact that nobody had any illusions about how far the Community had fallen behind in certain aspects of its development, particularly in dismantling barriers to the free flow of trade other than customs barriers; in removing frontier controls; in eliminating all restrictions on the right of establishment of firms or companies anywhere in the Community; in ensuring the free movement of services and capital; and in coping with trade monopolies. The reason for this approach is simply that there is no doubt that working against deadlines under pressure provides the Community with the most effective means of moving ahead and making progress. Plainly medicine can teach the Community a lesson in this respect. It does a patient no good to allow him to lie back and do nothing until his health is fully restored.

The Subject-Matter of Integration The issues involved here have

99

again been interpreted with the elasticity outlined in the aims of the Treaties and intended by their original negotiators. If I were to single out the most significant decision of The Hague Conference, I should point to the agreement to hammer out a plan in 1970 for the establishment by stages of an economic and monetary union based on the harmonization of economic policy and aimed at creating a 'Community of stability and growth'. In other words, this decision explicitly recognizes and defines economic union as the next essential stage on the road towards full integration. The Conference also declared that the time was ripe to grapple with the question of reforming the Community's Social Fund within the wider framework of bringing about an extensive harmonization of different national social policies. Moreover, the Conference called for more intense action on the part of the Community in the technological field. It demanded a common agricultural production policy, so as to avoid surpluses or underproduction of certain goods and to stabilize the market in agricultural products. It again expressed its interest in the European University. And the foreign ministers of the Six were asked to submit proposals on possible steps towards political union by the middle of 1970.

The Institutional Structure The most important agreement in this field was to make a start in giving the Community the constitutional power over its own finances. The Community is to be provided in stages with its own financial resources, and budgetary control by the European Parliament is to be strengthened.

The Geographical Size and Membership of the Community The Hague Conference not only re-affirmed the geographical enlargement of the Community as a basic principle of the Treaty of Rome; it also agreed to the opening of negotiations with countries which wanted to join, and it stated that such negotiations should be conducted with 'the Community'. Agreement on this point removes the most dangerous source of trouble and crisis for the Community.

Naturally we should have liked The Hague Conference to have done much more still, particularly by insisting on special attention being paid to all measures designed to establish a true internal market within the Six, because a true internal market is, after all, the core of the Economic Community. National differences in

100

taxation and legal systems must be rapidly abolished. So must administrative differences and frontier controls of all kinds. Only then can we be certain beyond the slightest shadow of doubt that the existence of the Community is an irreversible fact and that it can no longer be shaken by recurring crises. Only the inescapable logic of a fully-integrated and complete internal market, free of all restrictions, compels us to move forward, to advance; and it was this consideration that prompted all who wanted full political union to seek to achieve their end by way of economic-political communities like the Coal and Steel Community, Euratom, and EEC.

We should also have welcomed clear directives and encouragement in promoting policies in the fields of transport, regional development, competition, and energy.

Again, no one can be unaware of significant omissions in the communiqué of The Hague Conference concerning important aspects of the Community's institutional structure. We search in vain for measures actually to restore majority voting in the Council of Ministers, or to introduce direct election to the European Parliament. There is no provision for strengthening the position of the Commission, for example, by having it invested with its powers and functions by the European Parliament, or by defining its role in negotiations with countries seeking membership.

Finally, most of the dates fixed for the completion of the talks laid down at The Hague Conference smack of diplomatic compromise, that is to say, they lie too far in the future. Problems which could be rapidly resolved are left over to be disposed of later in the 1970s, although there must surely have been every encouragement to make up for lost time by speedier action at this stage.

We can, therefore, but hope confidently that the fresh impetus which The Hague Summit Conference brought to the task of building a united Europe will also make itself felt in all those spheres of our work not dealt with at The Hague, and that this will happen before more precious time is lost.

Chapter Five

European Economic Policy

I. UNITY

Economic union is the central purpose of our work following the end of the transition period of the Common Market, as laid down in the Treaty. In speeches we have been fond of comparing the grand objective of European unification to a three-stage rocket: customs union, economic union, and political union. However effective we have been in taking such rhetorical liberties, what we were saying was not, strictly speaking, correct either in theory or in practice. For from the very beginning, even in stage one of our rhetorical rocket, politics played a part; after all, the establishment of a customs union involved national customs policies which form an important part of national trade policies. And the establishment of an economic union cannot be brought about without fusing national policies in a wide range of essential areas. In fact, an economic union means that economic frontiers must be abolished, that a common system of laws must be established, and that common policies must be hammered out and put into practice. All three objectives were and are pursued simultaneously and not consecutively, and all three are essential today if we are to be successful in creating conditions within the whole Community similar to those prevailing in an internal national market; if we are, in fact, to create a Common Market in the true sense of the term and to achieve the fusion of the national economies of the member-states. Only if we do that can we start the chain reaction which gives economic integration its sense and purpose; only then do we begin to reap the benefits that are bound to flow from allowing enterprises to be set up in the most suitable locations of their own choosing; only then can there be a more effective use of the division of labour, a more pronounced specialization in the manufacture of goods or of parts, an advance in mass production and a reduction in costs: only then, in short, can there be a general rise in the standard of living.

102

The emergence of some economic frontiers can be traced back to before the First World War, but a substantial number of them are a consequence of the severe economic crisis following the First World War which undermined the world's economic system as we had known it up to then. During the nineteenth century and up to the First World War, national frontiers were generally speaking not of very great importance. They only became important and led to the breaking up of the economic unity of Europe when the countries of Europe began to give absolute priority to setting economic targets exclusively in terms of their internal national markets, a trend that coincided with and was strengthened by the increasing intervention by the state in economic affairs. It seemed to matter little that Europe's economic landscape was a single entity and that breaking it up was, to put it mildly, senseless.

The economic frontiers which arose as a result of these trends take all sorts of different forms. There is the classical type of economic frontier, the customs tariff, between different states. Customs tariffs between the Six were abolished on 1 July, 1968. At the same time there came into force the common external tariff of the Community of the Six on imports from non-member countries. The abolition of customs barriers within the Six and the establishment of a common external tariff had to go together, because if the member-states of the Community had been left free individually to fix their own tariffs on imports from non-member countries, there would inevitably have been unfair and unjustifiable diversion of trade. Since then there have been further advances, particularly in the harmonization of customs laws. But although the Customs Union is now in existence, it does not mean that we have yet achieved a true Common Market. To do that depends on the progress we make towards economic union.

Customs barriers are not the only forms of economic frontiers dividing Europe's economic landscape. Indeed, the disappearance of tariffs within the Community has made the other barriers more visible. There are still barriers caused by the existence of different taxation systems. This is particularly true of taxes which affect the flow and volume of trade, like turnover and consumer taxes. Where such differences exist, member-states try to balance them out and to create equal and fair conditions of competition by devising schemes of tax rebates and tax-equalization payments. Such

103

schemes inevitably lead to checks at frontiers, and these can be done away with only if taxation systems and tax rates are harmonized.

Similarly, barriers exist because of different administrative laws and systems. There are differences in the provisions regarding the maintenance of public order; different national technical safety regulations; different rules for the protection of plants and of public health; and, again, none of these can be enforced without examination at the frontier. As a result, customs officials have not disappeared; they are merely known by a different name. This state of affairs is not only a nuisance for all concerned, it also offers a strong temptation quietly to circumvent the requirements of the Customs Union. Again, the solution is to harmonize the regulations involved and so to make controls and checks at frontiers superfluous. For controls and checks make the flow of trade more difficult and raise costs. What is more, they also have an unfortunate psychological side effect: they accentuate differences between members of the Community; they make strangers of people who are meant to be partners.

The physical presence of frontier posts is not the only obstacle to the free movement of trade and business within the new expanded and unified Community area. There are other, invisible barriers, caused by differences in the national legal systems and in national administrative procedures. Nationals of one country receive different treatment in another member-country from that they receive in their own, and one set of circumstances can be subject to different sets of rules and procedures in each of the member-states. This can and does amount to discrimination and is particularly noticeable outside the pure field of trade in goods. The Common Market means more than the free movement of goods: it also means the free movement of people. To be specific, it means the freedom of workers to take jobs anywhere within the Community; it means the freedom of businessmen to set up enterprises where they see fit; it means the liberalization of services (transport in particular) and of capital. Economists summarize these four elements somewhat drily as 'the liberalization of the factors of production'; convinced Europeans refer to them as 'the four freedoms'. But if they are to be realized, then our legal systems must be cleansed of anything and everything that could lead to discrimination. Such a development would, to begin with, appear to open up but a comparatively small area of progress merely by providing greater equality in commercial competition – not that that is to be despised – but the long-term consequences of such a step would be immeasurably more far-reaching. New standards of equality would emerge which would prevail throughout the Community. National legal systems and administrations would then treat in the same way not only transactions carried out in their respective territories, but also Community transactions. The worker who takes a job in another member-country of the Community would no longer be a stranger, nor would the businessman who opened up an enterprise outside his own country. And matters would not stop there. The citizens of the Community would become equal before the law of each of the member-states. Moreover, the urge to create fairer conditions of competition within the whole area of the Common Market would carry us further still. It would stimulate the wish, indeed it would compel us, to bring our various national laws and legal systems more in tune with one another. Naturally this can come about only by close co-operation within the Community. We see the gradual evolution of this process in its highest, most developed and concentrated form in the Community laws issued under the Treaty or under the legislative powers conferred by the Treaty.

Even here we are dealing only with a part of what needs to be done. It may even be the less important part; for it is, so to speak, built into the structure and constitution of the Community; it will continue to function virtually automatically, and help to contribute to the gradual integration of the economies of the member-states. But there is another part which makes an essential contribution to the attainment of the objectives we have set ourselves: politics. The political contribution to the unification of Europe is not automatic. It does not function of its own volition. It alone can provide the essential element of dynamism to our work. The Six must exert their political will to set target dates. Target dates provide the future outline of the Community's economic activity. They not merely preserve and consolidate what has been achieved; they also open up new perspectives and lay the basis for future changes. They help to create a common economic policy by surmounting old values and putting in their place new targets pointing us clearly in the direction of the goal of European unity.

Of course, this trend in economic development is not new nowadays, particularly in our Community. It means that the economic policy of the Community manifests itself in two forms: on the one hand, there is a common economic policy (at least in so far as there are no important exceptions to its implementation) which we call our 'medium-term' economic policy, to differentiate it from policy measures to cope with trade cycles; and, on the other hand, there are special policies to deal with specific areas of economic activity.

The way in which these special policies are being formulated and applied reflects the economic and political philosophy of our times and, more particularly, of our European civilization. A free market economy may be a basic principle of our policies and actions, but it must be a free market economy which is aware of and recognizes the social consequences of the effects it may produce. Consequently, it has become generally accepted that the state has a right, indeed a duty, to intervene when necessary. This means that the state confines itself not merely to laying down broad guidelines for the economy – an economy largely governed by the interplay of market forces – by, for example, changing discount or exchange rates, but that it also actively assists certain sectors of the economy. The question, of course, is what those sectors are, and the answer is that there is and can be no criterion which is universally applicable. For public authorities, when they decide to intervene, do so for strictly pragmatic reasons and for particular purposes, and their only criterion is the public weal. This is the essential difference between state intervention in economic matters in the West and between the planned economies of the East, but it is not the only difference. In the West the points at which the state may decide to intervene may touch on vast, almost global, areas of the economy, like agriculture, transport, trade (especially foreign trade), handicrafts, and, more recently, industry, branches of which require particular attention because of their considerable difficulties in adapting themselves to modern conditions; but the state also intervenes, from time to time, in specific, restricted areas of the complex economic process. It will intervene in factors affecting production, like employment, working conditions and wages, or in settling details in re-development of under-developed regions, or in regulating trade cycles. As I have pointed out, special economic policies are determined on

106

a pragmatic basis, and it is only when the state formulates those policies that the areas of state intervention at any particular period of time become clear. In this context mention must also be made of the national currencies which, although they play such a prominent part in our economic and political life, stand slightly, if proudly, apart from the general scheme of things. They are placed in the care – though not the exclusive care – of that distinguished club of organizations known as the Central Banks.

Naturally the different forms of state intervention in economic affairs affect the work of the Community. It is worth noting that the Treaty appears to add yet another dimension to this problem; this has a bearing on the extent to which the economic policies of the Community can be integrated. The Treaty sets out four different methods by which its members are to bring about closer union among themselves. In the first place, some aspect of economic policy can be declared to be 'a matter of common interest'; this applies to rates of exchange and, in the last resort, also to any measures dealing with trade cycles. Secondly, there are provisions for 'co-operation'; these apply in the field of social policy. Thirdly, there are rules for 'co-ordination' which are meant to apply generally to the whole field of economic policy. And fourthly and finally, the Treaty lays it down specifically that there should be 'common policies' for foreign trade, agriculture, and transport. This last requirement represents the closest form of joint European action in the economic field contained in the Treaty.

But it would be a mistake to attach too much importance to these somewhat precious and delicate distinctions of terminology. They are, first and foremost, evidence of the tough diplomatic bargaining that surrounded the drafting of the Treaty; they also reflect the reluctance of some authorities to see their powers and areas of competence reduced in any way. They can become important only when they interfere with the work of the Commission, and whether that happens or not depends largely on the attitude, the temperament of the people involved; that is to say, it is, in the last resort, a political question: it is, as in all federations, a question of the division of powers between the centre and the parts that make the federation. There has never been any practical reason for drawing such subtle distinctions, and there is even less now that the Community has become a more closely-knit entity. How, for example, can anyone justify the fact that matters of social policy – surely an issue which is central to the process of integration from both the political and material point of view – should be settled on the basis merely of 'co-operation'? It is difficult not to suspect that the various authorities responsible for administering social policy, which appear to be becoming more bureaucratic everywhere with every day that passes, are to blame for this lukewarm attitude. Certainly it is an attitude that compares very unfavourably with the active and extremely helpful political support of the trade unions for the European cause.

In any case, even such artificial distinctions about the degree of integration in different fields of activity cannot call in question two important conditions governing the work of the Community: the all-embracing competence of the Community over the whole area of economic policy, and the absolute necessity of close co-operation between member-states on all sectors of economic affairs. These points were discussed in the Treaty negotiations in 1957 at the Château de Val Duchesse in Brussels, and the heads of the national delegations, i.e. the authors of the draft Treaty, issued an explanatory statement which was undisputed and unanimous. Their statement read:

> The co-ordination of the economic policies of the member-states, which is laid down in Article 145 of the Treaty founding the European Economic Community, involves economic policies in the widest sense and meaning of that phrase; in other words, it includes economic policy, social policy, monetary policy, etc. To avoid the need for an inexhaustible list of topics covered by the Article, the French, Italian and Dutch texts will use the expression 'general economic policies'. For reasons of language differences, the German text of the Treaty will use the expression 'economic policy', an expression which must therefor be understood and interpreted in a wider sense than the text of Part Three, Title II, of the Treaty might otherwise be thought to imply.

The above statement clearly expressed the intention to view and treat the economic policy of the Community as a whole and to proceed with its gradual integration in its complex entirety and not piecemeal. Integration was not to confine itself either to certain

108

areas of economic activity or to certain methods of economic intervention. What the statement did not imply, however, was that the centre claimed exclusive authority in the field of economic policy. Far from it. The member-states were not denied authority or responsibility in the conduct of economic affairs. After all, even in fully-established federations, the states that constitute the federation each have their own ministries of economics, agriculture, transport, etc. What the statement does assert is that the federal system, which consists of both the central and the state authorities, is entrusted with complete and over-all competence in economic affairs. The thesis that the Treaty denies the Community authority to deal with any subject which is not specifically mentioned as falling within the competence of the Community is firmly rejected. Even matters of economic policy which are not specifically mentioned are to be tackled in accordance with the rules and regulations of the Community, provided such action is 'within the sense and spirit of the Treaty'. And whether or not that proviso applies depends not only on the relevant passages in the text of the Treaty, but also on its interpretation, on precedents or additions to the Treaty touching on the subject-matter under consideration. This approach was given fresh and welcome impetus by the decisions of The Hague Summit Conference of 1969 on 'economic and monetary union'.

In considering the substantial progress that has been made in evolving a common economic policy for the Community, it is of the utmost importance not to overlook the fact that, despite the existence of differences in political structure and outlook, in administrative traditions and theoretical and philosophical approaches to problems, integration could not have proceeded as far as it has if there had not existed a vast number of common ideas in the countries of the Community about what had to be done about the aims, purposes, and means of economic policy. Had there been no such common fund to draw on, the Community would never have been capable of working out as many solutions to its common problems as it has up to now. There are three central issues around which economic and social policies revolve everywhere: they are the control of an economy or economies based on the division of labour (which is a feature of our modern society, the control being exercised by the working of the price mechanism and

109

a system ensuring fair competition); the distribution of incomes (which is particularly linked with concern about the problem of full employment); and safeguarding a steady rate of growth (which especially involves policies designed to regulate trade cycles).

II. THE DEVIL IS IN THE DETAILS

1. *Competition Policy*

It is generally accepted nowadays that a free market economy is a basic principle of the Treaty of Rome. Such a liberal economic system – 'liberal' is here used in its modern meaning – does not exclude state intervention. On the contrary, it presupposes that the state provides a framework for the operation of such a system; for only an appropriate framework allows each section of the economy to exercise its freedom of action, in fact compels it to exercise that freedom. Competition is, so to speak, the 'motor' of the system, and the smoothness and precision of the 'motor' largely determine the standard of performance. It therefore requires constant care and supervision. But policies designed to ensure fair competition are not simply a form of police activity; they demand a constant effort to create and maintain legal provisions to secure fair conditions for competition and competitiveness. Of course there are distortions in competitive conditions, and these arise particularly when the starting positions of certain branches of the economy in different member-states are unequal. These inequalities gain in importance the more the national markets of the Six grow together, and it would be foolish to underestimate how tough a fight it is to eliminate these inequalities. Both the member-states and the Community must never lose sight of the fact that some enterprises, or even whole areas of economic activity, are determined to use every ounce of strength, skill and will to escape the impact of the strict rules, the duties and the burdens which free competition brings.

The Community's rules of competition are designed to open up the internal markets of the Six – this includes the dismantling of all internal economic barriers and frontier controls within the Community; to eliminate all practices which distort competition; to maintain an effective competition system; and to promote undistorted international competition. Much of this programme has already been completed; some of it has been half-finished; and work on the rest has hardly begun, if at all. Whether everything that could have been done has in fact been done has recently been questioned: the Community, and especially the Commission, has been criticized for not having applied within member-states the anti-restrictive rigour it has shown in dealing with trade between them. It has even been argued that the Commission has shown a tendency to condone restrictions which a network of industrialists demanded (here the 'Industrial policy' programme of the Commission is sometimes quoted). What have the Commission and the Community really done?

What is irreversible is the opening-up of the internal markets, chiefly by the dismantling of the customs barriers. As a result of a common Community customs system, enterprises are, in this important sphere of economic activity, no longer faced with conditions which distort free competition. Indeed, the removal of the tariffs has already brought about so rapid an increase in the volume of the flow of trade within the Community – an increase of a size which was hardly anticipated – that it gives one some inkling of the profound effect that would be produced once the other aims in the field of free competition were realized. There can be no doubt that immense reserves of production and productivity of both an economic and a political character still remain untapped in our old Continent.

Admittedly, we have so far on the whole not advanced significantly further than the removal of the customs barriers. There has been a decision to introduce a common turnover tax system over the next few years, although, to begin with, the different national rates of tax are to remain as they are. This is an important first step in the sphere of a common taxation policy, and it is likely to have as profound an effect on stimulating economic integration as the dismantling of the customs barriers. But the complete removal of all tax barriers is bound to call for greater efforts still on the part of everyone concerned. A removal of such magnitude can only be brought about in two stages: the first must be the establishment of a common tax system, and the second the approximation of national rates of taxation.

Only a few of the other pillars that support our complex system

111

for ensuring free and fair competition are visible. Most of them are hidden – at least from the casual observer; nevertheless they are essential, in fact indispensable, to the stability of the edifice. In this context mention must be made of the freedom of individuals or companies of any of the member-states to set up business or establish agencies or branches in another member-state. This 'right of establishment' makes a valuable contribution to strengthening the Common Market. The Treaty devotes a complete chapter, comprising Articles 52–58, to it. The language in which these Articles are couched is sober and dry, and only a jurist with great imagination can grasp the political and practical significance which lies behind the language. There, in those Articles, is laid down a path for the future whose authors have drawn their inspiration from the proud nineteenth-century liberal tradition of free trade. All restrictions on the freedom of establishment by a national of one member-state in another member-state are to be lifted. Moreover, member-states undertake to introduce no further measures which might discriminate against nationals of other member-states wishing to settle in their territories. It was on these broad guidelines that the far-reaching Action Programme of January 1962 was worked out. Its aim was to remove all restrictions on the freedom of nationals of the member-states to supply services and to settle anywhere within the Community by the end of the transition period.

The true magnitude of this aim only became evident once we got down to details. Despite delays, most of the directives – more than fifty altogether – submitted by the Commission to the Council of Ministers have been formally approved and promulgated; most of the remainder are in the process of being decided upon. As regards industry and trade, the decisions that had to be taken are now virtually completed, and the transition periods in which member-states were allowed to make the necessary changes – periods that were occasionally very generous indeed – have for the most part expired. Discrimination on the ground of nationality has now definitely and finally been abolished, and the member-states have carried out the necessary changes in their laws. As regards agriculture, a beginning is being made. The same is true of insurance, but again, unfortunately, the process is somewhat slow.

112

There still remains the problem, as yet virtually untouched, of the freedom for members of the liberal professions to settle anywhere within the Community, irrespective of nationality. The members of these professions, in particular, know what value to attach to freedom. They know what it can mean to them and to the European cause as a whole. To accord them the right of settling within the Community will therefore allow them to make their very special contribution to the unification of the Continent. The freedom or right of 'establishment' will in their case not only prove of importance in promoting a uniform European law for non-wage-earning trades, crafts and professions; its effect will also be felt in the relations of universities in Europe, in science, and in cultural affairs. Article 57 of the Treaty of Rome makes provision for the mutual recognition of diplomas, certificates and other evidence of qualifications, but it has not been easy to give it effect. Professional bodies and craft guilds had grown up over the centuries. In some cases their attitudes had become frozen in traditions which partially had their origin in the rigid medieval system of the division between the recognized estates of the age. So it is not surprising that it was not until 1967 that the Commission was able to submit its first directive in this sphere to the Council of Ministers, a directive which dealt with the mutual recognition of diplomas of architects. This directive was the first indication of what could be achieved by exploiting the combined intellectual resources and skills of the whole of Europe. But let no one underestimate the difficulties. The resistance which guilds and professional bodies will put up is bound to be great. But why should we regard it as so Utopian for a French lawyer to plead before a court in Duesseldorf or Frankfurt and to establish a practice there; for a Belgian economic expert to examine the activities of a daughter company in France; or for a properly qualified Dutch engineer to build locks and dams in Italy?

Admittedly the freedom to settle anywhere within the Community and exercise one's trade, profession, craft or business is not the same as being able to do so in practice. But until the freedom is guaranteed, people do not even have the chance to decide where they want to settle and earn their living. This involves not merely the removal of restrictions: it involves something much more positive – the right to receive such public assistance as may be

113

prescribed by law, and the right of free and unimpeded access to all and any available legal and administrative procedures. The Belgian police would no longer be justified in interfering with the way a qualified French mechanic from Lille installed a water-supply system in Roubaix. And by the same token a joiner from Luxembourg would be able to marry into the business of his French father-in-law in Nancy and carry on his trade in France, provided he had the necessary recognized qualifications. It is by steps such as these that the markets of the Community will gradually open up and integrate.

The work that still remains to be done in this sphere is immense, and it is virtually impossible to measure what has been achieved with any degree of accuracy – the more so, since nationals and non-nationals of member-states are no longer listed separately in the statistics of trades, crafts and professions (and rightly so). But the report issued by the Commission in February 1970 reflects the not inconsiderable effort that has been and is being given to this work. It also reflects the fact that although there have frequently been delays, the member-states have, as a rule, carried out their obligations.

The removal of tax barriers is an essential requirement for the completion of a true Common Market. The same is true of the removal of the still-existing physical frontier controls. Their existence directly affects the short-, medium-, and long-term planning of individual enterprises and, above all, the rational exchange and distribution of goods and products. The effect these controls have is often well hidden and camouflaged. They distort free competition and protect the vested interests not only of certain sections of industry but also of some branches of the national bureaucracies. The fight for their dismantlement will mean a hard battle. But it is a battle that must be fought – no matter how troublesome it may prove and no matter how little public acclaim or glory it may bring. If there is genuine determination to speed up at long last the tiresome procedure for crossing frontiers within the Community, then that purpose would be adequately served by a system of controls based on common standards and guidelines and recognized reciprocally by all the member-states. This could possibly be done where different national veterinary laws and legal provisions for the prevention of

114

industrial accidents are concerned. Such moves would certainly make the lives of Europe's long-distance lorry-drivers a lot easier.

In another sphere – in the different national policies which member-states pursue in encouraging certain industries or regions – the Community has been more successful. Here its views are gradually prevailing and winning recognition and acceptance for the provisions of the Treaty – which, incidentally, are quite explicit on the point. But it was a grim, up-hill struggle, and it is by no means over. Much still remains to be done, especially since the member-states plainly find it very difficult to surrender their individual authority over the allocation of subsidies and no longer to regard it as a tool of their national policy as a whole. In February 1971 the Commission had to ask the Federal German government to make changes in the indiscriminate guaranteeing of investment aids under the coal regulations in force in North-Rhine/Westphalia. As a matter of fact, there is no need for member-states to give up all authority in this field, especially where subsidies to certain regions are concerned. All the Commission must watch over in this connection is that such subsidies as are given do not distort competition.

One of the as yet unexplored and undeveloped areas on the map of what we might call economic union is the problem of the state monopolies and of the public enterprises within the Community. It will prove impossible in this area to frame common policies in numerous and by no means unimportant spheres such as tobacco, brandy and, above all, energy, without changing these monopolies to exclude any form of discrimination within the Community. Or, to put it the other way round, only common policies can bring about the necessary changes and adjustments. Article 37 of the Treaty, which deals with this particular subject, can unfortunately be described only as a 'lazy compromise'. It entrusts the member-states with responsibility for the necessary adjustments. The Commission is merely empowered to issue 'recommendations' which, by their very nature, are not legally binding. Shortly before the end of the transition period, by December 1969, the Commission had issued ten such 'recommendations', one to the Federal German Republic, four to Italy, and five to France. One of the most important keys to the solution of this problem must be the eventual removal of the exclusive right of control by the state monopolies in

115

all matters relating to import, export, and marketing. The question of the French state oil monopoly is being discussed within the context of framing a common energy policy.)

By contrast, a system of rules and regulations to ensure free competition in its narrower sense, in particular in the question of cartels, is growing slowly and steadily, like a tree. More than a decade after the Common Market Treaty came into force, the Community has succeeded in laying down new and firm standards for all laws and regulations relating to cartels, including the relevant national laws of the member-states. Every businessman today is aware of the fact that real competition based on efficiency is one of the basic aims of the Treaty; that consequently the limits that are being placed on existing restrictions or distortions of competition are emerging more clearly every day; and that there is legal machinery to enforce the rules safeguarding competition. What we are, in fact, watching is the evolution of a whole new branch of law with its own common norms, jurisdiction and methods of procedure, an evolution which is truly fascinating from the legal as well as from the economic and broad political point of view. It is an evolution that has been helped along by the combination of a number of circumstances. In the first place, the wording of the Treaty is clear and unequivocal on this subject, particularly the wording of Article 85, which explicitly prohibits all agreements designed to prevent, restrict, or distort competition. Secondly, the Commission was successful in working out a common and generally acceptable theory according to which competition was to serve a triple purpose: it was to serve as a source of prosperity, as a creator of wealth, and as a guarantee for economic freedom. That the Commission would be able to do this and win acceptance for its 'theory' was by no means a foregone conclusion. After all, it had to contend with deep differences in national legal thinking and in economic practice. Having worked out its commonly accepted 'theory', or 'philosophy', the Commission then proceeded to set up the necessary administrative infrastructure which enabled it to take and carry out the decisions to give effect to its 'philosophy'. It is an effect that is proving continuous and continuing. Thirdly, the European Court of Justice, which plays a key role in this whole process, has adopted the concepts of the Commission practically in their entirety, a trend that is clearly reflected in its decisions, which are couched in modern yet impressively authoritative language. Finally, progress in this field owes much to the growing volume of helpful contributions which academics have brought and are bringing to the relevant discussions and consultations.

To ensure that all measures designed to secure the maximum degree of competition are observed, breaches can call forth sanctions, and the Commission has shown itself fully prepared to make use of that most effective weapon when necessary. It has imposed on the members of a cartel of quinine manufacturers fines amounting to about two million German marks – roughly £230,000 – one of which was confirmed, in a test case, by the European Court of Justice, and has also fined the members of a dye-stuff cartel, and the twenty-five partners in a scrap-metal cartel in the Ruhr.

The institutional framework for ensuring the maximum degree of competition proved well fitted for the purpose it was meant to serve. The member-states are left with considerable rights of making their views felt in the formulation and execution of policies; the Commission is clearly designated as the body competent to draw up and submit decisions; and the European Court of Justice is invested with powers to supervise these decisions. Admittedly, it took a good deal of time to get things moving. The key regulation, Regulation No. 17, came into force only after four years of argument and debate, in 1962. All agreements liable to affect trade between member-states and designed to prevent, restrict and distort competition within the Community had from then onwards to be compulsorily registered, and it was for the Commission to decide which agreements fell within the permitted categories and which did not. This faced the Commission with the threat of being swamped by applications for clearance, a threat which it has barely mastered even today and which could have been averted if there had been a little confidence in the Commission. The first wave of applications for clearance numbered nearly 40,000. It was not until 1965 that the Commission was empowered to exempt certain types of engagements in restraint of competition from the general prohibition against cartels, and it was not until 1967 that the Commission could eventually use that power. Since then, simple exclusive dealing arrangements, which do not confer on the parties to them absolute rights in a given area, no longer require specific clearance. In May 1970, the Commission announced further exemptions for unimportant cartels, i.e. those that had only a minor effect on trade between member-states because their share of the market or the turnover of the participants is too small; this is to encourage necessary co-operation between small and medium-sized firms. At the same time the Commission asked the Council to empower it to make further exemptions (especially for research, specialization, and joint buying and selling) and to simplify certain procedures.

Experience over the years has shown that enterprises which have been approached or reproved by the Commission in matters affecting restrictions on competition have increasingly tended to avoid the point where the Commission must give a formal decision, or where the case must be submitted to the European Court of Justice for adjudication. In practice this means that, in their search for agreed solutions, the Commission and the enterprises concerned become engaged in understandably confidential and extended negotiations. No doubt this method enhances the authority of the Commission in shaping the system for ensuring free competition, but it is a method that lacks the element of public control, and makes criticism too easy. It would therefore be advisable if the Commission did not allow itself to be confined to this method but sought from time to time to hand down formal decisions; for these decisions not only settle disputes, but also serve as precedents and so provide guidelines for the future conduct of the interested parties, thereby helping to avoid disputes arising in the future. The first formal decisions were handed down in 1964, among them, in the autumn of that year, the decision in the Grundig/Consten case, a decision which has rightly become celebrated. The German and French enterprises had entered into an agreement under which the French firm Consten was guaranteed sole sale rights in France for all similar kinds of products manufactured by Grundig, and Grundig undertook to sell none of its products in France. In accordance with this agreement Grundig had instructed all its distributors and consumers in other countries of Europe to discontinue the export of Grundig products to France. After long and exhaustive enquiries, the Commission came to the decision that the agreement between Grundig and Consten constituted a breach of the prohibition against contracts restricting

118

competition, as laid down in Article 85 of the Treaty; moreover, the Commission instructed Grundig and Consten to stop forthwith preventing the import into France of products similar to those manufactured by Grundig.

The Commission's decision aroused much interest at the time and was the target of a great deal of criticism from some sections of industry. The European Court of Justice, however, fully supported the Commission in its attitude and interpretation and had this to say on the case: 'An agreement between a manufacturer and a distributing and sales enterprise which seeks to resurrect national trade barriers between member-states, could . . . run counter to the fundamental aims of the Community. The Treaty, setting up the European Economic Community . . . does not permit enterprises to create new barriers of this sort.' The European Court of Justice went on to say: 'Since the agreement which is the subject of this dispute seeks to exclude Grundig products from the French market and to maintain by deliberate and artificial means separate national markets within the Community for products of a well-known and widely-marketed make, the agreement must be held to falsify and distort competition within the Common Market.'

The significance of this decision of the European Court of Justice in determining the climate in which competition is to evolve hardly needs stressing. The European Court, in its judgement, was positive where the Supreme Court of the German Reich, in its celebrated decision of 4 February 1897, was negative – negative in the sense that it opened the way to the formation of cartels. The Supreme Court of the Reich gave priority at the time to the freedom of parties to enter into contracts as they wished; the European Court of Justice, on the other hand, gave priority to the maintenance of free competition within the Common European Market, and its judgement continues to act as a leaven in this whole complex sphere. Nowhere is the ferment it is still causing more clearly felt than in the frequently heated disputes in the Federal German Republic about the validity of agreements which link re-sale price maintenance with prohibitions to export. Such prohibitions, it is argued, are allegedly essential to ensure that agreed re-sale prices are adhered to. For example, it was on the basis of the European Court's decision that the Commission was able eventually, after lengthy and weary discussions, to compel changes in the structure of sales syndicates of artificial fertilizers (nitrogen). On the other hand, the Commission has given it as its view, in a number of its decisions, that it regards exclusive dealing arrangements as useful so long as they are not linked with agreements between enterprises to divide and allocate markets or fields of business activity, or to give any enterprise exclusive and absolute rights to manufacture, trade, or carry on business in a given area.

European industry is gradually adapting itself to this new set of circumstances. For example, the biggest enterprises in the photographic industry in Europe eliminated all restrictions on the export or re-import of their products within the Common Market from their business arrangements as from 1 January 1970. In doing so, they removed restrictions on competition to which the Commission had taken exception.

The Commission does not, however, see its role in handing down decisions in this sphere merely as dismantling agreements in restraint of competition. It has, at the same time, stimulated and encouraged co-operation between enterprises, extending beyond national frontiers. One of the ideas which was generated within the Commission and which was put into practice, was to draw up what one might call a 'co-operation primer'. This 'primer' sets out in detail how enterprises within the Common Market can usefully work together in order to increase their competitiveness within the rules of international law, trade, and custom. Naturally, the limits set to co-operation are regarded as too narrow by the branches of the economy affected. But surely it is one of the great advantages of a body of legal rules and regulations, based on precedent, that it is flexible. Perhaps this process of development by evolution could be simplified without losing any of the certainty which legal rules must possess if they are to be effective and enjoy respect.

While the decisions of the Commission and of the European Court of Justice in interpreting Article 85 of the Treaty of Rome are gradually giving effect to the provisions it embodies, the application of Article 86 is presenting the Commission with considerable difficulties. In fact, the Commission finds itself in a position similar to every authority which tries to impose fair rules of competition in an oligopolistic market in which there are a limited number of suppliers who tend to react to changes in other suppliers' prices by changing their own prices. Article 86 of the Treaty prohibits any improper exploitation by one or more undertakings of a dominant position within the Common Market. This Article was first used in 1971. In March, the Commission had drawn the attention of the American firm 'Europe-emballage' to certain aspects of its activities which gave rise to the charge that it had misused its powerful position in the canning market. Europe-emballage appealed to the European Court of Justice. In June, the Commission took a decision against the Berlin group GEMA (*Gesellschaft für musikalische Aufführungs – und mechanische Versichfaltigungsrechte*), on the grounds that it discriminated against nationals of other member-states; bound its own members too closely; hindered the liberalization of services in music publishing; extended copyright to works in the public domain; and discriminated against non-German gramophone records, tape-recorders, and projectors. Thirdly, in a series of very significant decisions, the European Court of Justice went beyond its ruling on the Grundig-Consten case, and laid down that trade-protection laws must be administered in conformity with the competition rules of the Rome Treaty: this was in connection with the market-sharing aspects of the decision in the 'Sirena' case and the preliminary ruling in the dispute between the Deutsche-Gramophon-Gesellschaft and Metro-SA-Grossmarkte, Gmbh. & Co. H.G. But even before Article 86 led to definite formal decisions, it proved effective in furthering competition. The Commission has repeatedly received complaints from small and medium-sized enterprises, particularly concerning the boycotting of supplies, and whenever that has happened it has never hesitated to take action immediately; the enterprises charged with exploiting their dominant position have always at once stopped the practices which led to the complaints against them. This of course was one reason why there were for so long no formal decisions by the Commission on Article 86. But even without such decisions, undertakings of all kinds – whether they be big and powerful or whether they stand in need of protection – become increasingly aware of the circumstances in which the Commission will intervene on the grounds that an enterprise is being unfairly and improperly forced out of business. In December 1965 the Commission issued a memorandum on the subject of mergers. The memorandum made it clear

121

that the Commission intended as a general rule to treat any which would lead to a monopoly as an improper exploitation of a dominant position of the market – which would consequently be prohibited, because complete exclusion of competition in even one sphere of a free market economy amounts to abuse of power within the free market economy as a whole.

There remains the basic question of mergers as such. The need to speed up the process of concentration within the Community varies from industry to industry. In some branches it would be useful, in others desirable, and in still others absolutely essential. But in certain cases it could be positively harmful. The Commission and industry as a whole are at one in their conviction that, despite the so-called 'American challenge' – the *défi américain* – the correct solution in every case is not concentration at any price. The largest undertaking is by no means always the soundest structurally. Having said this, however, it is a pity to have to point out that almost none of the conditions for mergers across frontiers as yet exist in the important areas of company law and of taxation. Quite early in its career, the Commission began to work towards the establishment of a European company law. In 1967, a committee of leading experts under the chairmanship of Professor Sanders, from the Netherlands, drew up a first draft; but the work of the experts met a great variety of national opposition. In June 1970, the Commission proposed to the Council a draft regulation for a 'European Company' which in many respects differed from and went further than the experts' proposals. In its details, there were clear parallels with German law, and in particular with German company law, which at that time was the most advanced in the whole Community. Under this plan, a 'European Company' could be formed only with the participation of companies from several member-states, either through a merger between them, or through a holding company or a joint subsidiary. Where the capital comes from is immaterial; but for the time being there is no provision for a national company to acquire the status of a 'European Company' by itself. Corporate and personal holdings are permitted. The structure of the 'European Company' would include a General Meeting of Shareholders, a Board of Management, and a Board of Directors. Since works councils exist in several member-states, a European works council is also envisaged, and the Board of

Management must secure its agreement to any important decisions affecting employees, such as the basic conditions of hiring and dismissal, training, working-hours, and holidays. The employees appoint one-third of the Board of Directors, but can renounce this right by a two-thirds majority (a concession to the Communist trade unions). Some workers' representation may be professional trade unionists from outside. Finally, the 'European Company' would have the power to conclude collective agreements. The draft regulation also includes strict rules to protect outside shareholders and the creditors of dependent companies.

For the purpose of taxation, the 'European Company' would be subject to the national law of the country where its real headquarters were. It would not, that is, have any specially privileged position: indeed, the Commission would like to see applied here the basic principles of its 1969 proposals – that company profits should be taxed in the country where the company is really established, but that there should be the option of being taxed on 'world profits', i.e. of deducting from taxable profits in the Company's fiscal domicile any losses sustained abroad.

It is to be hoped that the Council will soon find a European solution to these problems.

If the member-states stick to their present attitudes, the industries as well as the consumers in the Community will be the losers. Competitors from the United States have long been in the habit of regarding the Community as a single entity and extracting all the benefits offered by its freedom of siting enterprises anywhere within it. And they have done so through companies which command enormous capital reserves. In the meantine, an attempt is being made gradually to harmonize the different national company laws by a system of conventions between the member-states, but at best this can only be a makeshift solution. It in no way meets what is needed – to bring together the industrial resources of the Common Market and make them more competitive.

Even industrial copyright laws in the member-states make for different market conditions in various parts of the Community. Since 1962, therefore, there has been an effort to unify patent law. After long stagnation, this task was taken up again in 1969. A new series of preliminary draft proposals for an agreement on general European patent-sharing procedures and for an agreement on a

'European patent' for the Common Market were made by the experts in April and June 1971; conclusions are expected in 1973, and it is thought that a European Patents Office could begin work in, say, 1976. Nineteen European states are negotiating about the former agreement. This should make it possible to demand protection for an invention by one procedure in all the signatory states, although by means of a series of national patents. The aim is one of rationalization. The purpose of the second agreement is integration – to establish an independent Common Market patent system, making it no longer necessary to accumulate national patents in order to ensure protection throughout the Community. On this task, only the member-states of the Community are engaged. But both projects would share the same European patents office, with a registry and a complaints department. Meanwhile the conditions for obtaining patents, which at present differ in strictness from one country to another, need to be made uniform.

2. Monetary Policy

Monetary policy is the touchstone of the Community. It did not require General de Gaulle's use of monetary policy as an instrument in the pursuit of France's national interests, as he saw them, to prove that monetary policy means politics in its full and true sense. The right to mint coins has always been recognized as visible proof of national sovereignty, and the mythology surrounding money accentuates even today the problems of those attempting to evolve common monetary policies for the European Community.

Every reliable and recognized interpretation of the Treaty of Rome leaves no doubt on the point that the co-ordination of economic policy rightly includes co-ordination of monetary policy. In fact, in a free market economy such as that of the European Economic Community, monetary policy is one of the main methods by which the economic process as a whole can be guided and controlled. The way in which the economy works depends to a large, not to say decisive, extent on the creation of money; on the amount of money in circulation; on the value of money both in internal national and in external terms in respect to foreign currencies; and on the movements of money. This involves not merely technicalities like payments, or the foreign exchange, or capital markets. It is a matter that touches virtually every aspect of

124

politics: taxation and budget policy; measures to control the trade cycle; economic growth; and foreign as well as internal policy as a whole. The control of these closely-knit spheres of political activity adds up to a considerable amount of power, not least because it determines the standard of living of every individual and of society as a whole. The way that power is exercised is, therefore, laid down most meticulously in any economic arrangements which are made in any state or community. Central banks, in particular, are as a rule given a certain measure of independence of the political authorities nowadays, at least as far as some of their functions are concerned, in order to guard against and diminish the impact of mistakes that might otherwise be made. To maintain the value of money is of prime importance. Indeed, it is one paramount objective of monetary policy.

If national economies are to be fused, as the Treaty of Rome envisaged, then it is a condition as well as an effect of this process that monetary policy will be affected at its most sensitive points. How is this fact to be taken into account in bringing about economic integration? Should we aim at a monetary union, a common monetary policy, and what form should such a union, such a policy take? On a great many occasions the question is also put: should such a change in the structures of the separate national monetary systems be used in conjunction with the other methods needed to bring about economic integration, acting – as it were – as a kind of 'motor' to the whole process? Or should it come at the end, to 'crown' the process of integration, so to speak? The question may seem pompous, but it contains a very simple problem, the problem of when the transition is best made. To put it in a different way, how long can the old national monetary structures remain untouched while economic and political circumstances are changing rapidly all around, without causing damage to the monetary or economic systems or, indeed, both?

The Treaty of Rome does not answer in any detail all the questions which arise in connection with a unified monetary system. The chapter of the Treaty which deals with monetary policy bears the title 'Balance of Payments'. According to Article 104, each member-state shall pursue 'the economic policy necessary to ensure the equilibrium of its over-all balance of payments and to maintain confidence in its currency, while ensuring a high level of

125

employment and the stability of price levels'. In order to facilitate the achievements of these objectives, the member-states shall co-ordinate their economic policies (Article 105). They shall for this purpose introduce a policy of collaboration between their appropriate administrative departments and their central banks. A Monetary Committee with consultative status is to be established in order to promote the co-ordination of the policies of member-states in monetary matters to the extent necessary to ensure the operation of the Common Market. Article 107 places the general obligation on each member-state to treat its policy with regard to rates of exchange as 'a matter of common interest'. Article 108 lays it down that member-states are obliged to grant 'mutual assistance' should one of their number run into balance-of-payments difficulties; at the same time the Article outlines the procedure by which such mutual assistance is to be granted. Where a member-state runs into a sudden balance-of-payments crisis, it is – according to Article 109 – authorized provisionally to 'take the necessary protective measures' on its own initiative; but such measures – so the Article provides – must cause the least possible disturbance in the functioning of the Common Market.

In practice, the problems raised by monetary policy and the way in which these problems have been tackled have taken us far beyond the bare outlines of the provisions laid down in the text of the Treaty. If we are to come to any conclusions about what needs to be done in future, then we must examine the way in which all the problems connected with monetary policy have developed, in terms of their effect both on the Community and on relations with the outside world.

In making this examination, one can clearly distinguish seven periods:

1. The first period begins in 1958 and ends roughly in the spring of 1961, when the German mark and the Dutch guilder were re-valued. In those years the Community was almost completely absorbed with its own internal affairs; it was concerned with getting its administrative apparatus going; with setting up its Institutions; with hammering out a common agricultural policy; and with working out, in sessions which involved much hard bargaining, a time-table which allowed a more rapid reduction of internal customs barriers than originally contemplated. Such dis-

cussion as there was on monetary policy took place almost exclusively in the Monetary Committee. The Committee began its work by taking stock of the situation. Its findings appeared in 1962 in a paper entitled 'The instruments of monetary policy in the member-states of the European Economic Community'. Apart from that, the Committee began pin-pointing and defining some of the important problems and decisions that would have to be faced in the early stages. It soon became obvious even then that economic integration, as laid down in the Treaty of Rome, presupposed as a matter of principle the stability of exchange rates between the currencies of the member-states; admittedly, as the fourth annual report of the Monetary Committee pointed out, adjustments in exchange rate should not be excluded in all circumstances during the transition period, particularly not where such adjustments were of substantial help to the Community in fulfilling other important aims. The Committee also recognized it as desirable that the member-states of the Community should adopt a common attitude in international discussions on monetary policy. In July 1961 the Monetary Committee submitted its important 'Report on current problems of international liquidity'. These were problems which were to occupy those responsible for matters affecting international monetary policy until 1969, when agreement was at last reached at the big financial and economic conferences held in London, Rio de Janeiro, and Stockholm. As a matter of fact, the member-states of the Community had, as early as 1961, reached 'virtually complete agreement' among themselves on the points of view they took at the negotiations on the conditions on which the resources of the International Monetary Fund were to be increased; but, on the whole, the way in which the member-states conducted their political affairs in practice left much to be desired – although there was, in the years that followed, a great deal of talk about co-ordinating monetary policy. For example the question of revaluing the German mark had been discussed for years; it had also been thrashed out in the Monetary Committee. But when the mark was eventually revalued, it was done without complete prior co-ordination within the Community.

2. The Community moved from the first stage of the transition period to its second stage on 1 January 1962. The move marked a significant step forward; it also marked a change in the nature of

the problems facing the Community. Most important of all, the establishment of a common agricultural market was now in sight, and the separate national markets were rapidly becoming more integrated. These developments created a new situation for the formulation of a common monetary policy as well as of joint measures for dealing with the problem of trade cycles. The European Commission lost no time in drawing attention to the action these new circumstances demanded. Its action programme, published in October 1962, which outlined what should be done, stated that the member-states would have to agree to fixed exchange rates between their respective currencies at the end of the transition period at the latest, if an economic union was to be set up. This was a view that has the support of quite a few experts on monetary policy. To quote from the Commission's action programme, 'fixed exchange rates by their very nature lead to economic union because it will be of no concern to a national of any of the Common Market countries in which currency his assets are held . . .' (Number 128, Paragraph 2). The proposals put forward by the Commission were moderate, although the targets which these proposals were ultimately to achieve were ambitious. The Commission wanted, in particular, to stimulate more active and constant consultation on monetary policy and to give more concrete form to the obligations, laid down in the Treaty, for 'mutual assistance' in balance-of-payments crises. To quote again from the Commission's action programme:

the establishment of a monetary union could be the aim of the third stage in the development of the Common Market. The finance or economic affairs ministers of the European Economic Community, meeting as a body in the Council of Ministers, would at the appropriate time frame the conditions on which the budgets of the separate member-states as well as of the Community were to be drawn up, and determine the over-all amount of the national budgets and that of the Community; they would also decide in broad terms the conditions for financing the budgets. A Council composed of the presidents of central banks would become the organ´of a central banking system on a federal pattern (Number 138, Paragraph 2).

In its memorandum of June 1963 the Commission made more

concrete proposals. Time was pressing, because the Common Market was making rapid progress. The Commission stressed that the growing interdependence of national monetary policies and of integration within the Common Market obliged all concerned to co-operate more closely in matters affecting monetary policy. The progress of integration would be endangered if the monetary policy of one of the member-states were to move away from the general principles and broad guidelines of monetary policy followed by other member-states. To avoid this happening, the Commission proposed that a committee of the governors of the central banks of the European Economic Community should be set up. The Commission also proposed that the member-states should undertake to consult one another before making changes in their foreign exchange rates. Co-operation in the area affecting policies to be pursued by the banks of issue, foreign exchange policy, and financial policy, was to be institutionalized by setting up a complete and comprehensive system of consultative organs, so as to avoid any possibility of gaps in the continuous process of consultation. The results of these proposals were modest. It took the violent eruption of Italy's monetary crisis in the spring of 1964 to make it clear to all concerned that concrete dicisions were long overdue.

3. The increasing dangers in the general economic situation had become evident as early as the summer of 1963. In the spring of that year the inflationary trends which had, up to then, been noticeable only here and there in isolated cases, had combined to form one mighty wave which swept over the Community before the Six were even aware of the danger. Furthermore, after 1963 at the very latest no member-state could afford to continue to remain indifferent to what policies affecting economic trends and monetary matters were being pursued in a neighbouring state. The Community found that the point had been reached where economic trends in one country made themselves felt in another country with ever-increasing speed. The explanation for this development is not difficult to find. It is a development which began as far back as 1959, when all European currencies became convertible. As a result it was easier to move money and capital, and the movement towards closer interdependence and integration of the separate national economies received an additional impulse. This would

have been the right and logical moment to transfer to the organs of the Community the means that existed for dealing with economic trends. But although the economics ministers of the member-states knew that they could no longer control economic trends, there was psychological opposition to any transfer of authority in this sphere. It was characteristic of the psychological climate in the Community at the time that Italy's first move – in her search for a solution to her monetary difficulties – for support of the lira was to turn to the Americans and not to Brussels; overnight the president of the Italian bank of issue flew off to New York. In consequence, a good opportunity of making progress in the field of monetary policy in the Community was missed.

All the same, the Council of Ministers was made more aware of its obligations than had previously been the case. For the first time there was talk of drawing up a catalogue of obligations for European economic policy and trends. Agreement was reached in April on a joint recommendation to the member-states to take measures to establish and ensure internal and external equilibrium in their economic development. Significantly, none of the member-states was prepared any longer to sacrifice one of the advantages of the Common Market by isolating and shutting off its national market. On the contrary, the recommendation stated that the maintenance of a liberal import policy both within the Community and in relation to non-member-states was to be regarded as an essential element in stabilizing the levels of prices. States with balance-of-payments deficits were advised to discuss their problems with other member-states in the Monetary Committee; in future Community members were to seek common solutions and work out joint aid programmes for their problems, and common solutions and aid programmes were to be implemented, where appropriate. This first positive action in this field achieved a measure of success, although the danger of inflation did not abate for some time.

At the same time, the Council of Ministers tackled the initiatives submitted by the Commission in 1963. The Council decided to set up the Committee of the Presidents of the Central Banks. The task of this new Committee was to be to discuss jointly the broad guidelines of central banks policy; to exchange information regularly on the most important measures bearing on monetary policy; and promptly to study and examine those measures. The Council of

Ministers also decided that there should be consultations, with the Commission present, on all questions relating to national and international monetary policy and on budget matters, in particular before any change in foreign exchange rates was contemplated or implemented. All this represented a beginning, and the decision on common grain prices (in December 1964) confirmed, soon afterwards, that we were on the right road. Admittedly, the process of consultation did not work as well as it should have. It failed to take account of the mutual confidence which is essential if consultation is to work effectively. If there is a situation – as there was when France devalued – where the head of the French Cabinet was not informed of the decision, then one can hardly expect the Council of Ministers and the other five member-governments to be so informed. At the same time one is bound to ask what the Council of Ministers thought it was trying to achieve in setting up the consultative system as it at present exists. Surely the Council did not intend the example set by Germany to be generally followed. Germany, it may be recalled, permitted itself the luxury of making the up-valuation of the mark an election issue.

4. The next phase lasted from 1964 until the autumn of 1967, until the spectacular devaluation of the British pound. This period saw the Community's great political crisis of 1965, which was sparked off by the proposals for the future financing of the common agricultural policy and was not resolved until the beginning of 1966. This period also saw the great international arguments on monetary policy, above all between France and the Anglo-Saxon powers. Furthermore, the consequences, in terms of monetary policy, produced by the common agricultural market emerged during this period. Agricultural prices within the Community had ceased being expressed in terms of national currencies as far back as 1962; instead they had been expressed in units of account which were linked to gold. These units of account were equal in value to the dollar and until recently remained so. This arrangement seriously impaired the ability of the member-states to pursue an independent exchange-rate policy, because changes in exchange rates between the member-states inevitably ran into virtually insuperable difficulties. It was only after years of discussion and argument that these problems were dealt with in a regulation issued in May 1968. Its aim was to maintain and secure the con-

131

tinued existence of the common agricultural market even after possible changes in the exchange rates, and at the same time to strengthen co-operation in the sphere of monetary policy within the European Economic Community.

Monetary policy continued to be discussed intensively on an international basis throughout 1965. The European Economic Community played its part in these discussions. Robert Marjolin, the Commission's Vice-President responsible for monetary policy, observed in March that the European Economic Community would enjoy substantially greater freedom of action – and on a world-wide scale – if it acted more as one unit in questions of monetary policy. He explained his observation in more precise terms by pointing out that the Community should seek to find common norms, particularly as regards budget policy, credit policy, and perhaps also incomes policy. The Community, he stressed, had to become a real entity as far as the movement of capital was concerned. The means by which monetary policy is carried out had to be harmonized. The member-states had to stand and act together ever more closely where questions of international liquidity reserves were concerned, and their co-operation in international currency transactions had to be increasingly strengthened, until the point was reached when the reserves of the separate countries could be regarded as parts of common reserves. In other words, the Commission had not lost sight of the high targets it had set itself in its programme of 1962, which laid down what should be done in the years ahead. An addition had rightly been made to this programme, namely that progress in the direction of a monetary union would be of decisive importance not only for the Community itself but also for the future of the international monetary system. Once the Common Market reaches such a degree of cohesion in matters of monetary policy that it appears as a single unit to the rest of the world, then it will become much easier to find equilibrium in international monetary matters.

The difficult position in which the pound sterling found itself from 1964 onwards increasingly dominated international financial discussions. The stages of this painful process are well known: in the autumn of 1964 the British Government introduced a special surcharge on imports into Britain; in September 1965 vast credits were made available by a number of issuing banks and the Bank for

132

International Settlements; these credits were renewed in 1966; then, at the beginning of September 1966, a further operation was launched to support the pound. None of these measures really proved effective and successful. During the same period the American balance-of-payments position worsened. Furthermore, the discussion and disagreements over what to do about the shortage of international liquidity – then and in the future – were revived.

A whole series of monetary conferences in 1967 eventually brought this phase to an end. The guiding theme at all these conferences was the so-called 'special drawing rights': the idea was to overcome the shortage of foreign currency reserves, which some central banks were experiencing, by the creation of 'special drawing rights' on the International Monetary Fund – in other words, the creation of a new kind of money usable only as between central banks. This was the first time in the history of money that an attempt was made intentionally to control the world's supply of foreign currency reserves on a long-term basis. As a first step the Group of Ten reached agreement, after considerable difficulties, at their meeting in London in July 1967 – and not, let it be noted, until after the divergences of view between France and America had once again led to a flare-up. Then, at the meeting of the International Monetary Fund in Rio de Janeiro the new plans were finally approved. Admittedly, storms still lay ahead in 1968, and there was vehement controversy when it came to agreement on the necessary changes in the statutes of the International Monetary Fund. In these conferences the countries of the European Economic Community presented a united front for the first time, particularly in controversies with the Anglo-Saxon powers (even though France continued to play its own special role) and they knew how to put across their case effectively. In the debates leading to the changes in the statutes of the International Monetary Fund, they succeeded in winning for themselves the right, although they might find themselves in a minority, of blocking decisions in important world monetary matters, including questions affecting the allocation of special drawing rights.

5. The next stage – up to the end of 1969 – brought the crisis in the development of a European monetary policy, a crisis both in the classical and medical sense; it also brought the decision on the

further evolution of the monetary policy, following on a veritable test, to the point of destruction. Even the beginning of that stage was dramatic: the British pound was devalued by 14·5 per cent on 18 November 1967. A mass of economic and political conclusions and mistakes, as well as an accumulation of mishaps, in the course of the summer of 1967 had made the decision to devalue inevitable; there had been the Middle East crisis in July which had led to the closing of the Suez Canal; there had been increases in interest rates in America, and substantial transfers of money from London to New York; the Labour government had lost a good deal of ground and internal political prestige as a result of a series of by-election defeats – and finally there had been the dock strike in Britain.

In the meantime Britain had in May 1967 renewed its application to join the European Economic Community. General de Gaulle had let it be known early on that he was not positively disposed towards Britain's renewed application. Nevertheless, the European Commission was instructed to express a view with regard to a possible enlargement of the Community. In its opinion of 30 September 1967, the Commission had to devote considerable space to the role of the pound sterling as a world reserve currency (even though that role was no longer universally recognized). The Commission made its diagnosis under the impact of what had recently happened. Was the stability of the pound not likely to be exposed to the same endless upsets in the next few years as it had been in the past decade? A renunciation on the part of Britain not to invoke Article 108 of the Treaty, under which member-states are obliged to grant mutual assistance to a member in balance-of-payments difficulties, could not offer the Community sufficient security. Nor would the existing arrangements which the Bank of England had made with a number of central banks provide an alternative to joint Community action in this field. Finally the Commission pointed out that Great Britain could not allow herself to be manœuvred into a position where she had to pursue conflicting aims:

The fact that Great Britain administers a reserve currency would mean that she would have to pursue economic and financial policies which would have to serve the aims of the Community and at the same time accord with objectives which are alien to the Community. No national currency could in the last resort accept the role of a Community monetary system to which the progressive co-ordination of the economic, monetary, and financial policies of the member-states is bound to lead (Number 100).

The world monetary situation continued to be disturbed. De Gaulle resumed his attacks on the prevailing world monetary system, above all, on the dollar. He particularly objected to the take-over of European enterprises by the Americans at a time when (in European eyes) dollar balances were in deficit. It may be possible, the General declared in November 1967, 'that the storms which have been unleashed at this time without any action on France's part and which have impaired the parity of the pound and threaten that of the dollar, may yet in the end lead to the restoration of the international monetary system which is based on the advantages of gold, its unchangeability, its impartiality, its universality.'

In fact, no sooner had the sterling crisis been resolved by the devaluation of the pound, than the dollar became the target of speculation. All sorts of measures were tried to cope with this situation – substantial deposits of dollars from the reserves of the members of the so-called Gold Pool (the USA, Great Britain, Switzerland, Belgium, Italy, the Netherlands, and Germany); resolutions of close co-operation by the same Group as well as specific declarations guaranteeing support; a new balance-of-payments programme by the American President – but all of them proved fruitless. In March 1968 it was therefore decided to allow two prices for gold. All efforts to stabilize the free market price of gold were stopped. The fixed price of thirty-five dollars per ounce of gold was to be used by the issuing banks only for dealings between official currency authorities. They were charged to do anything in their power to maintain existing parities between currencies.

Up to this point the European Community had been spared the crises and convulsions to which the pound and the dollar had been subjected; it was affected only indirectly by the at times extremely keen demand for the German mark. Then, overnight, as it seemed, one of the Community's most important currencies was itself endangered, the French franc. May and June 1968 saw the abrupt outbreak of a great political crisis in France. As a result of the disorders, the riots in the streets, and the lengthy strikes, there was a massive flight from the franc. This forced the French government to control imports, in some cases by means of import quotas, and to re-introduce exchange controls. To begin with, these emergency measures had been taken in a somewhat disorderly fashion in terms of the rules binding the members of the Community together, and it was only after strenuous efforts that the Council of Ministers and the Commission succeeded during June and July in turning what had been done into a mutual-assistance action for a country in balance-of-payments difficulties, in accordance with Article 108 of the Treaty. The summer saw the beginning of a period of calm, a calm about which the French government admittedly harboured no illusions.

The most memorable day, however, in that stormy year of 1968, was 9 September. That was the day on which Britain had to say farewell to the great role it had played in the past in international monetary policy. A session of the presidents of the issuing banks in Basle cleared the ground for the gradual liquidation of the sterling area without thereby causing any disruption of the world's economy. The sterling area was the last concrete link between Great Britain and most of the countries which had once belonged to the great British Empire. All the governments and issuing banks of the Western World assumed joint responsibility in this process of liquidation. From that moment onwards the Bank for International Settlements and twelve central banks have guaranteed the standstill agreement between Britain and the issuing banks of the sterling area.

But the calm was not to last for long. Storms broke out anew in November 1968. A fresh massive wave of speculation was building up throughout the world. It banked on the revaluation of the German mark and the devaluation of the French franc. The 'Group of Ten' (of the ten countries with the most important currencies) was hastily summoned to a meeting in Bonn, and the Federal German Government announced that, in order to avoid revaluing the mark, it would reduce taxes and duties on imports into Germany by 4 per cent of their value, and that it would increase taxes and duties on exports from Germany by 4 per cent.

136

The purpose of these measures was substantially to reduce Germany's huge trade and balance-of-payments surpluses without resorting to revaluation. France was promised new credits of two milliard dollars. Contrary to widespread expectations that France would devalue, de Gaulle refused to do so. Instead, he introduced new and stringent restrictive measures. The Commission, which had always declared itself opposed to changes in the parities of currencies within the Community because of the consequences such changes would have on the common agricultural policy, expressed its regret that the member-states had so far still not shown themselves prepared to co-ordinate their monetary policies more closely. The Commission 'is convinced that the solidarity of the Six, fitted – as it must seek to fit – into the framework of international co-operation, is an unavoidable basic condition for reconstructing a stable orderly international monetary system.'

The Commission had by now come to adopt a sharper tone. This was already evident in its memorandum of February 1968 addressed to finance ministers of the Community, and again in its two memoranda of 5 December 1968 and of 12 February 1969. Unless the economic policies of the member-states were better co-ordinated, the parities between currencies would be directly endangered. At the stage of development which the Common Market had by then reached, changes in the parities of currencies would have serious repercussions in giving effect to common policies, particularly to the common agricultural policy. But there could be no avoiding the fact that effective co-ordination of national economic policies depended for its success on the creation of a mechanism to enable the member-states to work together in the field of monetary policy. What was needed was a permanent system of mutual assistance in monetary policy, and such a system had to become reality.

Moreover, the memorandum of February 1969 took up the ideas underlying the action programme laid down in 1962 and presented them in a more pointed form. 'Consequently the Community cannot stand still at the point of development it has reached up to now. Either the Community succumbs to the pressures – already evident – which are likely to divide it, so that its unity is eroded, at a point in time – paradoxically – at which the customs union has after much stress and strain become reality, and the advantages derived from a large unified market are growing constantly as a result of rapid technological progress; or the Community is successful in harmonizing the different national economic policies in a satisfactory manner within the framework of its existing institutions . . . The Community accordingly faces a fundamental decision. It must make this decision without delay if it wishes to take advantage of possible courses of action which are still open to it, otherwise the equilibrium within the Community could be seriously disturbed and compel the Community to adopt undesirable solutions.'

The proposals on the subject of monetary policy aimed at the very heart of the problem. There was to be joint consultation before any member-government made an important decision affecting economic trends. The medium-term aims of national economic policy – above all, matters affecting rates of growth and of price increases – were to be brought into harmony and unified.

True, were one to measure the concrete monetary proposals put forward by the Commission against the frankly imploring tone struck in this memorandum, then one could describe these proposals only as very moderate, even though they were considered merely as a first step. They amount to no more than short-term monetary support actions. Every participating country was to be bound to put up funds – up to a fixed top limit – at the disposal of other countries, in the case of balance-of-payments difficulties. The form of medium-term financial assistance was merely indicated; unlike the provisions for short-term assistance, it was not to take place automatically. The Council of Ministers accepted this plan of the Commission in principle in July 1969 and formally in resolutions issued by it at the beginning of 1970. On 9 February 1970 it received the blessing of the presidents of the issuing banks. It was the first decision of the European Economic Community in the monetary field. The plan is called the 'Barre Plan', and rightly so: it is not only in its form that it bears the imprint of Raymond Barre, the French Vice-President of the Commission with special responsibility for monetary questions, being couched in his inventive and fruitful language. Under this plan, the issuing banks are now in a position to mobilize one thousand million dollars, and, in certain given circumstances, at a later stage a second thousand million dollars.

138

6. In the meantime, history had begun to prepare the ground for a fundamental turn in the development of the Community. President de Gaulle had laid down his office in April. His successor, Georges Pompidou, and his Minister of Finance, Valéry Giscard d'Estaing, continued for a while to attempt to maintain the then-prevailing exchange rate of the franc, by having recourse to a variety of measures; but the franc could not be held. On 8 August it was devalued by 11·11 per cent. Once again the German mark became the object of fierce speculation. After the September elections in Germany the new Federal Government at first allowed the mark to float and later revalued it by 9·29 per cent. Both these changes in parity caused difficult problems for agriculture. The mechanism of the European 'unit of account' for agricultural prices had been created in the expectation of resolving this kind of situation, but this expectation proved deceptive: monetary union was still a long way off, and the consequences of the 'unit of account' mechanism – a rise in national agricultural prices in the case of devaluation and a lowering of prices in the case of revaluation – failed to have their deterrent effect. It was only after considerable exertions that the Council of Ministers and the Commission succeeded in preventing the break-up of the common agricultural market which had been set up with such enormous effort. They succeeded partly by delaying the rise in prices in France and partly by means of compensating payments to the German farmers.

The time had come to draw the lessons for Europe from this development – a development which had been so rich in surprises, disappointments, and damage. To make this assessment was basically not too difficult.

Our present world monetary system is based on the monetary conference held at Bretton Woods towards the end of the Second World War. The monetary system based on gold, with its fixed exchange rates for national currencies, had collapsed between the two World Wars. The aim of maintaining an equilibrium in one's balance of payments had in nearly all countries lost its priority and been replaced by other aims: full employment, a stable level of prices, economic growth. To ward off the disadvantageous consequences to their own balance-of-payments position, countries had recourse to flexible exchange rates, devaluation, exchange controls.

139

The result was international monetary chaos. To guard against this kind of situation, the International Monetary Fund was set up at Bretton Woods: the aim was, by organizing co-operation in the monetary field, 'to promote the stability of currencies, to maintain an orderly system of monetary relations between the member-states and to prevent competitive devaluations'.

Not that under this system the exchange rates between the various currencies were to be unalterable in every instance. But the general rule was the stability of exchange rates, and a change in parities was the exception, to be applied in cases of fundamental imbalance. As between the most important countries – the members of the so-called 'Group of Ten' – there have been only very few changes in parities.

But it is not only countries that are in deficit, it is also countries that are in surplus, which have good reasons in principle to keep their exchange rates unaltered. The large enterprises and operating units of our time need large markets, larger than those provided by their national internal markets. A revaluation of their country's currency adversely affects their sales prospects abroad and exposes them to the risk of losses.

Irrespective of whether at the present time changes in parity between the world's most important currencies are useful or not, the European Economic Community at all events needs fixed exchange rates within its area. The Common Market demands conditions which are as close as possible to those prevailing in an internal national market. The system of the common agricultural market works by means of 'units of account', and this assures equal prices for the most important agricultural products, equal market intervention prices, equal levies. Revaluations would therefore lead to losses in proceeds and income and so to the necessity of providing subsidies; devaluations would cause price rises and increases in production. This is one of the essential reasons which caused Germany to adopt a kind of 'substitute' revaluation. It is only in their relations with countries outside the Community that all the Community members, acting together, can alter their currency parities. This possibility must be kept open, and for that purpose an integrated monetary policy is necessary.

The Bretton Woods system was carefully thought out, and it also proved itself over a long period of time by the beneficial effects it produced. Why is it, then, that such a system was incapable of preventing the disturbing accumulation of crises which we have witnessed in recent years? Certain special causes apart, there is one general, fundamental reason: on the one hand, states have renounced their individual national rights to use the most important instruments at their disposal for securing their foreign trade balances (such instruments as customs, quotas, and restrictions on convertibility) and have to that extent entered into international obligations by joining organizations such as GATT, OECD, the International Monetary Fund, and the European Economic Community; on the other hand, they have continued to keep economic policy, particularly conjunctural policy, under their own national control. In the area of policy which remains under national control, however, countries do not pursue the same aims as in the areas in which they have renounced control. The Monetary Committee of the European Economic Community has noted specifically 'that the development in relation to the admissibility of price rises varies greatly as between the separate member-states. The same is true of the way in which member-states are prepared to deal with inflation imported from outside the Community, as well as of the adoption of appropriate measures for fighting such inflationary pressures.'

The third of the Council of Ministers' programmes for medium-term economic policy, in March 1971, suggests as guidelines for the German Federal Republic annual price rises of 2·0 to 2·5 per cent between 1970 and 1975, but 2·3 to 3·3 per cent for the other member-states of the Community.

Where national economic policies pull in even such different directions as these, there is bound to follow an ever-accumulating surplus of foreign exchange reserves on the one hand and, on the other, a steady, dangerous drain on the reserves.

The only means therefore that remain at the disposal of member-states to combat the disequilibrium in the balance of payments which is bound to arise from the pursuit of differing national economic policies, is a change in the parity of national currencies. Small wonder, therefore, that this is a weapon that has recently been called for whenever a crisis of this nature has occurred. But it is only the symptoms which are cured by this method. The differing national economic policies are not affected at all, and

141

since they continue to go their different ways there has to be a new adjustment of parities after a few years.

The transition to freely-floating rates of exchange also offers no way out of the problem. Admittedly, such a remedy would provide a certain technical automatic neatness: differing developments in economic trends, in prices and in costs would be continuously balanced out by corresponding alterations in exchange rates which would take place in the market. However, all the same reasons which led to the abolition of this system – which had prevailed between the two World Wars – at the Bretton Woods Conference, still argue against its adoption today. What would happen to the movement of parities between different currencies in the future would always be a matter of uncertainty, an unknown factor, and consequently long-term export dealings, foreign credits, and the acquisition of foreign securities would be made so difficult as to become virtually impossible. Moreover, the re-structuring of production and the employment position in the economically more stable countries would become dependent on the chance influx of capital, whether of a genuine or a speculative nature. Countries like the Federal German Republic, which are determined to pursue a policy of stability, would see a steady increase in the value of their currency as compared to that of other countries; in other words, a permanent revaluation. To put it in another way, the solution of allowing freely-floating exchange rates would be tantamount to establishing economic isolationism anew, and in the monetary sphere it would mean resurrecting the royal right to mint one's own coinage, albeit a right that would be exercised in a more modern context, in the form of the 'sovereign' right of each state to create its own inflation. It would do unforeseeable damage to the world-wide division of labour with which – despite the crises involved – the prevailing economic order has left us to cope.

In these circumstances, then, there remains but one answer to the problem: one must seek to bring about as much discipline as possible in the way states conduct their economic and monetary policies in all matters which are important from the point of view of foreign trade. And what matter is not relevant in this respect? This aspect of the problem has not been taken seriously enough up to now. The International Monetary Fund knows of no obligation that binds it to subordinate national economic policies to the requirement of maintaining an equilibrium in the world's balance of payments. Attempts to move forward in this field got stuck when they were launched in the OECD and mentioned in discussions about an Atlantic partnership. And what about the European Community?

Its hour has come, as it had to come sooner or later. Efforts on different planes within a wider framework to force nations to adopt a sensible way of conducting their economic and monetary policies have failed or were not even attempted. The Bretton Woods system would have been wrecked if its participants had been expected to adopt such a course. But that was due in the last resort to the fact that the classical form and structure of international politics are not suitable for mastering our problem. They are, viewed structurally, too loose, too dependent on the continued preservation of a consensus once attained, too much lacking in authority of their own, too much obliged to rely on the goodwill of the signatories to see that a treaty is kept – whatever the actual text may promise. All these excuses do not exist as far as the European Community is concerned. It at least has the strict minimum of structure and procedure to make possible the integration of anything it may wish to achieve in the sphere of economic policy. Everything the Community has achieved, so far, bears this out.

Is the world then, to look forward to an isolated (possibly an isolationist) solution to the problem by the European Community? By no means. The Community is already a factor making for stability in the world's economy. Were it to pull together the monetary policies and currencies of its members, its character as a community of stability would finally and firmly emerge. It would be quite inevitable that the trends towards stability, thus generated, would transmit themselves to the world outside, with which the Community has such close economic ties. Economic trends in the world generally would gain in stability. Consequently this consideration, too, impels the Community towards a decision: it is a condition for making the world economic system function better. Within that world economic system the Community would carry more weight, as well as enjoy more freedom of manœuvre – if that is wanted – than the sum total of its members today.

The breakthrough in tackling all these necessary problems took place at The Hague Summit of the Six held at the end of 1969.

President Pompidou provided the motive force. What he suggested went beyond what the Commission had proposed so far, both in its purport and in its precision (for example, his proposal to use the Special Drawing Rights of the International Monetary Fund to feed a European Reserve Fund). What was achieved in the economic and monetary sphere was – next to the decision to put an end to the paralysis in which the question of the enlargement of the Community had been for some time – the most significant part of the results reached at The Hague Summit and was one of the most important steps forward in the history of European integration. Paragraph 8 of the communiqué stated: 'The Heads of States and Governments

> reaffirmed their readiness to further the more rapid progress of the later development needed to strengthen the Community and promote its development into an economic union. They are of the opinion that the integration process should result in a community of stability and growth. To this end they agreed that within the Council, on the basis of the memorandum presented by the Commission on 12 February 1969, and in close collaboration with the latter, a plan in stages should be worked out during 1970 with a view to the creation of an economic and monetary union. The development of monetary co-operation should depend on the harmonization of economic policies.
>
> They agreed to arrange for the investigation of the possibility of settling up a European Reserve Fund in which a joint economic and monetary policy would have to result.'

Four important options were here adopted: procedure by stages; the goals of stability and growth; the harmonization of economic policy; and a common reserve fund.

The Council of Ministers of the Community got down to work immediately. Three formulations of the plan in stages, mentioned in the communiqué, were put forward by members of the Council: a Belgian one in January, a German one in February, and a Luxembourg one in March 1970. The Commission followed these up with a draft of its own in which the previously-made suggestions had already been taken into consideration.

The texts of the four drafts show a high level of agreement, particularly on fundamental issues. But at the same time there were

144

evident differences of opinion, which were to lead to a year's controversy in the Council of Ministers. It has become customary to schematize this as a contrast between 'monetarists and economists'. The more 'monetarist' countries were France, Belgium, and Luxembourg; the more 'economist' Germany, Italy, and the Netherlands. The difference quickly polarized as between France and Germany. For Germany, the most important issue – dictated by the German code of stability and growth – was to use external economic policy to assure domestic economic stability: hence, to give priority to the co-ordination of economic policies in the Community. France, on the other hand, sought first and foremost to establish monetary machinery that would overcome national balance-of-payments crises by Community means, and so presented monetary devices (like a pooling of reserves and a narrowing of the bonds of exchange rate fluctuation) as 'incentives' to coordination: but the Germans feared that, without binding, institutional guarantees for the goal of stability, the country in the Community most prone to inflation would determine the whole Community's inflation rate. Under the surface of this economically if euphemistically stated dispute about methods was concealed a political problem to which the laconic formula of the Hague communiqué offered no solution. That is, is the union that is sought irreversible? What institutions are to be set up, with what powers, and in what relationship to the existing institutions? What priority should be given to different economic aims, and is currency stability to come first?

On 6 March 1970, the Council set up an *ad hoc* committee composed of representatives of the Commission and the presidents of the Community Committees for monetary policy, budget policy, conjunctural policy, and medium-term economic policy, under the chairmanship of Pierre Werner, the Luxembourg Prime Minister. On 20 May the Committee produced an interim report, which, while explaining that differences of opinion still remained, already contained the essential elements of the final report, and which, on 8 and 9 June 1970, was unanimously adopted by the Economics and Finance Ministers meeting in the Council. The final report appeared on 8 October. It is the most important document in the history of European integration since the Treaties of Rome. In form and content, in view of the magnitude of the task, it is outstanding for its simple and practical logic, for its uncompromising objectivity, and for its unflinching political vision. 'Economic and monetary union', it concludes, 'works like yeast to bring about political union, without which it cannot be permanent.' The content of the Report is a compromise accepted by all the members of the group, and one which leans towards the economists' school of thought. The aim is a union which 'internally brings about full and irreversible convertibility of currencies, the removal of bands of exchange rate fluctuation, unalterable fixed parities, and full liberalization of capital movements'. Political considerations, it declares, militate in favour of a single currency. The union must at the same time be an economic union. It should make possible 'the guaranteeing of growth and stability in the Community . . . and make of the Community an entity of stability'. It must therefore be linked with 'parallel progress in, and later the unification of, economic policies'. That is to say, there must be parallelism between the creation of these fields of competence and the establishment of the necessary Community institutions.

The following institutions are proposed: 'a centre of economic policy decision-making' for tax and conjunctural policy, to be supervised by a strengthened European Parliament (whether this centre is to be the Commission or the Council, or both, is left open) and 'a Community central bank system' independent of outside instructions.

In a first three-year stage, co-ordination of national policies is to be improved. Responsibility for this is to rest with the Council, as always with the Commission present, and with regular participation of the president of the banks of issue. An 'Annual Report on the Economic Situation of the Community' is to be made and placed before the Economic and Social Committee as well as the European Parliament. Together with the existing medium-term credit facilities, the margin of fluctuation between the Community currencies is to be narrowed, at first on an experimental basis. By the second stage, if not sooner, a 'European Fund for Monetary Policy Co-operation' is to be set up. At the end of the first stage, a balance-sheet of progress is to be drawn up, together with an action programme for the two further stages. This is to be the task of a Conference of Governments, which will also decide on any necessary Treaty amendments.

146

It might have been hoped that the Commission would have felt able to lend to the great thrust of the plan the further unprejudiced impulse of its own support and authority. But the Commission is also an arbitrator – not only the motor of integration and the guardian of the Treaty – and the gulf between Paris and the Werner Committee was too great. Perhaps also the Commission felt itself compelled, in its legitimate function as the initiator of policy, to be original. At all events, with a somewhat reserved and critical statement of its opinion it drew rather into the background. It was therefore salutary when President Malfatti once more stressed, in the Parliament and the Council, the political character of the objective. The Commission's opinion was issued on 29 October 1970. Its influence on later events is undeniable. The upshot was a second compromise between that reached in the Werner plan and the point of view of the French. This compromise slowly took shape in difficult Council meetings in November and December and in the Franco-German consultations (provided for in the Franco-German Treaty of Friendship) in January 1971. Eventually, on 9 February, 1971, it was adopted by the Council in the form of a Decision and a series of Resolutions.

Broadly speaking, the Council adopted the first stage of the Werner Plan. Its decision on the co-ordination of economic policies, admittedly, was weaker than that called for by the Werner Report. At the same time, however, it followed the Commission's lead in giving greater scope to tax and regional policy in the first stage. The procedure for moving into the second stage is also in many respects based on the Werner proposals. That will be the time to decide whether Treaty amendments are necessary.

For the final stage, on the other hand, the Council only partly followed the Werner Plan. Its decision said nothing about the connection with political union, and its remarks about institutions are much less decisive. The future political structure of the Community thus remains in important ways uncertain, and has in fact been entrusted to 'incentives', or the force of circumstances. It is helped by the so-called 'time-limit clause' which the Commission managed to insert into the agreement, and which was based on a similar proposal by Karl Schiller: the monetary policy provisions and the medium-term credit facilities are valid for only five years, and only continue thereafter if there is agreement to embark on the second stage – a representative threat less effective than a preventive guarantee. It would be flattering to call this a 'plan by stages'.

7. The practical application of the plan began badly. In the first stage – although without any strict commitment – the Community countries' banks of issue were, from 15 June 1971, to intervene in close co-operation in order to narrow the margins of mutual fluctuation of their currencies' parity. But this first step was indefinitely postponed. What had happened?

After almost two years' peace on the money markets, a new monetary crisis had broken out. Unlike those of 1968 and 1969, it was not due to uneven development within the Common Market, but to a considerable inflow of dollars from outside, especially into the Federal German Republic. In 1969 and again at the beginning of 1970, the United States had pursued a restrictive money and credit policy, which enabled the European banks of issue also to fight inflation by restricting liquidity and maintaining high interest rates. But during 1971 this situation changed. For internal reasons, the United States switched its conjunctural policy over to expansion. The amount of money in circulation increased rapidly, and the American balance-of-payments deficit rose to 10,000 million dollars, which entered the currency reserves of the other industrialized countries, and increased the amount of money in circulation there, too. After all, what was the significance of a 10,000 million dollar payments deficit for a country with a gross national product one hundred times as great? Once again Europe had to fight against the inflow of liquidity due to the American deficit, which had been growing irregularly for the past fifteen years. This reduced it to virtual impotence against its own inflationary pressure, especially since it had had full employment since the beginning of the nineteen-sixties. The Eurodollar market, a product of convertibility, and for a large part fed by the creation of liquidity due to the American deficit, not only escaped from all control by the banks of issue: it also blunted the weapons of their money policy. At the same time, an abundance of IMF special drawing rights, to the tune of 9,000 million dollars, was allotted to the strengthening of the world's currency reserves. The vessel overflowed, especially in Germany, where – although there seemed no objective justification for a revaluation – uncertainty about policy stimulated so much speculation that 1,000 million dollars

148

suddenly poured in. Between December 1969 and the end of April 1971, i.e. even before the final wave of speculation, German currency reserves rose from thirty-four to sixty thousand million German marks.

On 5 May most money markets were closed. On 9 May, after twenty hours of discussion, the EEC Council of Ministers 'expressed understanding for the fact that some member-states were for a limited time widening the margin of fluctuation of their currencies although 'in normal circumstances flexible exchange rates are not compatible with the proper functioning of an economic Community', and it added that 'a revaluation of the EEC currencies is not justified'. With that, the Federal German Republic and the Netherlands let their currencies float. At the same time, Switzerland revalued the Swiss franc by 7 per cent, and Austria revalued her currency by more than 5 per cent. The direct effect on the Common Market was serious: the common market in agriculture was split into several partial markets, the new-born economic and monetary union was blocked, and solidarity was weakened. Out of the currency crisis came a Community crisis. How did this come about, and what can be done to remedy it?

The answer to the first question is that the present interests of the member-states are in conflict, and that their differences will lead to conflicting monetary policies so long as monetary policies remain national. The Federal German Republic, which unlike the other Community countries has a very large trade surplus, sees it as in its interest to damp down exports (to avoid importing inflation) and to fend off Eurodollars, whenever the German mark looks 'ripe for revaluation' owing to the country's external economic strength. Floating exchange rates meet both these needs – pressure on exports, and the diminution of export earnings. The other Community countries are neither courted by such a mass of speculative capital, nor do they have such a large trade surplus. If all the Community currencies were to float together *vis-à-vis* the rest of the world, this would lead all of them into a permanent revaluation and worsen both their position on foreign markets and their unemployment problems. For this reason, the German proposal at the Council of 8 and 9 May, to widen the funds *vis-à-vis* the rest of the world, while narrowing those within the Community, was supported by none of the other five Community

149

countries, although it was in conformity with Community principles. The interest of the other five, indeed, is to stave off speculative capital, but without revaluation. To this end, various technical measures were discussed, in particular the Belgian 'split market' system, distinguishing between commercial and 'purely' financial transactions, for which latter the bands are wider. After some hesitation, the Federal German Republic admitted such 'flanking controls', and in particular a 'cash deposit' system for certain amounts of speculative capital. The Commission went further. Indefatigable as always since the beginning of these events, it at once proposed a three-part procedure: the enlargement in the armoury of monetary policy; a joint control of the Eurodollar market; and the preparation of a reform of the international monetary system with the aim of broadening the bands *vis-à-vis* the rest of the world and narrowing them within the Community, not later than the next allocation of special drawing rights in the IMF. Its judgement was that the American payments deficit must in the future be regularly financed by joint credit from the international monetary institutions, instead of by unlimited accumulation of dollar holdings on the part of foreign banks of issue.

This is an emergency programme. Lasting peace will be achieved only with the permanent establishment of the European Economic and Monetary union.

3. *Conjunctural Policy*
In the summer of 1969 the European Commission declared in its memorandum on the economic situation: 'The Community has fallen into an inflationary situation, and efforts must be made to prevent these inflationary trends from becoming more pronounced in the months ahead.'

Is this declaration evidence of inadequacy on the part of the Community's institutions, the member-governments, and parliaments? Or are we confronted with an insoluble problem?

True, the wording of the Treaty on policy relating to economic trends (Article 103, paragraphs 1 to 3) can only be described as laconic:

1. Member-states shall regard their conjunctural policy as a matter of common concern. They shall consult with each other

and with the Commission as to any measures to be taken in the light of the prevailing circumstances.

2. Without prejudice to any other procedures provided for in this Treaty, the Council may, on a proposal of the Commission, unanimously decide upon the appropriate measures to take.

3. The Council shall, when appropriate, issue any directives necessary to give effect to the measures decided upon under paragraph 2. It shall do so by qualified majority vote, on a proposal of the Commission.

But all the same the Treaty does provide for (unanimously reached) 'decisions' (paragraph 3) and for 'directives' (reached by a majority) based on these decisions. Decisions have binding force; directives, on the other hand, are 'binding as far as their aim is concerned', but not as far as their form and means are concerned. Only one decision had been handed down so far and no directive has been issued. In the meantime, there have been repeated 'recommendations' and as Article 189, paragraph 5 of the Treaty states, 'recommendations shall have no binding force'.

The Commission devoted itself right from the very beginning to the task of creating the institutions and material conditions for evolving a conjunctural policy for the Community. It found that the Treaty had provided for a Monetary Committee which naturally concerned itself with conjunctural policy. It brought about the setting up as early as January 1960 of a Committee with special responsibility for watching over economic trends and trade cycles. This Committee is made up of high officials from the national administrations and from the Commission. Furthermore, the Commission encouraged the discussion of conjunctural questions at the conferences held by the finance ministers, and at meetings of the presidents of the banks of issue. Besides, the trend towards higher prices in the member-states made it impossible not to discuss such questions. It was recommended in December 1962 that greater precision ought to be given to the means for dealing with conjunctural policy. But as late as 21 January 1964 Robert Marjolin exclaimed in the European Parliament in Strasbourg:

'It is high time to take action to ensure that inflation does not become a permanent feature of our Community . . . We must find solutions to these problems if we wish to avoid serious

151

damage which could endanger the harmonious development of our economy and eventually also the process of European integration.'

Shortly afterwards, in February, on a day when there had been much struggle and argument about speeding up the removal of customs barriers, the then German Economics Minister, Herr Schmuecker, suddenly launched a discussion of conjunctural policy: he no longer had control over policy in such matters, nor had any other Ministers; if conjunctural policy within the Community was to be successful, then it could from now on be pursued only jointly on a common basis. What happened next seemed almost like a small miracle: all his colleagues agreed with him. Only a little later, however, in the spring of the same year, the Commission was compelled to go on record with the statement that the measures proposed by itself and the two Committees mentioned previously had 'not always been carried out to the extent that was desirable'.

It was not until April that the Council of Ministers at last agreed for the first time to issue to the member-states recommendations on certain aspects of policy affecting economic trends. These recommendations were seen everywhere as the beginning of a common approach to conjunctural policy, and so they were – at least at the start. Moreover, they proved a success. The situation had been bad enough. No one was any longer taken in by the excuse that what was involved was merely the growing pains of a young Community; an imbalance in the level of economic activity was there for all to see. In the German Federal Republic economic activity had soared to such a level of excessive boom that the 'coupon tax' had to be introduced to arrest the inflow of unwelcome money from abroad; in Italy, on the other hand, the lira was in difficulties.

In 1967 the cudgels were once again taken up jointly to fight the decline in economic activity, the recession. But these efforts were never more than sporadic actions, designed to deal with specific, concrete situations. As soon as these had been mastered, the will, the drive to tackle this problem on a broader basis, evaporated.

Why have these attempts not led to a common over-all control of

152

a European conjunctural policy? Why were the means of action, provided for in the Treaty, not fully used? There are two reasons.

The first is, as it were, objective. The question which economic policy has to resolve is clear and by no means new: how can economic growth, full employment, a sound balance of payments, and stability in the value of money all be assured at one and the same time? The answer to this question determines whether an economic system based on freedom, and on the free movement of men, goods, services, and capital, and market- and competition-orientated, is credible or not. The answer, however, can up to the present be described as only partially satisfactory. True, the fight against unemployment appears to have been solved in theory and to some extent in practice, in contrast to the situation which prevailed in the thirties. There has also been progress in understanding, in theory at least, the links between growth and currency stability; and the analysing of economic trends has become ever more accurate. But in practice the control of economic forces is still incomplete. That is hardly surprising, nor is it meant as a reproach. The means of influencing the level of economic activity are very extensive, the various methods numerous: there is money and credit policy, financial and budgetary policy, income policy, and import policy. Moreover, in this matter we are concerned not with mere mechanical but with predominantly psychological factors, and these cannot be calculated beforehand: how does a businessman react to indications of economic trends and to methods used to implement policies affecting the level of economic activity? Is his reaction one of courage or of anxiety? On top of that, there are the changes which the creation and evolution of the Community are bringing about. It is not merely the currencies which have become convertible within the Community: fluctuations of economic activity tend to adjust themselves one to the other. Economic movements have greater force. Businessmen plan and invest in terms of a larger market. All this complicates the question, the more so as we are going through a period of evolution. There can therefore be no doubt that we shall have to pay still more for our apprenticeship. But the problem will be solved, provided we recognize clearly what it is we are tackling and go about it in the right way, treating it not as an object of economic policy to be dealt with from time to time when occasion arises, but as a fundamental

153

problem indissolubly bound up with the existence of our new Community.

It is here that we come to the second and graver difficulty. As we have already noted, the political objectives affecting levels of economic activity are not uniform in the six member-states of the Community. The whole world appears to be reconciled to a 'certain' decline in the value of money taking place all the time. But how great a decline is acceptable? There are considerable differences of view on this point, and they, in turn, have considerable consequences. Since 1963 industrial production in the Community has increased by some 60 per cent. But consumer prices have risen at the same time, in some cases steeply: from 1963 to the end of 1970 by more than 25 per cent in the Federal German Republic; by 30 per cent to 35 per cent in France, Belgium and Italy; and in the Netherlands by more than 50 per cent. This presents those responsible for the national economic policy of each member-state with a serious decision. Is it not too high a price to pay for economic growth and full employment? What is the limit to which one can go? This is the first question that must be tackled, because – not although – it is the most difficult question. It is a question to which, right at the beginning, there must be found a common answer. With good reason, the European Commission reproves France for its foreign exchange controls, the Netherlands for its price-control system, and Germany for its claim to currency-equalization levies. It rightly regards all these measures as retrogressive steps, taking the Community away from the degree of integration it has already achieved, and as obstacles on the road towards economic union.

The time has therefore come for making a forceful decision. It should prove no more difficult to reach such a decision than were the agreement to speed up the establishment of the customs union, the creation of a common agricultural policy, the Kennedy Round, or other great achievements of the past. The threat of disintegration comes from different quarters today from those of ten years ago; the failure to establish common policies on the level of economic activities constitutes one of the most serious threats. The state of permanent crisis in the monetary sphere makes the problem more acute. Faced with this situation the Commission has rightly discarded the method of issuing 'recommendations', since this method invariably brought one far too close merely to seeking agreement on the basis of the lowest common denominator. More is needed.

A measure of progress was achieved when the Council of Ministers directed the member-governments to consult with one another before making any decision on all important conjunctural-policy matters. The Council issued this directive on the basis of a proposal by the Commission in February 1969 (the Barre Plan) which is also of special interest from the point of view of monetary policy. Consultation usually takes place in the Monetary Committee, the Committee with special responsibility for watching over economic trends, and the Budgetary Committee; but every member-state and the Commission can ask that consultation take place in the Council of Ministers, and in such cases the Council is promptly convened. The experience of the French devaluation and the German revaluation has taught us how valuable this procedure is. It is an experience that should give fresh impetus to reaching a decision on the most important point of all: the setting of concrete common targets. In the meantime, the developments in the Community, initiated by The Hague Conference, have sharpened awareness of the fact that the state of the economy and the level of economic activity have also become a common phenomenon touching the whole of Europe. The consequences flowing from this are reflected in the growing sense of freedom and lack of inhibitions with which plans are being drawn up, particularly in the spheres of taxation and budgetary policy and of the capital market, where useful starting-points for action already exist. It is good that the banks of issue have begun to play a more active role in Europe as a whole. They have co-operated in the short-term monetary support system which was outlined in the Commission's memorandum of February 1969. There are, of course, certain explanations for their reserved attitude up to now: the divergence of political objective in monetary matters within the Community; furthermore, they must take into account their need to collaborate outside the confines of Europe, for the reason that the amounts of capital, which are moved around where there are violent waves of speculation, are enormous. But these are not reasons for restraining oneself from becoming involved in Europe. The independence of the banks will not suffer within a European framework. Far from it.

155

The Monetary Committee also has not been inactive. It is endeavouring to develop possibilities for medium-term financial assistance in case of disturbances occasioned by a balance-of-payments disequilibrium. In every sphere, then, the various steps that have to be taken are emerging more clearly. But it will be a long time yet before one can imagine there being a 'European law of stability', according to the pattern of the Federal German Republic, containing an inventory of all the instruments for controlling conjunctural policy: the constitution of reserve funds by the public authorities and the social insurance institutions to balance out fluctuations in economic trends; implementation of the budget in such a way as to combat cyclical downswings in the economy; the requirement to give adequate consideration to the level of economic activity in framing the budgets of public authorities, including those of the railways and the postal services; credit restrictions for public authorities whenever those should become necessary; depending on the prevailing situation, higher or lower advance payments of tax; variations in the rates of depreciation allowances; where appropriate, too, the raising or lowering of taxes; a common market for public contracts.

The plan to bring about an economic and monetary union by stages will help to start the evolution of a common European conjectural policy.

4. *Fiscal Policy*

As regards a taxation policy, the Treaty contains only the most timid starting-points, less – as we can confirm on the basis of our present experiences – than the minimum for which the establishment even of an economic union calls. The beginnings of a Community tax are its proposed share of the TVA. The normal revenues of the Community – apart from the allocation to it of customs duties and levies – are contributions by the member-states. But taxes are not only sources of income. They are also a factor in economic policy; that is essentially the reason for the ever-recurring tendency to follow the French example and unite the ministries of economics and finance. (The brilliant linguistic device *finances* makes this fusion easier.) Admittedly there is a chapter in the Treaty headed 'Fiscal Provisions' (Articles 95–99). But, significantly, it follows the chapter dealing with 'Rules of

156

Competition'. In terms of the Common Market, the chapter on 'Fiscal Provisions' is formulated in the most limiting kind of language. The wording is designed to ensure primarily that taxes should no longer be allowed to interfere with the flow of goods across internal frontiers within the Community and to distort competition. The Treaty does not even spell out the fiscal consequences of the provisions for the free movement of capital, laid down in the Treaty itself. One could almost say that the fiscal provisions in the Treaty are a part of internal commercial policy. Different turnover taxes, consumption levies, and other indirect taxes should no longer be discriminatory in character. But there is no mention of direct taxes, of income and corporation tax.

In strictly juridical terms, therefore, the Treaty has 'gaps' which must be remedied by the way the Treaty is applied, in the sense of the over-all concept underlying the Treaty – that is to say, the unification of the separate national economies, as expressed in the preamble to the Treaty.

Accordingly, fiscal policy as a whole has, right from the beginning, been an object of common Community effort. Indeed, the sum total of the tax burden is decisive as far as competition is concerned. It has become a predominant factor in determining where to locate an enterprise or business, more important often than the availability of water or power, of workers or raw materials. In this context, it is not merely a question of tax levels as such, but frequently of directives concerning valuation and depreciation. Fiscal policy can act as a brake; it can paralyse, indeed kill, initiative and imagination. It can, however, also stimulate, release energies and give fresh impulses. It therefore exerts ever-increasing control over the extent to which prosperity develops, and over the opportunities that may exist for growth. Consequently, fiscal policy – like economic and social policy, and next to them monetary policy and matters affecting the level of economic activity – is one of the spheres in which the Community must take political action. Admittedly, there is a long road to travel from recognizing these problems to arriving at concrete decisions. For there is no doubt that notions of national financial sovereignty will be gravely affected, and problems, federal in nature, of finding a balance in financial questions between the Community and the member-states are already coming into view over the horizon.

157

After long and painstaking preparatory work, the Commission was in a position in June 1964 to propose that the different turn-over-tax systems within the Community should, to begin with, be changed into an value-added tax system which should be alike in all member-states. Such a system makes it possible to balance out and neutralize unfair competition, which is bound to exist as long as tax frontiers continue to exist. The next step is to be the harmonization of rates of taxation, which would make it possible to get rid of the nuisance of balancing out the effects of different national taxation systems at the frontiers. In April 1967 the Council of Ministers issued the first two directives on the value-added tax. They provide that all member-states are to introduce the value-added tax by 1 January 1970. The Council, however, agreed in December 1969 that Belgium should not have to carry out this difficult change-over until 1 January 1971 and Italy until 1 January 1972.

By the beginning of 1970 the consumer-tax systems were also to be harmonized and to be adapted to the needs of the Common Market as a whole. Taxes which yield substantial returns are of particular concern here, such as taxes on tobacco, mineral oil, alcohol, and beer. The solution of this problem presents great difficulties. For it cuts into sensitive areas of fiscal traditions which have grown up over the years, and into political and social conditions, affecting property, both of the member-states and of individuals. It also changes the massive room for manœuvre which the states enjoy in fiscal matters. It sets new conditions for whole wide areas of economic activity: one has only to think of the tax on mineral oil and its application in formulating traffic or power policy. But if market conditions resembling those prevailing in an internal national market are to come about within the Community, then it is absolutely essential that these important excise duties should be adjusted and brought into line.

It is also from this concept that the plans for an economic and monetary union, following The Hague conference, are proceeding. Accordingly, the Commission has presented a precise plan for fiscal harmonization. It provides for the removal of all tax barriers – unfortunately not until 1978: the differences in rates of the value-added tax are to be brought into line, step by step, until they are within a margin of about 3 per cent of one another; a common

158

tax-assessment basis is to be decided upon as early as 1973. Furthermore, the large consumer taxes (the excise duties on mineral oil, tobacco, and alcohol) are to be harmonized to the extent of eliminating any distortions of competition that may still exist, and this is to be achieved in two phases: to begin with, by bringing the structural differences into line, and then by dealing with different rates of tax.

Progress has been slower in the adjustment of taxes which serve as pointers for the capital markets. But in July 1969 the Council of Ministers issued a directive which dealt with indirect taxes affecting the accumulation of capital. It provided that the tax on securities was to be abolished and that at the time the corporation tax, which is raised on the capital resources of companies and therefore indirectly on the shares issued by them, was to be harmonized; this harmonization is conceived in such a way that corporation tax will for all practical purposes be the same in all the member-states. At the same time the arrangements necessary to give effect to these directives were to come into force on 1 January 1972.

But there is more still that needs to be done. One simply cannot succeed in drawing on the common available sources of capital without developing a common capital market, and this development is still trailing behind the stages of evolution it should have reached. The Commission has rightly warned about this. As far back as November 1966 it worked out a comprehensive plan for a common capital market for the Community in a report which is called the 'Segré Report', after the official responsible for dealing with this subject. But hardly anything has happened since then. For this reason, private initiatives are all the more useful. Well-deserved attention has been paid to the arrangements for co-operation made in autumn 1970 by a number of European banks: the Gruppe Deutsche Bank, the biggest German merchant bankers; the Amsterdam-Rotterdam Bank; the Société Générale (Brussels); the Midland Bank Ltd (London); and the group formed by the Commerzbank (the third largest of the German merchant banks); the Crédit Lyonnais, the second biggest nationalized French bank; and the Banco di Roma. But the national capital markets continue to remain isolated from one another, particularly as a result of different national fiscal regulations: there are divergent regulations on taxes on income from capital which in some cases lead to double taxation, and every country also has its own foreign exchange regulations for nationals and foreigners. The aim must be, especially in this sphere, to establish a strict neutrality as far as taxation is concerned. Direct taxation ought not in any way to influence where capital is invested within the Community, and there ought to be no discrimination, as a result of taxation, between investors from different member-states. The programme of the Commission for gradual establishment of an economic and monetary union lists all the taxes which still restrict the free flow of capital, in the sphere of direct taxation and also of the corporation tax. A memorandum by the Commission of May 1970 sets out the most compelling reasons for tackling this problem. But there is still resistance, particularly on the part of Germany.

Great efforts will therefore have to be made in the sphere of fiscal policy. Solely to bring the different rates of taxation within the Community into line with one another is an unusually difficult task, although this has now a firm basis in the plan for economic and monetary union. The Council's decisions for the first stage include an impressive array of concrete measures, among them the second phase of tax harmonization, that is the unification of the basis of assessment.

But it is already widely recognized that a turnover-tax system which does not distort competition and is, in other words, 'neutral' from the point of view of competition, is not enough by itself. One must also take direct taxation into account and go even further, to the harmonization of the regulations governing the assessment of taxes. Among other things, this means that countries whose revenue today largely depends on the yield from indirect taxes – above all, Italy – must make an effort to increase the revenue yield from direct taxes. It means, too, that countries whose position is the other way round and whose tax revenue today is derived mainly from direct taxes – as is the case above all, in the Netherlands, but also in the Federal German Republic – must make a move in the opposite fiscal direction. Finally, it will be necessary to guarantee tax neutrality (that is to say, no discrimination on the basis of taxation) where enterprises enter into amalgamations and fusions across the frontiers of the member-states of the Community. Without such a reform it will hardly prove feasible to create European companies capable of competing in the world at large.

Fiscal policy in the Community consequently provides a good example of the way in which all important aspects of economic policy interact one upon the other, and it illustrates how such interaction generates impulses which make for progress. The negotiations on enlarging the Community have also worked in the same direction.

5. *Medium-Term Economic Policy*

In seeking to evolve and formulate medium-term economic policy the Community entered virgin territory. This particular aspect of the Community's activities was simply to be called 'economic policy'. For the expression 'medium-term' serves only to point up the distinction between making short-term conjunctural policy and recognizing that one can, if necessary, plan ahead reliably for the medium-term.

True, the new settlers in this virgin territory have not yet been able to bring in any record harvest, but the first yields are good. To start with, the ground had to be cleared of roots and undergrowth; swamps of false prejudices had to be dried out; rocks of misunderstanding and of rigid, hardened habits of thought had to be exploded. The adventure of the Common Market demanded new methods of economic thinking and conduct, new forms of common action.

The Treaty refers to these new things only vaguely; moreover, it expresses itself in traditional formulae. Article 2 calls for the 'progressive approximation of the economic policies of the member-states'. According to Article 6, the member-states shall co-ordinate their respective economic policies 'in close collaboration with the institutions of the Community'. According to Article 145, the Council 'shall ensure that the economic policies of the member-states are co-ordinated'. In short, therefore, the Treaty contains only clauses couched in broad, general terms. It was surprising how rapidly, after a successful start had been made in building a Common Market, it came to be felt that there was a need to breathe life into these clauses.

Common action began with the use of a common language, of common terms which could be common only if they reflected

161

common thinking. It was essential to build on the existing vocabulary – above all, of course, on the vocabulary of scientific terms. After the horrors, in the Western World, between 1920 and 1950, of the German inflation and the great world economic crisis, after the succession of failures to combine central direction of the economy with political freedom, no one any longer disputed the existence of functional links between certain academic concepts and opinions, particularly where monetary theory and theories on economic fluctuations of boom and depression were concerned. We were able to draw considerable benefit from this. Moreover, these economic analyses found general acceptance, irrespective – on the whole – of fundamental political convictions. If these analyses had already been available in the thirties, Europe would probably have been spared many horrors.

The situation and the practical problems involved began to emerge more clearly in the course of a dispute which was provoked by the 'action programme' for the second stage of the transition period of the Community, submitted by the Commission in October 1962. At the turn of the year 1961–2, the Community had entered the second stage after the first bout of marathon sessions of the Council of Ministers, which had gone on for weeks. The Commission had to lay down guidelines for what was to be done in the sphere of economic policy over the next few years, guidelines for itself, for the Community, for the member-states and for the economy. Unfortunately parts of this programme – for example, the chapter dealing with 'Monetary Policy' – have up to the present still lost none of their topical interest.

The controversy was sparked off by a chapter entitled 'Economic Policy' which for the first time laid down the basic outlines of a short-term and medium-term economic policy, its methods and means, required for a supranational community of states. Number 109 of the Chapter stated that 'the consolidated programme of economic policy' also had to lay down 'what division of the estimated gross national product would be desirable or acceptable as between the large economic sectors of the Community: agriculture, mining, manufacturing industries, transport and service industries'. Germany expressed its anxiety that figures, once laid down, as 'desirable' under the plan, would soon be followed by political proposals designed to ensure that the figures laid down would, in

162

fact, be treated as targets under the plan which had to be met. The argument between Brussels and Bonn, between the Commission and the Federal German Economics Ministry, between the German Minister for Economics, Ludwig Erhard, and myself, was at times violent. Nowadays it is only comprehensible to someone who took part in or witnessed the lively dispute on economic policy which took place in the Federal German Republic between 1948 and about 1953 and in which Erhard eventually emerged as the victor: the victory was not without significance in the purely political sphere. The controversy reached its climax and conclusion in the debate between the two of us before the European Parliament in Strasbourg on 20 November 1962 when Erhard declared: 'What we need is not a programme tied to plans, but a programme that promotes stable conditions.' This took us to the very heart of our dispute, or, to be more precise, of the misunderstanding between us. For it was exactly a policy aimed at producing stable conditions that also formed the basis of the Commission's action programme. Its purpose was to pursue not a planned economy but a policy with purposeful objectives and not without any objectives at all. In everyone's interest, the details of these objectives should be generally known.

But the controversy proved useful. It contributed to elucidating the issues involved on both sides. An expert opinion, published by the Scientific Advisory Council of the Federal German Economics Ministry at the beginning of 1964, made a particularly useful contribution in this context: what was needed – the Council pointed out – was to estimate likely developments over the whole field of the economy for several years ahead, in order to formulate and coordinate political measures on economic and structural trends on a more rational basis in Germany. Admittedly – the professors added in the expert opinion they submitted – it would be dangerous to make the attainment of these estimates obligatory and thus give them a measure of compulsion which they should, by their very nature, not possess. The same kind of optional medium-term economic estimates were also recommended by the German Advisory Council for the European Economic Community. The Commission welcomed the Council's expert opinion. The views and criticisms expressed in it pushed against open doors. At the same time, the Federal German Government withdrew its

163

reservations about estimates on medium-term economic developments.

In the meantime, the Commission had already made it clear to the Council of Ministers in its recommendation of July 1963 that it harboured no intention of limiting the freedom of decision of enterprises, particularly in the area of investment. Furthermore, the danger was to be avoided of treating proposed estimates and plans for the future as 'growth targets' for the Community. There remained the delicate subject of dividing global, overall estimates of future economic development as between large sectors of the economy, a subject on which there was much lively controversy. The sting was to be taken out of the controversy by insisting that any 'examinations of what should and should not be linked together economically' should serve internal purposes only and should not be published. The Commission had left no doubt on the point that conditions in which competition could flourish must be maintained and strengthened, and that this was one of the aims of the Treaty. It had also made it clear that it could not close its eyes to the numerous interventions in many spheres of economic activity by the member-states. This state of affairs presented the Commission with two sets of questions: firstly, were certain interventions by the member-states useful and admissible, especially when they limited competition and distorted the functioning of free market-forces; and, secondly, were public interventions, which might at a given moment have been considered necessary, still rational?

Nobody nowadays any longer denies the need for a medium-term economic policy. The question has ceased to be a matter of dispute. Economic decisions taking a longer view are bound to be more rational – that is the firm incantation, the '*cantus firmus*', sung in support of a medium-term economic policy. There is a need to avoid such measures as are taken being taken too late to be effective or failing to take account of other sectors of the economy, or even being contradictory. An economic community feels this compulsion more strongly than any other economic body, in view of the fact that an economic community is committed to the free movement of goods, persons, services and capital, and the right of establishment. Should such a community disregard this compulsion, it is bound to make errors in its use of scarce productive resources.

In April 1964 the Council of Ministers agreed to the establishment of the Committee for Medium-Term Economic Policy which was formed later that year in December 1964. Its task was, in particular, 'to formulate a draft for a programme for medium-term economic policy'. This programme was to set out the broad outlines of the economic policy which it was intended to implement, and to ensure its co-ordination. Further, the Committee was to examine the medium-term policies of the member-states and their compatibility with the programme. It is also entitled to work out points of view on its own initiative and to submit them to the Council of Ministers. The member-states collaborated actively in the Committee's work; high national officials, responsible for preparing economic policy in their respective member-states, were despatched to sit in on the meetings of the Committee and its sub-committees.

Naturally, no rapid and spectacular results could be expected from these labours. It takes time to harmonize thinking on economic policy, on concepts, on the vocabulary of terms used. In addition, as a result of the crisis in 1965 and 1966, France temporarily ceased to take part in the work of the Community, including the work of this Committee, and so the Committee was unable to submit its first programme until May 1966. This programme was adopted by the Council in April 1967. The second programme, which was meant to supplement the first, was submitted as early as March 1968 and, after a thorough and probing debate in the European Parliament, received the approval of the Council of Ministers, without a change being made, in December 1968.

Medium-term economic policy seeks to put all available and measurable economic data in relationship to one another and to base on them, 'to project into the future', certain plans for the years ahead. Admittedly, economic development can be calculated ahead only to a very limited degree, above all, because it is human beings who make the decisions – human beings, who, among other things, also allow themselves to be guided by irrational motives. But both of the first two programmes already reveal the surprising extent to which numerous data are known and are capable of being recognized. As a rule, however, only public authorities can produce all the accessible data – like changes in the potential labour

165

force or the demand for certain goods and services. Yet these data ought to be prepared and made available as quickly as possible to those who have to make decisions in the economic field – to governments or parliaments, to employers or employees. To use a dangerous, yet illuminating term, one would say that medium-term economic policy is 'an aid to decision-making'. Only by employing it in this manner can it exert an effect in depth. It is neither a weapon that can work miracles in economic policy, nor a book of prescriptions through which one thumbs to discover the right medicinal dosage to cure economic ills. The deliberations and planning ahead will become progressively less abstract in character: to bring a policy of growth into harmony with a policy of stability will, for example, be a continuous and highly concrete, down-to-earth task.

The method is already apparent in the first programme. Naturally it rests on certain assumptions to make it work – assumptions on the development of conditions that make for growth and expansion, and of supply and demand. For that reason, it is also pointed out that the estimates and calculations on future development cannot be treated as setting targets; they are merely quantitative indicators. Employment policy and policies on vocational training, public finance, and regional development are themes in the first programme which point the direction in which medium-term policy must evolve. An incomes policy, on the other hand, belongs to those areas of economic activity with which medium-term policy can come to grips only with great difficulty – if, indeed, it can be expected to do so at all. As things stand, medium-term planning still appears to be at its most effective in coping with the economic policies of public authorities; but even here the estimates set out in the programmes will constantly have to be corrected and adopted. In any case, the successes this approach has had in all the member-states, including the Federal German Republic, are encouraging.

If the first programme was still concerned with defining what a medium-term economic policy in a Community of states meant in fact and what it could achieve, the second already dealt with how it could be carried out in practice. In the years between the two programmes the Common Market had become more closely integrated. All national economies revealed weaknesses on a regional

166

basis as well as in particular branches of the economy. The movement of enterprises from one part of the Community to another had begun a process that in particular cases often proved painful. Competition with other industrial states – with America and also, ever more strongly, with Japan – had increased. Quantitative forward planning by itself was no longer enough. Consequently, European economic policy is concentrating, in a way that is becoming more marked all the time, on a task that bears the name of 'sectional structural policy', that is to say, industrial policy which devotes itself continually to the problems of certain regions or branches of industry. The principle behind it is that economic policy cannot confine itself to the great 'global' issues, to determining only the broad over-all economic data; it must also contribute to the work of seeing that the details involved in the process of integration and adaptation takes place under the most favourable conditions possible. At the same time, enterprises must not be relieved of having to adapt themselves to the constantly-changing demands of supply and demand; their task in this respect is only made easier. It therefore follows that the second programme defines the strengthening of the Community's capacity to complete as the decisive factor in determining what sectional support-measures there should be. In principle, then, all measures which might have the effect of transferring the costs of one sector of the economy to another have to be avoided. Guarantees are to be granted only in exceptional cases where they can be specially justified. No effort is to be made to keep going enterprises or lines of production which are not competitive.

The third programme, drawn up at the end of 1970, and covering the years 1971–5, shows very clearly the links on the one hand with medium-term financial aid (the Barre Plan) and on the other with the monetary part of the plan for economic and monetary union, for which national policies need to be concerted. It therefore contains, as already agreed upon in the Council at the beginning of 1970, global quantitative indications. These are intended to bring national targets into line with the real possibilities of the now interdependent national economies, and thereby to prevent member-states being forced into emergency measures and parity changes as a result of balance-of-payments crises. Thus the national projections are to be made 'compatible' one with another. These data are to be checked against guidelines for national and Community policy. The main problem is that of differing rates of inflation, and hence of arriving at stability within the Community. Structural policy is again extremely important: that is, the completion of the larger market by the removal of the remaining barriers and the adaptation of labour supply. Also in the foreground are measures to harmonize credit and finance policies. To this end, there is a need for compatibility between economic budgets, a system of warning indicators, the establishment of permissible margins for cyclical movements, and the synchronization of national programming procedures.

This work is not only proving beneficial to the evolution of economic policy; it is also important from an institutional point of view. Within the space of a few years there has grown up a continuous and continuing dialogue between those in positions of responsibility. This is a process which is new for Europe and which is in itself of inestimable value. Never before has there existed so precise and complete a knowledge of each other's economic affairs and projects as today. All have learnt to speak a common language in matters of economic policy. All have recognized and accepted their interdependence. All have understood that their own problems have for some time past also become the problems of their partners. They know that the painful processes of adaptation, though unavoidable, can be directed and controlled, and that this is easier within the framework of the Community than it would be if each state acted on its own. They also know that to base economic policy on reason is no longer Utopian and, at the same time, that a large community encourages a higher degree of rational thinking, which guarantees the maintenance of the capacity to compete. One of the results of the constant interchange of views and information – and this is far from being one of the least important – is that all those involved have become more firmly convinced than before that the economic policy of the Community can never be anything but a policy governed by the interplay of market forces.

Owing to the procedures it has adopted and the results it has achieved, the 'medium-term economic policy' of the Community has smoothed the way for economic and monetary union. It will be an important factor in realizing the plan by which this union is to be brought about in stages. Setting common overall economic guidelines for the medium term will act in effect as a warning system which will register any deviations from the guiding principles. This, in fact, is the basis of a 'common economic policy'. Indeed, as economic union proceeds, the systematic separation of medium-term economic policies will gradually disappear.

6. *Social Policy*

The provisions of the Treaty of Rome on social policy – like those on transport policy, monetary policy, and other matters – clearly bear the mark of the controversies during the negotiations leading to the conclusion of the Treaty. In other words, they bear the mark of the past. They reflect not so much the 'nature of the subject matter', the objective requirements of a European policy as circumstances and conditions created by historical accident which blocked the will to reform. The text of the Treaty does not seek solutions for the difficulties, but mirrors the difficulty of finding solutions. The greatest of these was the French desire for 'social assimilation', which meant the extension of its expensive social system to the whole Community. This French demand was not based purely on considerations of social policy: France feared that its high social charges would place it at a disadvantage in competing with other member-states. It cost much effort to reach a compromise; the heads of government themselves had to intervene during the final phase of the negotiations at the end of 1956 and the beginning of 1957. Agreement was eventually reached by adopting the term 'harmonization', a term which is weaker than 'equalization'. This way of going about things is symptomatic of a conservative attitude which strikes one as peculiarly strange in social affairs, where much of the motivation springs from strong human and dynamic forces. The national social systems have all become technically very rigid. As a result the national social technocrats defend them in good faith (which can only be described as dangerous) not only against progress in the European field but also, inside their own countries, against any reforms which are not put forward by the specialists and technocrats themselves.

Consequently, the Treaty does not point a direct route towards a true 'common social policy'. It uses the concept only in relation to vocational training, in so far as it provides that the Council of Ministers should lay down 'general principles' with the aim of promoting the harmonious development in this field; these principles were decided on in 1963. Otherwise the provisions in the Treaty are meagre. Problems – admittedly important ones, such as the freedom of people to take jobs anywhere in the Community, and the remuneration of female workers – have been tackled only in isolation and then resolved in legally binding form by means of clear juridical provisions. As for the rest, the Treaty advanced no further in the sphere of social policy than outlining a programme (Article 118, paragraph i, also Article 120) or rules of procedure (enabling regulations). It does not tackle the problem of the competence of the national authorities on a broad front. The chapter of the Treaty dealing with social policy speaks only of 'collaboration' of the member-states. Naturally this does not restrict the general principle of 'co-ordination', which is laid down for the whole of economic policy and also includes social policy. But, apart from the special areas which have already been enumerated, the competence of the Commission is expressly limited to studies, to the giving of opinions, and to the preparation of consultations – the weakest form of initiative.

Modest though the help is which the Treaty provides to launch a common social policy, it is interesting to note how the European ground-swell, slowly but irresistibly, washes over the national sand-banks. Despite all the differences in national social 'techniques' – which in their variety recall the many different forms of agricultural protectionism – there do, all the same, exist a great many common factors in social matters: these arise not only from facts and circumstances, from needs and from interests, but also from concepts of social value and from trends in social policy. Let us draw particular attention in this context to social security: to the trend to extend the protection afforded by insurance, and to improve the payments made under insurance schemes. Social expenditure has risen enormously in all the member-states of the Community, and considerably more rapidly than national income. The margin between the different social systems has thereby been narrowed at the same time.

True, the Treaty largely left the harmonization of social systems to 'development' with a certain air of fatalism. But all the same the attitude this approach reflected was more than an easy way of wishful thinking. It was inconceivable that the mighty current, which was driving the member-states of the Community in the direction of greater unity, freedom (including the greater mobility of economic elements), equality, progress and, above all, security, could fail to carry social policy along with it and, instead, leave it untouched as a kind of island belonging to the past. Those responsible for drawing up the Treaty, could therefore confidently content themselves with entrusting the Commission merely with actions of an indirect nature – apart that is from imposing on it the duty of promoting collaboration between the member-states and of carrying out specific tasks in respect of the freedom of movement of workers and of the remuneration of women. The Commission has done much to use the language of the Treaty in a constructive way, driven forward by the conscientious and tenacious efforts of Giuseppe Petrilli, one of its members, and of his successor, Vice-President Lionello Levi Sandri. Furthermore, one could rest assured that there would gradually come about a common usage of terms, a common language which would be bound to lead in the short or the long run to a common basis for reaching decisions and taking actions. Institutionalizing the talks on questions of social policy could not fail to bring fruitful results, not only as far as the exchange of information was concerned but also in helping common concepts of value to evolve. No less was the confidence one could have in the trade unions, whose European sentiments have long been well and truly proven. Their views are heard, and not only in the Economic and Social Committee. Finally, the Commission is bound to set out in a special chapter of its annual report how the social situation within the Community is developing. It devotes considerable space to this chapter because it deals with the theoretical aspects of the subject, as well as with what is being prepared and with what has been achieved. The chapter must, according to the Treaty, be comprehensive. It covers the following themes: employment, labour laws, conditions of work, vocational training as well as further training, social security, prevention of injuries at work and of occupational diseases, protection of health, freedom to organize unions or associations, and collective negotiations between employers and employees. The documentation which the Commission has gathered together over the years on all those themes and published represents an important collection of material which is descriptive as well as analytical and stimulating.

It is no accident that the only piece of social policy which has been properly worked out and not merely set forth in the form of a programme – the freedom of movement of workers within the Community – is laid down in the part of the Treaty entitled 'Foundations of the Community'. This is the part that deals with the 'four freedoms'. To be sure, the theory of social policy grew up and developed within the framework of the science of economics, particularly in the theory on incomes and the policy on incomes. Then, in the course of the last half-century, it has gradually emerged and freed itself from that framework, until today it has reached the point where it is an aspect of the whole of economic policy. In this evolution the equality of competition within the Community has played and is playing an important role. Thus it is perfectly natural that the Treaty should deal with the freedom of movement of workers from the angle of the mobility of the factors of production. It is equally understandable that in the sectors where provision is made for 'common policies', there should also be provision for dealing with the special social problems of these sectors (in the sectors of agricultural policy and of transport policy). What has happened shows clearly that the process of integration in the sphere of social policy, as in others, compels the Community to solve not only the problems it found at the start but also and equally those which arise as an inevitable consequence of integration.

Finally, it is not only in the actions the Community takes in matters of policy affecting economic trends that elements of social policy – such as incomes, wages, and employment – are deeply involved. Social questions also play an important role in the first medium-term economic programme as well as in the second, which largely concentrated on policy relating to the structure of the economy: these are problems of employment; advice on careers for and training of the young; training, adaptation, and further education of adults; the establishment of labour exchanges and decisions on the methods they should employ to carry out their functions; the creation of new jobs by means of locating enterprises in certain areas.

The freedom to take jobs anywhere within the Community involves much more than just freedom of movement. It means that there should be no discrimination against non-nationals from other countries in the Community, as far as employment, pay, and other conditions of work are concerned. It involves the right to apply for work, to look for work in a country other than one's own, and also to remain there subject to certain conditions. All employees from countries in the Community are eligible for membership of the unions in the country in which they work and can be elected to the bodies which represent the staff in the enterprises employing them. They receive the same legal treatment as the nationals of the country where they work, in all tax and social matters. They can ask the members of their family to join them, they have the right to lodgings and the right to acquire real estate. A second aspect of the freedom to work anywhere in the Community is the task with which the legislative authority of the Community has been charged under the Treaty. It is a task it can discharge either by itself – drawing the consequences from those principles guaranteeing social security – or by authorizing the Commission to implement what is necessary. In practice this means that a non-national from a country in the Community will enjoy the same status as regards social security as a national of the country where he works.

Thus not only is the 'priority of the national labour market' abolished and its place taken by the 'priority of the Community labour market' (in preference to the labour markets of countries outside the Common Market), but also new common factors are emerging in the sphere of social policy: all nationals of all member-states of the Community are to be treated in the same way. This sweeping freedom of movement of workers was brought about in three stages – the first in 1961, the second in 1964, and the third in 1968 – and came fully into force on 1 July 1968, one-and-a-half years before the end of the transition period of the European Economic Community. One of the most spectacular points in the programme which is to lead to the integration of Europe was thus attained. On the basis of this success alone, the Community could claim the right to call itself the 'European Economic and Social Community'. The consequences in terms of constitutional policy are incalculable. Do they point to the beginning of a common

173

European 'citizenship'? Rather in the same way as in the Community's monetary policy, a distinction is now drawn, for the purpose of anti-speculation measures, between nationals of the Community and nationals of non-member-countries. Certainly economic and social motives have caused a breach to be made in what had previously been regarded as being part of a national state's exclusive preserve of internal policy.

By contrast, there is as yet no common policy on wages nor on collective agreements on rates of pay. In this sphere, particularly, one can expect the increasing degree to which economic conditions in the Common Market are becoming unified to stimulate the process of harmonization, the more so in case of further progress towards economic union. The only firm and concrete requirement is that male and female workers should receive equal remuneration for the same work (Article 119 of the Treaty of Rome). It is very near to being fully realized; it is worth drawing attention to the fact that the practice of treating female workers separately in collective agreements on rates of pay has virtually disappeared, and that, generally speaking, the wage rates for women have risen more markedly than those for men. This, too, represents a step forward which would not have been taken by now without the existence of the Treaty of Rome.

The most important social problems with which the advancing process of integration has to contend – problems which are partly created or accelerated by integration – are those of adaptation: this is evident, for example, in agriculture, in mining, in shipbuilding, and in the high-technology industries. Their solution demands a capacity to adapt – in other words: mobility. We have already talked of mobility in the geographical sense. Occupational mobility – the capacity to change jobs and acquire new skills – is more important still, since a man prefers changing his job (and does so more easily) to changing his outward circumstances of life. Occupational mobility is so important that there are, as we have seen, provisions in the Treaty itself laying down general principles for carrying out a 'common policy' with regard to vocational training. There is an old German proverb which was used to admonish the young in the past: 'What young Johnny does not learn now, John will never learn'. Its meaning has long been overtaken by events. In a future, the beginning of which we are already seeing around us, training will, next to technological advances, be the second most important factor of progress. The Commission has rightly stressed this point in its memorandum of March 1970 on industrial policy. Training and further education will accompany man throughout his whole life. For changes in the techniques of work and moves from the occupation one has learnt, to another occupation up or down the career ladder from the rung to which one had become accustomed, will be normal features of a working life. Statistics already bear out this trend very clearly. It is also evident in separate branches of the economy and in different occupations.

The most important instrument for dealing with the need for adaptation in the Community is the 'European Social Fund'. Its purpose is to increase the possibilities of employment for workers in the Common Market. At the request of a member-state it makes good half the expenditure incurred for occupational retraining, for resettlement allowances or for such aid as workers may receive whose employment has been reduced or terminated as a result of the conversion of a concern to other production. The nature of the Fund is therefore that of a bank of compensation which operates in the interests of social policy. Member-states have shown a marked inclination to draw out of the Fund more or less exactly what they have paid in – a procedure which in France is known as *juste retour*. The Fund is administered by the Commission with the aid of a Committee composed of representatives of member-governments and of trade unions and employers' organizations. Up to the end of 1970 the Fund had paid out roughly the equivalent of 550 million German marks, the largest part of which went towards retraining, and a small proportion towards resettlement.

The Fund has, within its limits, worked satisfactorily. But even in the early years of its existence there were demands for its reform. The Commission first put such demands forward in 1965, but they at first met with no success. The Treaty itself expressly provides that the Council of Ministers may, after the end of the transition period on 31 December 1969, unanimously decide on new tasks to be entrusted to the Fund within the framework of its fundamental aims, after the Commission has expressed its opinion and the Economic and Social Committee has been consulted. In accordance with this provision the Commission submitted a detailed opinion which amounted to a fundamental re-orientation

175

of the Fund. The aim was to set up an instrument capable of pursuing a dynamic policy of employment, of responding to the changes in the structure of the economy of the Community and to such adaptations as these changes required.

In fact, conditions have changed considerably since the Treaty was drawn up: those in positions of responsibility are concerned less nowadays with unemployment than with underemployment – which is not easily recognized for what it is – and with the lack of flexibility to adapt to new circumstances on the part of the apparatus of production. The prevailing arrangements were felt to be inflexible, quibbling and unwieldy. They reacted only after the event and therefore missed the opportunity of effectively shaping events. They were concerned on a narrow basis: in the main they cope only with the unemployed and with those who are plainly underemployed. They dispersed the resources at their disposal over too wide a field. They denied the European Social Fund any kind of initiative of its own and any chance to use its own judgement. They worked indirectly: only member-states could request and receive funds. By contrast, action which is spontaneous, dynamic, comprehensive and direct holds out the promise of making it possible to respond to the needs of adaptation by taking initiatives in cases where intervention appears singularly suitable. So in fact what was needed – and what the Community Labour Conference in Luxembourg at the end of April called for – was an instrument of employment policy for the Community, which would complete the Community's structural-policy provisions.

On the proposal of the Commission, in July and November 1970 the Council made fundamental reforms in the European Social Fund. Now, it is no longer restricted to the attack on unemployment. It is engaged in preventive measures, and no longer merely automatic, but acting according to criteria laid down by the Council in accordance with the employment situation. It now has a role in Community decisions affecting labour markets, as in regional policy and structural policy, but also trade and tariff policy. During a transitional phase, it has the task of helping to correct lasting situations (here Italy was the main concern) in sectors, branches of the economy, and groups of firms that are out of balance, to assist those whose employment situation is unsatisfactory (the jobless, the underemployed, the handicapped, the

176

older workers, women, and young people). In this respect the Fund is still a compensation fund. It puts up 50 per cent of the costs borne by those responsible for employment policy. And its aid is for human beings, not investment assistance: its purpose is to facilitate retraining, continuation-schooling, and resettlement.

At this same November meeting the Council also agreed to set up the 'Permanent Committee on Employment' which had been under discussion since 1965 – the most important outcome of the conference that April between the Community institutions and the Community-level representation of employers and trade unions. The Committee's purpose is consultation on questions of European employment policy. Employers and trade unions are represented equally on it through their Community-level organizations: on the employers' side, UNICE (Industry, handicrafts, trade, and insurance), COPA (agriculture), and CEEP (public enterprises), and on the trade union side the European Federation of Free Trade Unions, the European branch of the World Confederation of Employees, the Joint Secretariat of the CGT (French) and CGIL (Italian), the CIC (white-collar workers), the German Employees' Trade Union, the CFTC (French). The Committee has been at work since March 1971.

At the same time the Council took up some German proposals of April 1970 for the introduction of an annual Social Budget on the German model, and the preparation of the harmonization of social security by a comparison of the range of insured persons, to begin with by means of practical investigation.

Finally, at the end of March 1971, the Commission published a Memorandum on the 'Preliminary establishment of a programme for a Community Social Policy', in order to open up a wide-ranging policy debate. Its main consideration is the problem of employment, to be dealt with by improvement of the Community labour market. Transparency of the market, free right of settlement, the organization of migrant labour, the establishment of new labour exchanges, and vocational training – these are its main starting-points. The Commission deplores the existence of lasting wage disparities and sees the divergent financing of social security benefits as a serious distortion of competitive conditions. It also raises such questions as decision-sharing by employers and trade unions, European collective agreements, European working

177

and apprenticeship conditions, and safety standards. Finally, it places great emphasis on living conditions outside the place of work. Housing policy (a familiar preoccupation of the Coal and Steel Community), leisure conditions, family policy – what the Commission calls 'the demands of civilization' – all have a bearing on competition policy, since differing national standards can distort costs. From all these considerations, the Commission is led to propose an overall programme for the environment.

All these rapidly-growing activities reveal that the dynamic force of the social considerations that have, so to speak, grafted themselves on to the Community, will carry it forward. Moreover, it is one of the intellectual and moral forces, one of the hopes, which propel Europe forward on the road to progress.

7. *Agricultural Policy*

Agricultural policy provides one of the most exciting chapters on the diverse branches of European economic policy. In no sphere were the labours facing the Community of such Herculean dimensions. Nowhere else has so much courage and iron determination been brought to bear on the problems involved. As the common agricultural policy evolved, grave conflicts broke out – conflicts which even called into question the fundamental political nature of the Community itself. What had to be faced was the variety of facts and circumstances that existed as we began our work; the profound changes that economic conditions were undergoing; and the magnitude of the targets that had been set. The challenge of dealing with the specialist and technical tasks involved therefore called for the highest degree of unremitting industry, knowledge of the subject-matter, imagination and lack of prejudice. The European Agricultural Policy is one of the decisive theatres of war in the struggle for a political union, a union that is to be established by way of a common economic and social policy. Historically it is associated with the name of Sicco Mansholt, then Vice-President of the Commission responsible for agriculture.

It was no more possible for us at European level than it is in individual national economies to avoid intervening in agriculture. The reasons for this have already been mentioned. Even less was it possible to leave responsibility for agriculture in the hands of national policies. If the rest of the economy is being Europeanized, then agriculture must follow the same path. For it is an integral part of the economy. It is also a consumer of products of other branches of the economy.

As far as the German Federal Republic was concerned, the preparation for the Treaty setting up the European Economic Community coincided with stormy controversies about agricultural policy. The post-war period of hunger had been forgotten, and agricultural production had once more got under way. Nevertheless, there was discontent everywhere. The spectre of 'unrest' on the land was constantly brought to everyone's mind. After the end of the war, in the early 1950s, Germany had, to begin with, to find a substitute for the food and agricultural organizations of the former Reich. In their place it set up a new system for regulating the market, with authorities for the import and the stockpiling of foodstuffs, while the arsenal of protectionist weapons was increased considerably. German industry, buoyed up by the demand to make good the losses of the past years – a demand of such immense proportions that it defied all accurate measurement, and provided with general fiscal and investment aids, had no difficulty in rapidly and successfully restructuring its production. German agriculture, by contrast, carried the heavy burden of a heritage, going back several decades, of a wrongly-conceived price policy, and grave distortions in its structure. Its methods were in many instances not up-to-date, and there were far too many people working on the land – despite the fact that there had begun to be a pronounced drift away from the land after the war, to the horror of many of the leaders of the farmers' unions. The then German Minister of Agriculture, Heinrich Luebke, soon recognized the basic fault and called for structural reforms in German agriculture – a theme which many were not used to hearing discussed. He made a good beginning of considerable importance in the right direction but, looking back, one has to admit now that he did not get very far. After the so-called 'Rhoendorf Conversations' in 1951, which are a well-known landmark in post-war German politics, German agricultural policy found itself in a blind alley. Instead of coming to grips with adapting to the needs of the market and with the problems of modernization, discussion revolved almost entirely around issues which were wrong and irrelevant in the light of what was necessary. To some extent this is still true today.

179

What was frequently ignored was the fact that the revolution in agriculture had begun long ago. The extent to which production and productivity increased – in Germany, too, but not only there – exceeded expectations. The pace of modernization has over the years lost none of its force. Under its impact social and economic structures that went back decades, even centuries, collapsed. There was enormous pressure to invest, and to invest rapidly, and such pressure could have harsh consequences. Where money had been rashly expended without working out the details, the result frequently was that those involved ran into debt. There is one problem, however, that agricultural policy still faces everywhere throughout Europe – in Germany as well, though to a lesser degree – and it is this: despite improved productivity, despite enormous technical progress and despite increased production, the income per head of those working in agriculture cannot keep step with the rises in income of those working in other branches of the economy. No matter how uncertain all statistical calculations may be about the precise degree of 'disparity', the gap remains and may even be growing wider.

It was in these circumstances that the EEC Treaty was formulated. It laid down new criteria for the discussion of agricultural policy, introduced new methods, and offered new opportunities. True, there had been intensive discussions immediately after the war to see whether a supranational agricultural policy would be feasible. There had been talk of a 'Green Pool'. But only when a common policy had been laid down in an organization firmly and securely embedded in a European constitution was it possible to resolve questions which the separate nation-states, acting on their own, had found increasingly insoluble. It was not until there was a Treaty that it became possible to get rid of a concept of agricultural policy which had become ever more sterile because it was seen only in protectionist terms.

The solutions, based on the Treaty of Rome, cover three main subjects. The common agricultural market means free trade in agricultural products within the Community. A preferential system of levies protects agriculture at the frontiers of the Community. Interventions in the market, export rebates (for exports to countries outside the Common Market) and part of the costs of improving the structure of agriculture are to be financed jointly; a special fund with considerable resources at its disposal has been set up for the purpose. In the early stages of evolving a common agricultural policy, the accent was largely on marketing and price policies. At too late a stage it has shifted to matters affecting the structure of agriculture – that is to say, to improving the balance between such factors as the amount of ground under cultivation, the number of people working on the land, and the total of capital invested.

The fundamental political decisions are contained in Articles 38 and 40 of the Treaty. Article 38, paragraph 1, states: 'The Common Market shall extend to agriculture and trade in agricultural products.' And paragraph 4 of the same Article reads: 'The operation and development of the Common Market for agricultural products must be accompanied by the establishment of a common agricultural policy amongst the member-states.' Article 40 mentions the possibility of developing European marketing arrangements. It is they which today determine the day-to-day business of agricultural policy.

The new European agricultural policy, like all agricultural policies, could not leave certain facts and circumstances out of account:

1. Agricultural prices have the double function, in a more marked manner than those of other branches of the economy, of providing private and public income and not merely of indicating the state of the market. In agriculture, moreover, people live where they work.

2. The consumption of certain foodstuffs does not rise in proportion to the rising national income; on the contrary, its proportion falls. The sales opportunities for such foodstuffs remain limited.

3. Agricultural enterprises are subject to many different kinds of difficulties in adapting themselves, which partly arise out of the nature of agriculture and are partly historical and partly psychological.

4. Several sections of European agriculture are for various reasons incapable of competing on the world market. Consequently, if European agriculture is to be kept in being, it is indispensable that it should be shielded by a system of preferences, and relatively high protection.

181

5. High protection enforces the trend towards self-sufficiency, saturation of the market, and over-production which is the result of technical progress but is also connected with 'artificially' fixed prices or an inelastic price system.

In the part dealing with agricultural policy, the Treaty confined itself to laying down a broad framework of provisions rather than detailed regulations, more so than in other parts. It even left certain fundamental options open. It did, however, provide that before the organs of the Community began their work of implementing agricultural policy, a conference should be held, at which the Commission, member-governments, and farming associations and unions were to state and to exchange their views. This conference met in Stresa as early as July 1958, a few months after the Commission had taken up its work in Brussels. It was greeted with great hope. The press wrote: 'The future of agricultural policy has begun.' In fact, the conference did turn out to be a success, not least because of the close collaboration between Luebke, the German Minister of Agriculture, and Sicco Mansholt – the dominating figures at the conference.

The broad outlines of a common agricultural policy emerged more clearly. It was recognized that agriculture was a part of the economy which contributed to the integration of the whole. Protection against non-member countries was reinforced. All the same, no one could anticipate the extent to which the formula that the Community had to 'protect itself against distorted competition from outside' was to be applied subsequently. The final communiqué pointed out that 'a close and balanced relationship had to be established between structural-improvement policy and market policy'. A balance was to be sought between possibilities of production and of sales, and subsidies which were contrary to the Treaty were to be eliminated.

The conference held at Stresa marked the end of the preparatory phase. The years that followed – above all up to and including the 'Mansholt Plan' – saw the development of a common agricultural policy and can be divided into a pattern of five periods:

1. The first lasted from 1959 to the end of 1962 and contained three events of outstanding significance. In the autumn of 1959, the Commission presented the first proposals on agricultural policy, which were approved by the Council of Ministers on 30

June 1960. December 1961 and January 1962 witnessed the first marathon discussions on agricultural policy; the fact that the subject matter of the discussions was closely related to the acceleration in eliminating customs barriers between the Six and to the politically important transition to the second stage of the Common Market played a considerable role in the marathon. In January 1961 the first marketing arrangements were decided on, and agreement was reached on the system of financing. This meant that the foundations had been laid for a common agricultural policy; from the practical point of view, a system of levies had been established, and, from the institutional point of view, management committees had been set up in which the administrations of the member-states and of the Commission work together to carry out policy decisions.

2. The second phase coincided, in the political sphere, with the first set of negotiations on Britain's application to join the Common Market, negotiations which were broken off in January 1963. De Gaulle's first ultimatum to the Six, in the course of which he stated that 'the Common Market could disappear', was followed by discussions on what marketing arrangements should be made next, and November 1963 saw the beginning of violent disputes on a common price system for grain, which did not end until December 1964; at the same time the Western world had to grapple with the problems of the Kennedy Round.

3. The third phase was marked, above all, by the deliberations on the financing of a common agricultural policy, which led to the spectacular departure of the French member from the Council of Ministers. It seems that in the summer of 1965 the French Head of State recognized the political nature of the Community. The crisis was brought to an end in Luxembourg towards the end of January 1966 in a way that cast no glory on the aggressor. The question of financing and the remaining price and marketing arrangements were decided on in May and June 1966.

4. In the fourth phase the common markets for different food-stuffs began to function, one after the other, and the common price systems came into force: 1 July 1967 saw the introduction of common cereal prices and of common markets for processed products; 1 April 1968 of common milk and beef prices. As a result the development in agricultural policy remained in step with the

evolution of the customs union and of the body of rules designed to bring about the free movement of workers within the Community.

5. The 'Mansholt Plan' entitled 'Agriculture 1980', which the Commission submitted towards the end of 1968, opened up a new chapter. Its importance cannot be appreciated – even provisionally – without first making an interim assessment of the state of European agricultural policy.

To begin with, the achievements:

(a) It is evident that a common agricultural policy and common agricultural markets are feasible objectives. Only a few years ago, there were still many who obstinately doubted this proposition. To take the matter even further: agricultural policy need not act as a brake on European union, but can, on the contrary, serve as a motor. That proposition, too, was frequently challenged. Admittedly, all this presupposes that the member-states submit to the common institutional rules, as laid down in the Treaty of Rome, and that the institutions of the Community do not use their authority in an unreasonable manner.

True, it could hardly be expected that a common agricultural policy, designed to serve a community of states, would work immediately. Such a policy is like an advance into entirely virgin territory so far as agriculture is concerned. Inevitably, there were bound to be periods of crisis, especially in the early stages. It was impossible to break up social and production patterns, which had in part been inherited from long ago, without causing suffering and distress. A common European agricultural policy, combined with the freedom of movement of workers, the establishment of a customs union and the beginnings of an economic union, has made a quite extraordinary contribution towards helping to make Europe grow into one unit, although it is difficult precisely to measure the value of that contribution. It is, for example, barely conceivable how Italy could have found a way out of the unhappy division that existed between its economically and politically active North and its merely vegetating South, without the opportunities the agricultural common market offers the whole country.

(b) It has not been refuted that it is possible to guide and control the prices of agricultural produce, even in so large an area as that of the Community. True, the burden of devising a responsible price policy, as regards both the internal Community market and the world outside, becomes constantly heavier. Once prices are too high and the Six become self-sufficient, marketing arrangements are no longer 'neutral'. They can no longer seek to attain and maintain a proper balance between supply and demand in the market-place; moreover, protection against the outside world fails to operate as it was intended to do. All the same, great though these difficulties are, and are likely to continue to be for quite a while, in the case of various agricultural products, there is no proof that a different system, based perhaps on quotas, would work better.

Against these observations must be set some failures:

(*a*) The institutions of the Community only appear to function satisfactorily. To be sure, the marketing arrangements are being applied with such perfect, silent smoothness as to seem almost sinister. The way in which the Commission, the management committees and the council of Ministers collaborate is beyond reproach, but only on a purely technical basis. On the other hand, the Council of Ministers has failed to handle price policies as they should be handled, as a result of the internal national political pressures to which each of its members is subject. It may well be that the fault lies in the fact that decisions by a majority vote are in practice avoided. Perhaps a decision would have been reached on checking the rising surpluses if one minister had not used his veto when it came to feed-grains, a second when the decision involved sugar prices, and a third when it involved the price for soft wheat. If the source of the evil lies in this way of doing things, then the whole question of how the Community exercises its legislative authority must be reconsidered.

(*b*) The first proposals submitted by the Commission had treated the restructuring of agriculture, agricultural marketing arrangements, and the social aspects of agricultural policy as one integral package. All these new policies were to be implemented step by step, but in unison one with another. The preparatory phase was to last until 30 June 1967. After that the common market in agriculture was to begin. These plans were to prove appropriate, despite all political upsets: the common market in grain and processed products did in fact start operating on 1 July 1967. It proved more difficult, however, to put into effect the over-all programme for agricultural policy in its planned stages. Nevertheless, the Commission was right to apply here, too, its well-tested 'pragmatic' method of seeking to give effect to what was good without waiting for what might be better.

The farmers, above all, had to be won over to this new bold policy. That has already meant years of effort, and it will mean many more years yet. Events in Germany provide a vivid example of prevailing attitudes. For far too long the farmers' association paid only lip-service to structural policy. In the political discussions that took place, it attached much more importance, on the whole, to price policy and to marketing arrangements. Furthermore, too many people simply could not bring themselves to believe that a common agricultural policy would be turned into reality so rapidly. Indeed, people played for time and used delaying tactics. As a result they entered into arguments and fought battles without rhyme or reason. For example, they fought on the issue of distortions in competition, a battle they lost because no distortions could be proved. In addition, the farmers were fed with all sorts of illusions: nothing could happen until the end of the transition period, cereal prices would not be lowered, and things of that sort. It was only at a late stage that it was recognized what an opportunity the Community offers in the sphere of agricultural policy.

Such opposition caused the Community to be pushed into involving itself ever more deeply in marketing arrangements and into treating the restructuring of agriculture as a mere adjunct of its activities. In the first regulation on finance, the concept of dealing with agricultural policy as a unit, as one package, was still preserved. But as time went on, price and marketing policy increasingly formed the centre of gravity of the practical political work that was done.

(c) There is another danger that is inherent in a price policy, as in a wages policy: namely that it comes to operate like an escalator which moves in only one direction – upwards. The Commission certainly recognized the dangers of too high a price level in the debate on cereal prices and therefore did not budge from its position in all the difficult discussions that took place. But in the meantime the reserves of production and of productivity (as a result, for example, of new strains) have proved to be even greater

186

than the Commission had foreseen or could foresee. It is impossible to see an end to this process, even where the production of cereals is concerned – not to mention other products such as milk. The unsolved problem of the agricultural surpluses has become one of the most dangerous burdens the Community has to shoulder. They are leading to charges on a scale which have already increased the amount of the Agricultural Fund in 1969–1970 to over £1,000 million.

The question at issue is not whether agriculture needs help. Everyone is agreed on that point. What is at issue is the form this help should take. Every citizen in the Community pays taxes from which his national budget subsidizes agriculture and from which contributions are made to the Community's Agricultural Fund. Must he, on top of the taxes, pay still higher prices in the shops which produce senseless surpluses, which in turn lead to still more senseless charges running into thousands of millions? Is there not a danger that the Community itself will gain the dubious reputation of being a senseless undertaking?

(d) We have also underestimated the consequences of the high protection surrounding the Community on agricultural production within the Six. As long ago as November 1959 the Commission pointed out that the price level of the Community had to be higher than that of the world market, because the conditions prevailing in the world markets were in many cases distorted. One had to take account of the fact 'that the conditions of production as well as the character of the agricultural enterprises in the Community were not the same as in the most important exporting countries of agricultural products outside Europe'. This principle is as true today as it was then. But the wall around the Community has become very high. The most recent set of figures, contained in the Commission's memorandum on reform, makes it clear how far the price level of the European Economic Community lies above that of the world market: in the case of hard wheat and oil-seeds, by 200 per cent; in the case of soft wheat by 185 per cent; in the case of barley and maize by 160 per cent; in the case of white sugar by 438 per cent; in the case of beef by 175 per cent; in the case of pork by 147 per cent; in the case of poultry and eggs by 131 per cent; and in the case of butter by nearly 400 per cent. Moreover, this high degree of protection against the outside world is underwritten by a

187

precisely-operating system of variable levies. Industry has always been denied the protection of such a system. All this, combined with the partially unknown amount of agricultural reserves of production and productivity, has led to an enormous increase in agricultural production, and caused important currents of trade to be diverted and, in some cases, even cut off. It is hard to blame the Commission and the Council of Ministers for not being able to calculate the precise extent of the reserves of production and consequently to assess accurately the full impact on trade with the outside world. It must also be conceded that Council and Commission were surprised by the rapidity with which whole groups of products from outside ceased being imported into the Community, while some outside countries abandoned the European Community as a market altogether – and did so at the very moment at which the extraordinary growth in prosperity made the Community a particularly interesting market.

Finally, it is only fair to point out that, in the course of the Kennedy Round negotiations, the Commission put forward a series of bold and highly original proposals for world-wide agreements which were aimed at eliminating agricultural protectionism. One can hardly find adequate words to express one's regret that these suggestions came to nothing – in the last resort because of the opposition of the United States. Certainly if they had been accepted, then all involved, including the United States, would have had to submit to a minimum of discipline in matters of agricultural policy and protection. But it would have been worth the price. Nor should it be forgotten that we would, in the course of such negotiations, have been induced to submit to examination our system of variable levies, and we would have done so to the extent that other states, particularly countries exporting agricultural products, would have submitted to similar examination. Still, for the time being, this opportunity has been missed.

The Commission, then, is in its new, ambitious, wide-ranging proposals guided not merely by what one might call constructive imagination but also by solid experience. The aim is to complete the common agricultural policy by European agrarian reforms. The political, social and economic targets set for these reforms can be compared in their scope only with the reforms which Stein and Hardenberg carried out in Prussia at the beginning of the last

188

century, reforms which included the setting free of the peasants. The aim of the reforms contemplated by the Commission is the restructuring of the Community's agriculture so as to bring it into line with the requirements of the age of the second Industrial Revolution. For this purpose, agriculture is to be thoroughly modernized and productivity consequently increased. Over-production of foodstuffs which are not competitive is to be limited. Superfluous labour is to be encouraged to leave the land, and the incomes and social situation of those who remain behind on the land are to be made comparable to those of workers in industry. At the same time the equilibrium between the markets of the various branches of the economy is to be restored, and the financial burden which the policy with regard to the agricultural market has brought about is to be reduced to a reasonable level.

These considerations, which many regarded as brutal, at first shocked public opinion, particularly that of the farmers. One was not prepared for them because public authorities and still more the professional organizations, had painted the situation in rosy colours. But once the first excitement had died down, the general objectives appear to have been accepted in principle. Who, after all, is against the idea of farmers who are free and capable of adapting themselves, of balanced markets, of prices which are reasonable both from the point of view of the producer and the consumer? Who is against the vision of a European countryside with all its different methods of cultivation offering an infinite variety of products? Who is against the elimination of butter mountains and similar surpluses, and against saving the thousands of millions of unproductive charges which over-production brings about at present? Who wants to see grants continuing to be paid for the destruction of fruit and vegetables? Who is against removing the irritation felt by all those affected by the present state of trade policy?

Still, general principles are one thing; the methods by which they are to be implemented, another. On these there was a great dispute. For example, Germany, which is in a comparatively favourable position as regards the structural problems of agriculture in relation to France and Italy, pays more attention than other countries in the Community to the long-term evolutionary process of adaptation which is likely to take place in agriculture

189

within the framework of growth of the economy as a whole, and which is bound to create the need for a larger labour force in industry, thus absorbing the labour no longer required on the land. The Commission would like to go further and speed up this evolution by a variety of incentives such as subsidies, aid for retraining, and other measures of social support.

There is a general agreement, however, that the traditional means which agricultural policy has at its disposal to achieve its ends are no longer adequate for coping with the immense task facing it at present. A task of such far-reaching, unique, age-old dimensions can be tackled successfully only if it is seen in the broad context of the whole of the economy, and if all the means of economic intervention are used. Regional development, transport policy, the best use to be made of the soil, training and retraining schemes, social policy, industrial and fiscal policy, must all be made to play their part if agricultural regions with lower yields are not to run to waste.

The Council of Ministers took its first policy decision on the Commision's proposals in March 1971 in Brussels – and in dramatic circumstances: there was a street riot sparked off by angry farmers. Meanwhile three new circumstances had arisen, changing and in a large part complicating the whole issue. Firstly, there was now a real likelihood that the Community would be enlarged. Secondly, world-wide inflation had grown to disquieting proportions, and in May 1971 it was to throw Europe into a monetary crisis which became a Community crisis. Finally, the long-standing Community plan for economic and social union at the Hague Summit conference in December 1969, had taken shape more and more, not least under the pressure of inflationary dangers.

The countries seeking membership of the Community have indeed agreed to accept the common agricultural policy, now augmented by market organizations for wine, tobacco, and fisheries. Three of them also bring to the Community healthy, modern, and efficient agricultural industries – difficult as it is to assess the precise development of the market and above all the self-sufficiency of the enlarged Community. But it is also to be expected that the already laborious process of decision-making in the Council of Ministers will grow even more difficult, at least at the beginning, in the transition period, in so far as some of the new member-states (Great Britain, Ireland, and Denmark) will have to raise their prices from the low world level to the Community level, and will be little inclined to make this process more difficult by additional price-raising decisions. Yet it is unthinkable that there should be a price freeze for Community farmers until 1977, the date when the transition period is due to end.

The farmers are especially hard-hit by world inflation, because they cannot pass on the increase in costs. So the yearly price-fixing debates in the Council grow ever more difficult. The dangers of inflation for farmers are now at least as great as those from cheaper competition abroad, from which they are sheltered by the common agricultural policy. Against inflation there is virtually no protection. Fresh in everyone's mind is the memory of what happened when the French franc was devalued and the German mark revalued in 1969: in one case an increase, in the other a fall in agricultural prices as expressed in the national currency, which led to cumbersome compensation arrangements. On the other hand, farm prices in 1971 were increased by about 4 to 5 per cent; and for 1972–3 the Commission has proposed a further rise of 2 to 3 per cent, together with measures in favour of efficient farms. But the farmers regard these percentages as quite out of the question: they look apprehensively at the scissor action of costs and profits, and at their continued and astonishing increase in productivity.

For some time, moreover, attention in agricultural policy, as elsewhere, has been focused on the beginnings of economic and monetary union. France insists more strongly than ever on the maintenance of the agricultural policy, and above all on Community preference and financial solidarity in market intervention and export subsidies. But louder than ever, too, are voices in the member-states which call for national leeway in agricultural policy to be widened, above all in the matter of subsidies. Common prices, it is said, can no longer perform their double task of steering the market and of giving farmers satisfactory incomes; the structural reform already undertaken, although already complemented by parallel measures in most member-states, cannot produce quick enough results.

In the Council's decisive marathon session from 22–25 March, 1971, the Commission put forward an idea whose original formula-

191

tion in 1968 had been twice revised, but whose essential elements had been maintained with unparalleled strength of will. In April 1970 it gave up any rigid classification of farms by size in favour of a more elastic formula whereby only farms capable of development, in respect of production or manpower, were to qualify for support. In February 1971 it added regional differentiation and social mobility, thereby securing a favourable reaction from the European Parliament. But its basic principle remained unshaken, that the price can fulfil its double function only if a balanced market is secured by means of structural policy – the lack of which was demonstrated to the point of absurdity by the fact that in 1969 the Community's farmers represented 13·8 per cent of the working population, but only 5·8 per cent of the gross Community product. In economic terms, this meant that, of the factors of production, manpower and acreage should be reduced, and the size of enterprises increased. With this basic principle, and its implementation, the Commission has carried through the essence of its ideas.

In the series of measures that constitute the Council's decision, the accent – at last – was placed on structural policy; at the same time, producer prices for 1971–2 were laid down. On the one hand, in order to reduce the farm population, financial inducements are offered, from public funds, to those who are willing to leave the land – life pensions for those between fifty-five and sixty-five, and retraining aids for younger farmers who wish to change their occupation. To discourage the extension of acreage in use, special re-afforestation and recreational programmes are planned. At the same time, with the aim of modernization, an aid system was introduced by the member-states, to be based on approved farm-development plans, and available only to farmers whose enterprises offer a normal income to two or more workers. They are to have a prior claim to unused agricultural land, financial aid, and security for loans. The farming advisory service and vocational training are also to be improved. Finally, producer co-operatives are to improve the marketing of agricultural produce; they are to be supported by an aid system comprising initial assistance, investment aid, and loan guarantees. The financing of this whole structural reform programme is basically to be covered, up to 25 per cent, by the European Agricultural Guidance and Guarantee

Fund, and also, in part, by the European Social Fund: this falls far short of the Commission's proposals. Since national financing is thus to play an important part, a survey is to be undertaken of all existing aids which run counter to the aims of the structural reform programme. The aim is to harmonize all investment aids, to abolish all other aids which affect production costs, and to work out joint criteria for the general aid system. Much of the Community's contribution will go to Italy: this is the start of a still-evolving European financial compensation system – a classical hallmark of all federations.

Practical measures of application deal with the details of this whole apparatus. Its concrete prospects were described in the European Parliament by Sicco Mansholt: of the 4·8 million farms in the Community, 400,000 qualify as 'modern' in the Commission's usage of the term; the heads of 2·5 million farms are more than fifty-five years old and therefore qualify for pensions.

The first campaign in the great reform is over. Its targets have been accepted. The results, naturally enough, are not to be expected in the short term. For, so long as agricultural policy is also a matter of price policy, there will always be new dangers from other battlefields on the flanks. These will only be eliminated when economic and monetary union, and with it a European monetary policy, has become an irreversible reality.

8. *Industrial Policy*

Few topics demonstrate so clearly the topical interest, the usefulness, even the necessity, the complexity and the political nature of the process of European integration as industrial policy, the most recent of the special branches of economic policy. All these special branches are exceptions to what is called general economic policy. Consequently, like the other special branches, industrial policy emerged in the form of an identifiable multiplicity of economic problems only when industry could no longer cope with the general philosophy and operation of a free market economy, and stood in special need of help from the public authorities. This need has increased greatly in recent times and has grown greater still as a result of the process of economic integration in Europe. Psychologically, the rapid progress made in evolving a common agricultural policy has given rise to a desire to see more attention paid

193

to other spheres of economic activity and so to redress the balance. One might compare this desire to a wish to catch up. In strictly practical terms – which are a much more important element in explaining the wish to see an industrial policy evolve – the process of integration, linked – as it effectively is – to the 'second Industrial Revolution' has created such massive problems of adaptation that not all sectors of industry find themselves capable of dealing with them on their own. The general rules governing the operation of a free market economy presuppose a certain measure of ability to look ahead and assess future developments, as well as a certain capacity to adapt to changes in economically important circumstances. Where more is demanded than that ability and capacity – as is the case, for instance, with the restructuring of agriculture – economic policy is expected to intervene.

In March 1970 the European Commission drew up a substantial memorandum on its ideas for an industrial policy, ideas which had previously not been defined in precise, concrete terms. The memorandum was drafted under the guidance of Don Guido di Colonna di Paliano, the Italian member of the Commission responsible for this subject. The Memorandum sets out the concept of an 'over-all strategy for industrial policy', and represents in this respect a counterpart of the Mansholt Plan for agriculture. It leaves no doubt not only that the productivity of European industry lies far behind that of American industry but also that the gap that has to be closed is still growing wider in absolute terms. The productivity of everyone engaged in industry within the Community is only 61 per cent of that of his counterpart in the United States. In Japan the comparative figures are 54 per cent, and in Great Britain 38 per cent. In the United States 35 per cent of the people working in industry are responsible for 40 per cent of the gross national product, whereas in the Community 44 per cent of those working in industry produce 44 per cent of the gross Community product. In the United States 61 per cent of those gainfully employed provide services, as against 48 per cent in the European Economic Community. There are still considerable differences within the Community; Germany's productivity, for example, is 50 per cent higher than Italy's.

The aims of the 'over-all strategy' outlined in the memorandum can be summarized as follows: to improve the productivity of

European industry and to increase its adaptability; to facilitate industrial co-operation in Europe; to provide European industry with better means of financing its operations; and – last but not least – to create a true Common Market in spheres where it does not as yet exist, such as the sphere of advanced technology, of building nuclear reactors, and in aviation. The Commission, in its memorandum, recommends the methods by which these aims might be achieved. It mentions the need for the fusion of enterprises on a European scale, (the third General Report of the Commission for 1969 contains interesting figures which clearly show how little has been done here). It also mentions that there should be financial relief for such fusions, through the European Investment Bank. Further, the Commission advises that there should be legislation on industrial combines (at present there is such legislation only in the Federal German Republic); that a uniform legal, fiscal and financial system should be introduced; that technical obstructions to the flow of trade should be removed; that there should be a European capital market; and that industrial enterprises should come together to found a 'European institute for management and training'. The Commission also recommends that there should be greater solidarity in external economic relations, particularly when it comes to export credits and other forms of support, to the supply of power, and to technological collaboration. The reform of the European Social Fund has added to this catalogue a new instrument for an active employment policy, which should help to make possible the necessary large-scale changes in employment structure. It is interesting to note that the memorandum also includes modern ideas of particular appeal to the younger generation, such as policies on the environment ('the preservation of the natural environment') and other objectives concerned with the 'quality of life' based on an indigenous civilization. Quite a few of these suggestions are not unlike those put forward by the French government at about the same time in the Council of Ministers.

The debate on the scheme outlined in this massive memorandum has only just begun in a Working Party on Industry set up by the Council. The main argument lies between the French and German governments and revolves around a basic conflict of approach: should industrial policy chiefly concern itself with interventions on the part of the state in this or that sphere of industry (in other words should it be *dirigiste*), or shall it devote itself to creating in Europe one uniform economic and investment entity, subject to the interplay of free competition? The themes which will form the subject at the outset will be the granting of public contracts – on this there is already a decision by the Council, reached in July 1971; the role of the European Investment Bank; the duration of export-credits; and policy and industrial statistics. To advise the Commission and the Council, the Commission proposed in April 1971 the establishment of a 'Committee on Industrial Policy', composed of senior officials from the Commission and from the member-states.

There are two outstanding factors which have to be considered in devising industrial policy in our age: on the one hand, there are certain traditional branches of the economy which are shrinking, as a result not only of economic trends, but also of structural changes – a process which it is sought to counter by pursuing what is called a 'sectional' restructuring policy; on the other hand, there are the so-called 'industries of the future'.

Among the traditional branches of the economy there are, first of all, mining, steel, some sectors of the metallurgical industry, shipbuilding, and sections of the textile and pulp and paper industries. All these traditional industrial sectors present problems which are at one and the same time of a regional and of a social nature, and the most usual method of seeking to deal with these problems is by providing some form of aid, particularly subsidies. The European Community has itself intervened in a number of such cases. Its intervention was, to begin with, concerned with Europe's steel industries; the Coal and Steel Community represents the most significant enterprise launched in the sphere of European industrial policy. Subsequently, shipbuilding, lead and zinc, and a few branches of the textile and pulp and paper industries required attention and action on the part of the European Community. The results did not always prove satisfactory. Needless to say, the point of intervening was not to avoid the structural alignments which the situation demanded, but, on the contrary, to assist the process of adaptation. It is in this sense that industrial policy stimulates the dynamic forces of the Community's economy.

The second factor involved is that of the industries of the

future. The problems they present are generally summarized under the heading of 'technology'. A decision reached by the Ministers of Science of the European Community gives a list of what is meant by 'industries of the future'. It includes the exploitation and dissemination of information, telecommunications, new methods of transport, oceanography, metallurgy, and pollution of the environment, as well as space-exploration and nuclear science. Most of these spheres of knowledge have to rely on electronics. That is a factor they have in common but it does not provide the basis for a comprehensive definition. Where the evolution of technology and natural science creates similar problems of adaptation, we are faced with similar questions which demand similar answers.

Indeed, nowhere are we brought face to face so directly with the future as in technology, with perhaps the possible exception of agricultural policy. Technology presented all countries with a challenge on a broad front – a challenge, moreover, that had to be met rapidly. As a result of the independence enjoyed by universities and high schools, scientific research and teaching are free, and the activity of the state is confined to providing finance. Applied research and technical development were chiefly the concern of industry, which tackled these problems with considerable dynamism and success. The state began to play a significant, even prevailing role because of its interest in armaments; for example, in the spheres of aviation and telecommunications. Incidentally, the state's interest over the whole field of scientific and technological development, far from diminishing, is actually on the increase. Its interest very quickly extended to all industries of the future.

The whole range of topics raised by the development of the industries of the future has become of immense topical, political, and – last but not least – European interest, as a result of the so-called 'technological gap', the great gulf that exists in science and technology between America and Europe. There is considerable disquiet in Europe that America enjoys a dominating position in the whole field of scientific achievement, and that consequently Europe is dependent on America, particularly in certain important areas of military activity. There is also disquiet about the 'brain drain' from Europe to America and the penetration of the European market by American enterprises, assisted by enormous com-

197

mercial and financial resources. It was soon recognized that the available reserves of men and means in Europe had to be pooled, and that the central problem had to be dealt with – the co-ordination of disciplines, of commercial devices, and of markets. And the recommendation of the Committee for Medium-Term Economic Policy of the European Economic Community fell on receptive ears when it pointed out: 'If the Community countries continue the practice they appear to have followed for the past generation, of being the chief importers of inventions and the chief exporters of intelligence, then they will condemn themselves to a cumulative form of under-development which will rapidly make their decline irreversible.'

This clearly poses the problem which Europe faces: it requires a common solution, a solution which sooner or later must include Great Britain. Its aim is not to make Europe protectionist, but to make Europe capable of being truly competitive. The purpose in constantly drawing attention to the superiority of the Americans is not to protect the present against the future. If such were the purpose, it would be naïve. The purpose is rather that, for the present and for longer than anyone can foresee, the rate at which we must progress depends on American achievements. What we seek is to become their equals in what we can accomplish. In other words, our aim is competition among equals; and in achieving that aim we shall realize one of the basic conditions which is supposed to determine the relationship of the two continents within the Atlantic partnership.

The state of technology – that is to say, of technical science, research and development – lies at the heart of the problem. Scientific research has been called the third factor affecting production in modern economy, after capital and labour. In fact, the reserves of the labour market in Europe have been virtually exhausted, and we can hardly expect further growth to be stimulated from that quarter. If we want to increase our productivity we therefore need to plan to expand our knowledge of the natural sciences and of technology. The contribution this could make is simply not capable of being measured accurately – despite American attempts to do so – but nobody denies its value. Japan owes its growth, which over the last ten years has been greater than that of any other country in the world, to concentrating on the most modern methods of production. It is because the Americans recognize the importance of scientific and technological research that both the state and individual enterprises there invest enormous sums in it; Soviet investment in this sphere is also on an immense scale. In Europe, which has about the same population as America, state and industry spend only a quarter of what the Americans spend on research. The number of natural scientists and technologists at American research centres is twice as great as in Europe.

It is therefore beyond doubt that any policy to stimulate the growth of technology must begin by encouraging research and development. The best way to provide the necessary aid – and it is a way that has proved itself – is agreements on research and development and contracts by public authorities. But at the same time such a policy must be implemented and co-ordinated within a European framework.

This policy must, however, on no account confine itself only to science. The term 'technology' has in the past been used in connection with the whole complex of problems which such a policy faces. It is a survival of an attitude which goes back to the days when all attention was focused on science, on research and development. There was indeed a period when programmes were designed to serve not economic requirements but achievements in pure science alone – were designed, in short, for science's own sake. This method of approaching the problem was not wrong in itself, because the gap in scientific knowledge had to be made up, to begin with. But it was incomplete. Since then it has come to be generally agreed that industrial policy must concern itself not only with technology but at least as much with practical technical matters – that is to say, with production or, to use the language of technology, with 'innovation', with the practical application of new scientific knowledge to manufacturing processes.

We must, however, also face the fact that Americans are quicker than we are in applying scientific discoveries in technical industrial processes. Here the human element plays a part. It is not merely a question of intelligence, but rather of determination and courage. In other words, it is a question of education, in the true, profound meaning of that word. For this reason the freedom to take work anywhere within the Community and the competitive-

199

ness it promotes are so important. The freedom to take work any-where must in this context be seen in its widest sense. It involves not only workers but also the leaders and managers of enterprises, research scientists and engineers, and particularly teachers and students. We stand in need of a 'common market of intelligence'. Would not such a 'market' – more than anything else – accord with the concept and the tradition of a university, the most magnificent form of cultural institution created by the European mind? How much further would we have advanced if an unholy alliance of reactionary and backward sections of the academic brotherhood – which unfortunately also exists in Germany – had not steered the original plan for a 'European University', as envisaged in the Treaty setting up Euratom (the European Atomic Energy Com-munity), into a blind alley! Let us at least hope that the present trends towards reform in the university can be harnessed to the creation of a true 'European University'.

We therefore also need a common market which is – as we have noted – essential for so many others things, in order to reap the benefit of 'innovation'. We must ensure that our limited material resources are used on a rational basis. That means that we must see to it that the available labour is properly distributed as between and within the various branches of the economy. There must be no duplication of the use of labour. Specialization must be encouraged. The European national economies are too small to permit each one to establish itself on its own in all the fields of modern technology at one and the same time. Besides, modern technological produc-tion relentlessly calls for the creation of very large enterprises, as American experience proves. It is therefore essential that European enterprises should work together and merge. It is at this point that our problem takes us to the project of creating an enterprise which is conceived and operates on a truly European scale.

Finally – and for the same reasons – the question of marketing the new products cannot simply be left to solve itself. Once again we can learn from the Americans: a large unified market must be created; indeed, we must evolve a common policy in allocating contracts by public bodies if the profitability of the new forms of production is to be assured.

In all these respects, one can hardly claim that things are as well-ordered in Europe as one would wish.

There is no true common market for the products of the industries of the future. This is an astonishing statement, but it is true. The great Common Market which was to embrace all types of products, and which owes its existence to the creation of the European Economic Community and of the European Atomic Energy Community, has developed virtually without making any impact on the previously prevailing conditions, in the atomic industry in particular. Admittedly, all customs duties on the exchange of nuclear products between member-states have been abolished since 1959; but one cannot seriously claim that there is any noticeable degree of co-operation even among the producers of the same types of nuclear reactors and fuels. The main reason is that invitations for tenders have, with one exception, so far been published only in the country concerned.

Consequently, there is no proper distribution of available labour resources. The same fear and the same ambition which cause Europeans to be afraid of becoming too dependent on America also constitute obstacles to co-operation within Europe. Where one expects resources to be brought together and used in some form of co-operation, one finds them divided and separated one from the other. For example, in 1969 two 'families' of tested, reliable reactors (water-cooled, water-moderated, and gas-cooled-graphite-moderated) were being developed separately behind closed national frontiers. One can explain this development historically on the grounds of the need to ensure adequate power supplies. But all the same, the market for power stations in Europe is extremely modest. There were in existence or in construction about twenty nuclear power stations, with a capacity of 6,300 MWe – as against one hundred power stations using a single-type of reactor (light water) in the United States. When one examined the types of reactors which had not yet proved themselves the situation looked even worse: there were three basic types, and there were four or two variants of each of these. Furthermore, one has to take into account that in constructing a power station, the stage from the very beginning to the completion of the working reactor alone costs 500 million dollars or more. The supply of this somewhat motley range of production-offer was shared in the European Community between a dozen firms which were in the business of constructing reactors. Of these only eight had then constructed a power station

201

with a capacity of at least 250 MWe. In America, there were four such firms, possibly there will soon be five – and the market there is nearly ten times as great as ours in Europe. In the aerospace industry the picture is the same. It covers only 15·2 per cent of the Community's needs (in the U.S. it covers 97·9 per cent). It is not cost-effective; 49 per cent of the turnover goes on development (in the U.S., 19 per cent). Co-operation is inadequate. Above all, there is no common market, and exports are too small.

Meanwhile, technology and economic logic have not failed to achieve some rationalization. At the beginning of 1971 half the nuclear power stations in the world were equipped with light-water reactors, which in the nineteen-sixties had been developed chiefly in the United States and the Soviet Union and in the nineteen-seventies were to dominate the market. A good third of the others were equipped with graphite-moderated, gas-cooled reactors, chiefly developed in Great Britain and France. The rest had mainly heavy-water reactors, chiefly developed with Canadian resources. But because in the nineteen-eighties 'fast-breeders' will rival and replace gas-graphite and light-water reactors, and because their development is very costly, collaboration has been initiated between the industries of Germany, Belgium, the Netherlands, and Luxembourg. Finally, in nuclear power-station construction, productive units are growing ever greater. For all these reasons, in July 1971 seven ten-year co-operation agreements were signed by German, British, Italian, Belgian, and Dutch reactor manufacturers; the French, who were invited, declined because they were too closely tied to American patents. Co-operation concerned primarily the exchange of patents and know-how, the construction and delivery of reactors to non-member countries, and the production and delivery of nuclear fuel. This was an important step towards equipping one of Europe's most essential 'industries of the future' to face the world market.

The Community's own atomic policy seeks to counter the fragmentation of effort, but so far it appears to have been effective chiefly within the different national frameworks. And so we find ourselves in the position of people trying to jump out of the frying-pan only to discover that they have landed in the fire. Every member-state is intent on attaining the maximum of self-sufficiency so far as the supply of power is concerned, together with the minimum of dependence on others. As a result of this attitude, member-states encourage their various branches of industry to combine and to establish what are virtually 'nationalized industries', though not in the strictly technical meaning of that term. This is done by granting contracts for research and by pursuing certain purchasing policies and other methods which produce more or less similar results. The trend is obvious. In a whole range of what might be described as a country's main industries – ranging from coal, steel, and aviation to atomic energy, car production, and computers – member-states tend to concentrate on one or two major national enterprises, which are naturally treated as important national productive assets. Nothing, however, is more conducive to national isolation than purely national subsidies. This is not the place to deal with the national problems which this evolution is bound to raise, a process which of course favours 'nationalization' in the formal, technical, sense. Enterprises which are too large in the narrow perspective of a nation-state are always bound to be a source of anxiety and to require cushioning by the state. From the broad European viewpoint one can certainly only regret this evolution, because it provokes national rivalry instead of promoting a common approach. There are differences in the way these large enterprises are treated in different member-states, and there are already indications that smaller enterprises feel a sense of grievance and disappointment at the way their bigger brothers are being treated. Needless to say, there are areas, such as ELDO and even Euratom, where attempts are being made to order matters on a common basis. But even there one cannot ignore the tendency that contracts for research and development are apportioned on the basis of the amount which member-states contribute financially to the common project. Not even in defence and in questions of armaments have member-states risen above national rivalries and differences of opinion in military strategy. Co-operation by itself is simply not enough – despite the one or two successes it has helped to bring about. Moreover, the truly fantastic escalation of costs makes it all too easy to find reasons for withdrawing even from objectives on which agreement to co-operate had previously been reached.

Even the magnificent concept of a great enterprise spanning all of Europe cannot be realized, because the systems of rules and regulations required are not what they should be. In trying to realize it, we meet a mass of unsolved questions and plans that have yet to be worked out. A legal framework of European dimensions is still missing for such a project. For some considerable time past, the European Commission has rightly been pressing for a European company statute, and to this end put forward a draft in June 1970. The differences between the economic systems in the various member-states also create difficulties, especially since some systems are close to what is called a planned economy and others are more 'liberal'. The European capital market is, in fact, far from unified, and remains divided and is therefore too weak to be effective. Finally, we have to contend with psychological blockages such as national susceptibilities and old or new national rivalries.

The consequences arising out of all this deserve the greatest attention. Since economics, like politics, abhors a vacuum, a vacuum that needs to be – but is not – filled by what is at hand is filled by something else. That something else is, in Europe's case, provided by American enterprises. These enterprises are, as a result of the experience they have gained in their own country, fully acquainted with the possibilities offered and the requirements demanded by a market of continental dimensions. They have the necessary financial means at their disposal, more than adequate in most cases for the purpose, and they are fully equipped to deal with the scientific challenge they face. Paradoxically, it is they who are realizing our Platonic concept of an enterprise designed and operating on a truly 'European' scale. European enterprises, aware of their own inadequate resources, at least seek a link with these American firms whenever the Americans do not virtually dominate the market – which is on the whole the exception. For example, six of the twelve firms building reactors in the Community have links with American enterprises by means of licences or technical agreements; AEG works with General Electric, Siemens with Westinghouse, the French with both. Although such a relationship wins a measure of independence for the Europeans, they find it difficult nevertheless to keep pace with their American partners, the more so since the Americans, who grant the licences, are themselves continually seeking to expand their markets and are therefore bound to work against similar efforts by the Europeans to whom they have granted licences.

In short, the prevailing situation is unsatisfactory from everyone's point of view. The member-states have to pour out very large and ever-increasing sums of money. Research alone cost all the member-states of the Community a total of 3,334 million dollars in 1967. These enormous costs are being incurred without, however, reaching the goal of becoming competitive on a world scale. Nor can the European customers be satisfied with the situation; there are, for example, the enterprises producing electricity by means of nuclear power, which are anxiously looking for secure guarantees for the future. Still more insupportable basically is the position of the enterprises constructing nuclear reactors and power stations; they have to put too much at risk and they cannot wish to see competitiveness degenerate into competition for public subsidies. Again something suffers: it is the negotiating ability of the Europeans. This is shown by the disappointing results of the negotiations with the Americans for the cession of delivery vehicles for a European communications-satellite system. Even the willingness of the Europeans to put up a thousand million dollars for the costly 'Apollo Follow-up program' failed to persuade the Americans to agree. It is hardly surprising that France is resorting more and more to bilateral co-operation. The state of the technological industry undoubtedly provides a classical argument for an integrated European economic policy.

What, then, is to be done? Do we have to start completely afresh? Is a European technological policy something that has still to be created and launched? Or are there already useful beginnings on which we can build?

The answer to these questions is all the more important because the complexities involved raise difficult political principles, as well as serious practical problems, in carrying out whatever course of action is eventually decided on. Quite apart from that, there is quite naturally bound to be opposition from special interests of a national, political, and economic nature. How can one achieve the greatest measure of effectiveness while applying the least pressure of *dirigisme*? How can one marry scientific freedom to the strictly practical needs of the economy? How can public authorities best co-operate with science and trade and industry? There has been no time so far to wait for answers to these questions to be worked out on a scientific basis; this observation is not meant as a reproach. One

205

had to get along in a relatively modest way as best one could, on an empirical basis, relying on such examples as different national ways of proceeding offered. In short, one had to improvise. The trouble was that these improvisations lacked uniformity.

Turning to traditional methods of international co-operation, one reached and continues to reach generally useful conclusions at this stage of preparatory examination of the problem. OEEC and OECD provide the best example, as well as acting as pacemakers in this sphere as in others, in pointing the way towards European unification. But we are on the threshold of a fresh critical phase, which involves the exploitation of new discoveries, 'innovation', production, and the sales of new products. In coming to grips with these problems, two things have rapidly emerged very clearly; in the first place, that the available resources can be brought to work together effectively only if plans are defined and projected on a relatively narrow basis, and only if there is a limited number of participants; in the second place, that a unified effort, even under these conditions, remains fragile. In the European Organization for Nuclear Research (CERN) it is the British who hold up development; in the European Space Research Organization (ESRO) it is the Italians; in the European Launcher Development Organization (ELDO), and in the European Conference on promoting telecommunications by the use of satellites (CETS), both – the British and the Italians – are jointly responsible for delaying progress. Only two relatively unimportant associations work satisfactorily: the European Nuclear Energy Agency (ENEA), a daughter organization of OECD, and the European Organization for Astronomical Research in the Southern Hemisphere (ESO). The disadvantages of this kind of inter-governmental organization arise to a considerable extent out of the multiplicity of different projects which are pursued and which stand in the way of effective co-ordination, so essential and indispensable if the available resources are to be used economically to the best advantage. In the final analysis, these disadvantages are due particularly to the fact that this type of inter-governmental organization depends for its funds on allocations from yearly national budgets, a fact which makes any long-term planning virtually impossible.

The other method is integration. Here we enter familiar territory. Indeed, we can put it more positively: the European Community has concerned itself with the problem we are facing, right from its beginnings, and has over the years accumulated a considerable treasure of valuable experience. Above all, however, it is pursuing an active policy in the field of technology. It has created its own institutions for the purpose, and its activities embrace all three stages of what is at issue: the scientific stage (research), the technical stage (production), and the economic stage (sales).

This policy of integration concerns itself with our problem in two ways: in the first place, as a result of the founding of the European Atomic Energy Community and, secondly – within the European Economic Community – as a result of the co-ordinartion of medium-term economic policy between the member-states. Since the fusion of the institutions of the three European Communities – of Coal and Steel, of Atomic Energy, and of the Economic Community – these two approaches to a European policy in the field of technology are becoming ever more closely interwoven. A beginning has been made in evolving a policy in the sphere of energy and energy supply, and this has contributed to the development of a broader technological policy. What has been achieved in the sphere of evolving an energy and energy-supply policy truly deserves to be called a 'common energy policy'.

The main aim in establishing a European Atomic Energy Community was to contribute towards the creation and growth of an atomic industry in Europe, based particularly on a broadly-conceived common programme of research. To begin with, the aim was pursued with a great deal of enthusiasm but, as time went on, difficulties gradually increased until there was finally a crisis. That crisis was temporarily resolved by a decision of the Council of Ministers in December 1968. The decision laid down a research and development programme for one year, but did not touch the long-term problems of nuclear policy.

There are several reasons for this crisis in the European Atomic Energy Community (Euratom). First of all, there was a defect in drawing up the treaty which created Euratom. As a result of this defect, too much emphasis was put on research and development, and industrial policy was neglected. Next, the political climate for co-operation within the European Community deteriorated, and consequently re-awakened and strengthened latent trends to look at problems in the atomic and nuclear field – as in others – in the light of national rather than Community interests. France's European policy bears a full – though not the whole – measure of responsibility for this. In any case, as a result of what was happening, the Commission made it quite clear in a 'White Paper' issued in October 1968 that the European Atomic Energy Community had been able to realize only to a very limited degree its ultimate aim – namely to create the basis for a productive and viable European nuclear industry. The reason was that it proved impossible to co-ordinate the separate efforts of the member-states, let alone combine such efforts in one unified plan.

Nevertheless, the institutions of the Community were successful in much that they did, within the limits of the work which was allotted to them, and it would be wrong to ignore these successes and the lessons they taught. When the treaty setting up the European Atomic Energy Community was concluded, Europe was, in the atomic field, in a state of under-development. In the meantime, it has become capable of competing in the world market as far as the construction of nuclear reactors is concerned. In other important fields such as space research, the availability of information and nuclear research, it is – apart from American – only European atomic technology which has succeeded in reaching the stage of being of consequence to the whole world – and this despite the facts that integration in Europe, which is confined mainly to research, is proceeding on a precariously narrow front and that there has been virtually no common industrial policy. Without going into the political reasons for and advantages to be derived from setting up Euratom, particularly for the Federal German Republic, it would be wrong to assume that the fact that Euratom was there was entirely unconnected with the successes of Europe's atomic technology.

Research work, organized on a Community basis, has in fact proved its worth. Team-work among Europeans is not only possible: it is producing good results. Equally, the somewhat flexible method of collaboration between the Community, the member-governments, science, and trade and industry has proved its worth. And, last but not least, the methods which Euratom adopted to help give a clearer picture of the measure of success which hazardous ventures were likely to have in the future are well worth following. These methods are of particular significance in view of the long time it takes for technological ventures to mature. There is basically only one way in which it can be made easier to reach a decision on whether a programme – once started – should be continued, altered or brought to an end – and that is to assemble all the important and relevant pieces of knowledge and experience and, once that has been done, to examine critically what is feasible. That means that we must apply to the solution of technological problems the same scientific method which has created for us what we choose to call the technological problems of our age. Euratom has, in accordance with the terms of its constitution, made the spread of scientific knowledge and the exchange of scientific experience one of its main tasks. In doing so, it has followed America's example, which clearly demonstrates that it is the rapidity with which information becomes available that is the essential factor in determining in which way any particular venture should be tackled. Euratom, accordingly, possesses a good information and documentation centre which works in close collaboration with smaller centres, both national and international; Euratom's information centre is the biggest of its kind to have an automatic documentation-retrieval system at its disposal.

The Summit Conference at The Hague in December 1969 sought to resolve the crisis into which Euratom had run (paragraphs 9 and 10 of the communiqué). The first attempt, a few days later, by the Council of Ministers to come to grips with the problem was very promising; the Commission and several governments, including the German government, followed up with constructive proposals. The Common Research Centre had been declining in importance for some years past. This process was stopped, and the Centre's existence was assured for 1970 and, should that prove necessary, for 1971. In the time thus gained, the Centre was to be reformed and put under modern 'management'. There were to be not only common programmes but also complementary programmes, with some, though not all, member-states participating, as well as private enterprises. There was also to be technological work of a non-nuclear nature.

This work fits into the framework of a comprehensive programme of technological collaboration which began in the sub-committee concerned with 'Scientific and Technological Research

Policy' of the Committee for Medium-Term Economic Policy. Collaboration under this programme embraces information, tele-communications, new methods of transport, metallurgy, environ-mental hygiene, meteorology and oceanography; seven specialist groups were formed to cope with this work. Non-members of Euratom were also invited to collaborate in these projects, namely the countries which are seeking to join the Common Market, as well as Austria, Portugal, Sweden, Switzerland, and Spain. As a result, two of the three innovations designed to restore Euratom to a sound and healthy state have already been recognized: the study of problems not connected with atomic science, and the collabora-tion of countries which are not members of Euratom. An example of the third innovation – envisaged in the programme – collabora-tion between some, not all, members of Euratom with a non-member – was not long in coming. It materialized when Germany, the Netherlands, and Britain concluded an agreement in March 1970 to explore the possibilities of gas centrifuges. According to the agreement, two installations were to be set up, one in the Nether-lands at Almeda and the other in Britain at Capenhurst. They were to develop and utilize the gas centrifugal process for producing 'light' enriched uranium. Their objective was and is to make Europe more independent in this sphere by ensuring the supply of nuclear fuel needed for the water-cooled, water-moderated nuclear reactors which most of our power plants in Europe use. Belgium and Italy have, not surprisingly, already declared their interest in the venture and their desire to participate. This broadening and greater flexibility is an example of what has recently been ex-perienced all over the world: nuclear science and nuclear industry are too small a basis to be the sole criterion of a large-scale research and development organization. This gives Euratom the chance of developing into the means of co-ordinating a global European research policy.

Following the initiatives conceived at The Hague Summit Con-ference of December 1969, and the expert opinion of the 'Four Wise Men' (Ailleret, Casimir, Maier-Leibrig, and Ruffolo) the Council and the Commission agreed in December 1970 that the Common Research Centre should be headed by a Director-General applying modern management methods. It is responsible for the preparation and execution of the programme. A Scientific

Committee made up of members of the centre and an Advisory Committee composed of representatives of the public interest, of science, and of economic affairs from each member-state works alongside it. The Council and Commission are responsible only for the financial framework. There was also a discussion and agreement, however, over concrete elements in the programme. But it appeared that the time was not yet ripe for a formal decision inaugurating a coherent research programme on the lines of the Memorandum laid before the Council by the Commission at the beginning of 1971.

Besides, a fresh danger now looms on the horizon. The Nuclear Non-Proliferation Treaty requires the European Atomic Energy Community to conclude an agreement within a short time on the control of atomic installations with the International Atomic Energy Agency in Vienna. France, which has not signed the non-proliferation treaty, is nevertheless opposed to having the Commission empowered to conduct negotiations in this matter.

France also refuses to respect the purchasing monopoly enjoyed by the Euratom Supply Agency, and has been taken to court on this account by the Commission. Meanwhile the Vienna Atomic Agency, in whose directorate the Federal German Republic is now represented, has agreed on the outline of a new control agreement. But before the Community negotiates with Vienna, it must agree on a common position. This whole episode is an unedifying spectacle of tactical manœuvres and temptations.

The European Economic Community right from the beginning concentrated on economics – that is to say, on industrial policy. Technology helped to prod the Community in the direction of facing up to general structural requirements such as, for example, the problem of making it possible to set up a company spanning the whole of Europe; of patents which were recognized throughout Europe; and of harmonizing fiscal laws. The Committee for Medium-Term Economic Policy consequently established a sub-committee, a working party for 'Scientific and Technical Research Policy', which in turn formed several specialist study groups and generated a most welcome spirit of initiative. In any case, the major part of the rules and regulations governing the Common Market meets the requirements of a policy designed to promote technology: a large market, the removal of economic barriers, the prohibition of national discrimination, the free movement of persons and services, the right to set up businesses and enterprises anywhere in the Community, and, more particularly, the pursuit of such projects as finding an appropriate legal form for setting up European companies and a European Patent Law. True, if we examine the whole complex of problems more deeply, we appear to come up against a dilemma which could subject the way in which the market is organized to a severe test. Any technological project takes a long time, from the first stages of research to the point of practical application until the stage of selling the end products is eventually reached; the costs involved in this lengthy process are very high. The funds must constantly be found as and when these expenses occur, while all the time the success of the project remains uncertain until the last moment. As a result of the forces of competition, however – whether on the national or the Community level or on the world market – the profitability of enterprises is determined by present successes and not by future expectations. All the questions this dilemma poses cannot be solved by how big a particular enterprise may be.

The progress made towards economic union provided further impetus to the work that was being done in this sphere. Admittedly, that impetus was soon lost – a victim of the crisis caused by the rejection of Britain's first bid to join the Common Market. It was not until December 1968 that the Council of Ministers decided that work should be resumed. March 1969 saw the first results. In that month the working groups submitted about fifty projects to the Committee for Medium-Term Economic Policy. The method of collaboration that was put forward is selective, in the sense that in each specific project only those countries interested should participate. Nevertheless, if one views all the projects as a whole, a certain balance should emerge so that each country gets a fair return, proportionate to what it contributes. This certainly eases the problem of the so-called *juste retour*. The projects deal with technological programmes; the work to be done at common centres of research; co-ordination in the allocation of public contracts to national centres of research or to industries; and the granting of financial support. Naturally, all these projects raise questions of organization, of collaboration and of methods of raising the necessary funds. Studies are to be announced on

212

information and documentation; the education and training of scientists; concerted actions on a broad European basis; common definitions of terms; and the production – as well as the supply and distribution – of new tools and instruments. In short, the problem is being tackled in all its breadth and its manifold aspects, and it is being tackled with as much drive as imagination.

The main significance of the policy objectives pursued by the European Community does not, however, lie in details of this kind. It lies in the fact that technological collaboration in this context is not merely the result and the expression of a limited measure of *ad hoc* usefulness, but is part and parcel of a comprehensive combination of economic and political interests which are closely interlinked. These links not only touch certain specific technological categories; they also affect the whole of industry. It is the inadequacies and the intolerable shortcomings of the present situation that call out for the evolution of an industrial policy. Furthermore, the whole of the economy is affected, because the whole of the economy suffers so long as the present situation continues. Indeed, since the Economic Community is the main part, as well as the instrument, of the policy of bringing about the unification of Europe, aspects which are not directly concerned with economic affairs must also be taken into consideration. Defence has incalculably close links with technology. Armaments are just as much a question for defence policy as for economic policy. Experience shows that if technology is to develop on its own within a European framework on the scientific, economic, and political level, there will be difficulties in overcoming the obstructions which have so far confined technology to the national framework. These obstructions may spring from vested interests, or from habits that have grown up over the years, or they may be emotional. It seems necessary to organize links on a larger scale, in order to ensure that particular national interests are subordinated to the common needs of Europe as a whole. Rightly, each country which joins in demands its share of success – in the form of jobs which may become available; by participating in business transactions; and by deriving such benefits as it may feel it should have from the advances that may be made. One further important consideration must be that, where the attempts to combine resources and effort are confined to technology, it is only rarely that more

213

than two countries can be brought together. Bilateralism, however, is something different from integration (as is very obvious in Anglo-French collaboration). Two European countries on their own do not possess sufficient resources or markets to ensure, even in the medium term, the development of a technological project of European calibre which promises to be competitive for a long time ahead.

This survey of the evolution and state of Europe's policy in the field of technology clearly shows up three traits: the novelty and the unique nature of the problem, its immense size and the realization that we are only in the very early stages, or, to put it another way, that the state of development we have reached up to the present, both as regards organization and methods, is still primitive. But at the same time, the survey shows how pressing is the need to gather and bring together policy in this field on a European basis.

9. *Energy Policy*

Agriculture, as we have noted, faces two sets of problems which it must tackle at one and the same time. The same is true of energy policy. As in agriculture, the dynamic aspect of integration must make its impact on two levels, that of space and that of time: on the one hand, policies which were conceived for geographical areas that have up to now been separated economically have to be unified; and on the other hand, the time factor demands that the new common authority emerging from this process, must – even as it evolves – cope with the truly revolutionary restructuring the energy industry must undergo.

The revolution in the energy industry is enormous in scope and violent, not to say explosive, in its nature. In this it resembles the revolutionary change in agriculture. But that is not the only point of comparison between agriculture and energy. The spheres in which policies have to be co-ordinated, and the conditions in which this has to be done, are not unlike in agriculture and energy. Both provide classic examples of spheres of economic activity where public authority has to intervene. Both present technical economic problems, and their solution involves important political considerations. A miner's wages carry the same political significance and implications as the price of bread. We have talked

214

of the political danger of unrest among the farmers. 'Unrest in the Ruhr' – a spectre that is often conjured up – is no less menacing. The mining industry finds it no easier to adapt to the rapidly changing requirements of the market than does agriculture. But finally, in both agriculture and energy, market forces asserted themselves though not without disputes, the use of pressures, and tactical political manœuvring. The changes in the energy industry represent a victory for the consumer, particularly in the Federal German Republic. A factor which contributed to this victory to no small degree was the policy of importing oil which, though it included high taxes, was nevertheless on the whole liberal.

The upheaval which took place in the energy market can be very exactly dated. The Treaty setting up the European Coal and Steel Community, even the sections of the Treaty on the Saar dealing with coal, were drawn up against the background of an energy shortage. Coal was in short supply, and it was expensive. Although, as a result, efforts – and successful efforts – had been made for years to reduce the use of coal, it was still possible to talk of an energy shortage as late as 1956/57; extra shifts still had to be worked in the Ruhr coal mines. Then, in the autumn of 1957, virtually overnight, market conditions changed. Heavy oil and natural gas began their triumphal progress, and within ten years the sources supplying energy were radically altered. It was a process that proved difficult for the coal industry. True, the German mining industry, for example, had always had to contend with a certain measure of competition (with British coal), but competition had never been so fierce as, for instance, in the automobile industry or in textiles. Sources of energy were, after all, regarded in many cases as a 'treasure belonging to the nation' which had to be looked after at whatever cost. Now, however, whole groups of customers who had previously bought coal dropped out completely: the railways, inland water transport, a large proportion of private homes, of industry, of enterprises and of plants producing electricity. At the same time, the need to rationalize the coal industry led to a situation which, again, was not unlike that in agriculture. It led to concentrating on competitive coal seams and pits and it thus mobilized substantial reserves capable of further rationalization. In nearly all coal-producing regions of the Community output per shift rose to a

215

level which it had previously been thought virtually impossible to reach. The same was true of the progress made in mechanizing the mining of hard coal, 80 per cent of which is mechanized today. Oil and natural gas have increasingly competed with coal as a source of power, above all, in France, Italy, and the Netherlands, and also to a growing extent in the Federal German Republic, and this form of competition has truly haunted the economics of energy and its supply. It is a process which has not yet ended, although it is likely to evolve somewhat more quietly in future. One can foresee new irruptions in the energy industry towards the end of this century, when nuclear energy becomes competitive in wide areas of the industry, above all as a result of the development of so-called 'fast-breeder' reactors.

The magnitude of the changes that have taken place emerges clearly if one examines the relevant figures. Between 1950 and 1970, the consumption of hard coal used for supplying energy in the Community dropped from 74 per cent to 23 per cent. In the same period the consumption of oil used for energy in the Community rose from 10 per cent to 58 per cent. As a result of this change, however, the sources of energy which had to be imported into the Community, also rose – from 25 per cent to 57 per cent; this by itself is a trend that has to be watched closely from the political point of view. Simplifying matters a little, one can say that the European Economic Community imports nearly as much for producing energy as it imports of agricultural products. In 1968 the Community imported materials for producing energy to the tune of about twenty-four milliard German marks, a sum equivalent in value to roughly 10 per cent of the Community's total imports. And all the time the demand for energy continues to rise steadily. The total consumption of the Community has in the past ten years risen from around 420 million tons, calculated in terms of units of hard coal, to about 670 million tons, and it is estimated to rise to around one milliard tons by 1980. Energy makes up 12 per cent of industrial production, and the resources invested in energy in the form of power plants constitute 15 per cent–20 per cent of all industrial investments. That gives the energy industry considerable weight both economically and politically.

But while the Community has worked out a complicated system for regulating its trade with the outside world in agricultural

216

products, there is virtually nothing comparable in the field of energy. There is only a policy – on the whole liberal – with regard to the import of oil. This is a policy which is pursued by every member except France. The comparative lack of any trading policy in the sphere of energy is all the more remarkable because trade in this sphere has long been part of foreign policy in general. Questions relating to the supply of oil are referred to in all treaties with the Soviet Union. Oil plays its part in the relations between France and Algeria. France and the Federal German Republic are making efforts to build up joint energy enterprises. In the Middle East, France is strenuously looking for oil, particularly in the region of the Persian Gulf. Europe's oil supplies are very sensitive to whatever happens throughout the Mediterranean area in general, above all since the closure of the Suez Canal. All oil suppliers in the Federal German Republic have concluded agreements among themselves, laying down quotas for the supply of heavy heating-oil. In the spring of 1971 came new demands from the oil producers of the Mediterranean and the Middle East. Not only did it become obvious that the age of cheap energy in Europe was over: it was also clear how vulnerable the Community is when it faces the united front of Middle East oil producers (OPEC), in other words how valuable it is to have assured supplies. Hence greater attention is now turned to nuclear energy – only to find that the Community is entirely dependent on the U.S. Atomic Energy Commission for its supplies of enriched uranium, although admittedly the conditions it imposes were relaxed at the beginning of 1971. More attention is also paid to coal, although no longer in the way it used to be. In October 1970 the Commission prolonged the policy of adaptation subsidies – although more carefully scrutinized than hitherto – for a further five years; their removal would only have made uncompetitive twenty million tons, out of a total production figure of 177 million for 1969. But the objective is not only to restructure the coal industry: it is also to secure energy supplies. For this reason the Commission proposes the joint financing of stocks and losses arising from the need to ensure secure supplies. In addition, the search is on everywhere in the world for uranium deposits, and people are looking for oil and natural gas in the North Sea. All these efforts – and others in the same sphere, including the Nuclear Non-Proliferation Treaty – are of great

217

significance as far as foreign policy is concerned. They contain opportunities as well as dangers. In any case, they demand that there should be action on a common basis, a European foreign trade policy for energy.

The price at which energy is available is an increasingly important factor in determining whether a national economy, or a combined economy like that of the Community, maintains its competitiveness on the world market. The European Community is far and away the greatest importer of materials required for producing energy, but it has not so far exerted the political power this position confers. This statement of fact is not made in order to assert a measure of political ascendancy or to assign too much significance to Europe's dependence on imports. What is at issue is much more simple: it is that Europe could have cheaper energy and at the same time safeguard, more securely than at present, its interests in the Mediterranean, the Middle East, or in Africa (which, after all, lies at our front door) if it were to unify its foreign trade policy on energy to a greater extent than at present.

If only energy policy on a purely national basis at least carried conviction! But far from it. In most countries it appears as a bastion of public intervention – moreover of the wrong kind of intervention. It serves as a stage where the struggle for political ascendancy is fought out and where the wrong political and economic decisions are almost invariably made. All this would not matter if energy policy did not affect nearly every aspect of the economy. It has a bearing on social policy, on conjunctural policy, on regional development, on competitiveness, and, above all, on taxation and finance. As a result, energy policy, conceived and pursued on a purely national basis, becomes complex and difficult to comprehend. Consequently, it turns into a plaything of vested interests and becomes an area in which only specialists and technicians can operate.

Moving away from energy policy on a narrow national basis, the Community was, although only gradually, to assume responsibility in the sphere of energy and its supply. To begin with, it lacked an adequate institutional framework. Indeed, there are few aspects of the way in which the Community is ordered which demonstrate more clearly the vital importance of adequate institutions for the tasks in hand. There existed no Community authority competent to deal with a common energy policy, until 1 July 1967, the day on which the institutions of the three European Communities were fused. Up till then authority had been divided not only between three treaties, i.e. three Communities, but also between three Councils of Ministers, and, especially, between three Executives: the High Authority of the Coal and Steel Community (for coal), the Commission of the European Atomic Energy Community (for atomic energy), and the Commission of the European Economic Community (which was responsible for the other sources of energy, oil and gas).

Admittedly, efforts have not been lacking since 1956 to prepare and develop a common energy policy. But the action that followed has been limited. It has not, in its nature, been Community action. It has been piecemeal. To begin with, there was the report of 'The Three Wise Men' of May 1957, on 'A Target for Euratom'. The report was correct in the motives on which it was based, appropriate in the political aims it pursued, and daring in the conclusions it drew. But events soon overtook the diagnoses on which the report rested, and failed to confirm many of the trends it predicted. To underline the assertion that 'Europe has lost its independence as regards materials needed for producing energy', the report had estimated that Europe would – as early as 1967 – need to import about 200 million tons in terms of units of hard coal to cover around 30 per cent of its total energy requirements. In fact, 330 million tons were imported to cover 52 per cent of total requirements. The figures foreshadowed for 1980 in the report were indeed already reached twelve years earlier. The costs of imports in 1967 were estimated to amount to four milliard US dollars. In fact, they ran to five-and-a-half milliard dollars, but even so the EEC at the time still enjoyed a balance-of-payments surplus. Furthermore, at that stage nobody could foretell that Europe would become less, and not more, dependent for its oil on the Near and Middle East, areas where conditions tend to be unstable. In 1958 86 per cent of Europe's oil was imported from those areas; in 1968 only 52 per cent. This represents an increasing diversification in the sources from which Europe draws its oil supplies, a trend that is continuing. In addition, the rapid development of atomic energy was, according to the report, to provide

219

Europe with a new source of energy and thus reduce its dependence on the outside world. In fact, development in this sphere did not follow the lines envisaged, and proceeded more slowly.

In other words, the situation with regard to the materials needed for producing energy changed dramatically only a few months after the publication of the report of the 'Three Wise Men'. Coal stocks rose rapidly; by the end of 1958 they had risen to thirteen million tons in the Federal German Republic alone. This trend reached its first peak in October 1959, when 12 per cent of the Federal German Republic's yearly coal production was put into stock, a higher percentage than had ever been put into stock during the world economic crisis.

The great landslide in the economics of the energy industry was upon us. It was in this period that the three European Executives began formulating a common energy policy. The first significant attempt in this direction was contained in their memorandum of June 1962, which was a useful beginning. It enumerated a number of aims which nobody disputed in principle but which, when pursued together at one and the same time, proved more difficult to realize in practice: they were that energy should be cheap; that alternative sources of energy should be made increasingly available; that a steady supply of energy should be assured on a long-term basis; that the consumer should have a free choice as to what type of energy he wanted; and that the Common Market should be treated as a single unit. The estimates contained in the memorandum were already more realistic than those in the report of 1957, but they were still not realistic enough: coal consumption in 1970, it was estimated, would 'probably' not exceed 35 per cent of the total energy requirements of the Community, but in 1968 it already made up no more than 28 per cent and in 1970, 23 per cent; and oil which, it had been estimated, would make up 50 per cent of the total energy consumption in 1970, already reached 56 per cent in 1968, and 58 per cent in 1970. The memorandum submitted a definite plan for the future, tied to a time-table. According to this plan, the coal industry was to adapt itself to the new market conditions by means of subsidies; preparations were to be made for creating a common market for energy production and supply; no obstacle was to be put in the way of extending the use of oil; and

220

systematic support was to be given to the development of nuclear energy.

This memorandum led to the 'Protocol of an Agreement Relating to Questions of Energy' which was approved by the Council of Ministers of the Coal and Steel Community in April 1963. 'Fair and just competition between the different suppliers of energy in the Common Market' was added as one of the objectives of a common energy policy – although exactly what was meant by that phrase was left open. Furthermore, the Council of Ministers laid down a trade policy which had not been set out in the Coal and Steel Community Treaty, as well as common rules and conditions of competition between the different suppliers of energy. All this represented a trend in the right direction but much, indeed most, of it, remained on paper only. In fairness, however, it must be pointed out that efforts to form three separate energy policies into one were bound to lead to futility until the three administrations of the three Communities were merged. Moreover, there were constant disputes on matters of detail – above all, on questions affecting coal – in the Council of Ministers of the Coal and Steel Community. And even then what was involved was mostly the question of approving measures which the member-states had already taken and which could hardly at that stage be revoked. These measures concerned subsidies, fiscal arrangements, and equalization systems.

On the whole, it was inevitable that the institutions of the three Communities should, despite all efforts to co-ordinate their approach to matters of energy, think in terms not of a common over-all policy for power but in terms of the coal industry, of oil, or of nuclear energy. A real change of attitude could and did come about only when the administrations in Brussels and Luxembourg had been merged. From that moment onwards a lead could be given in evolving a common energy policy. Stock was taken of the situation. Officials acquired the habit of thinking in common terms and objectives. All problems were approached on a common basis, and their integral unity defined. It was as a whole that the problems involved were presented and tackled.

The results were not long in coming. In its memorandum of December 1968 on the 'First Guide-lines for the Common Energy Policy', which was approved in principle by the Council of

221

Ministers in November 1969, the Commission did not spend much time in elaborating further on theoretical objectives; it merely stated that the aims of providing cheap energy through oil and of assuring energy supplies by exploiting internal coal and natural gas reserves were not irreconcilable and could be attained without resorting to extreme solutions. It placed more emphasis on them than on protection of the interests of the consumer. As for the rest, the Commission adopted the concrete language of the Treaty of Rome: it pointed to the creation of a common market in energy, that is to say it pointed to the Treaty provisions for the free movement of goods, the freedom to establish enterprises anywhere in the Community, the rules of competition, and the harmonization of taxes. The pragmatic method came into its own again; instead of striving after perfection, the Commission sought to keep an eye on the markets, watch what was going on, and, if necessary, make suggestions and recommendations for improvement. In December 1969 the Commission therefore proposed that enterprises engaged in production as well as in transport should be obliged to report all important investment projects; in the same way enterprises were to be obliged to report once a year their programmes for the import of oil and natural gas. There was to be direct intervention only if the Community's interest could not be asserted in any other way. What the Commission was after was that action should be taken on a continuous basis, which meant that there should be estimates looking ahead towards medium-term prospects, guidance for the future, and yearly studies of economic trends.

For a start this somewhat cautious method seemed likely to succeed; but we had to wait to see what happened. On no account must one think in terms of production targets and of estimates for extracting sources of energy. That method has hardly led to happy results. Plainly the risks of having supplies of oil and nuclear fuel cut off must, as far as possible, be reduced to a minimum; and a start has already been made on building up stocks on a common basis.

The Commission attaches particular importance to the provisions of Article 37 of the Treaty of Rome, which lays down that member-states shall gradually adjust any state trading monopolies so as to ensure that, when the transition period expires, there shall be no discrimination between the nationals of member-states as regards the supply and marketing of goods. Admittedly France was authorized at the end of 1969 to retain its system of oil quotas for another two years; yet at the same time it was advised to drop its quota restrictions on the import of crude oil from the member-states of the Community, and, moreover, to discard all measures of discrimination against member-states in setting limits on its oil imports. If there is to be fair competition, the main objective must be to assure all consumers of equal opportunities of access to the sources of supply. The energy industry in all its various aspects tends increasingly to concentrate on vast closely-knit enterprises. This tendency has to be watched, because it threatens free competition. If there is to be fair and equal competition in the sphere of energy and its supply, the different taxes and rates of tax in the Community must be harmonized. This is indispensable. Nothing can demonstrate more clearly how deeply any coherent comprehensive energy policy affects matters of transport and finance, particularly fuel taxes.

No less importance is attached to evolving a common trading policy for energy. The Commission believes that production in the Community's coal industry – essential if the Community is to be assured of energy, independent of imports from outside – can be maintained and the process of adaptation controlled only if imports serve common objectives. Any system of oil and nuclear fuel imports must in principle allow, indeed assure, the consumer his freedom of choice. To help bring this about, the Community's authorities must be informed beforehand of how enterprises plan to supply themselves with the energy they need. In this way the power-supply programme of the Community as a whole can be co-ordinated. Equally sensible is the idea of laying down common guidelines for investment projects in the energy industry, which are always expensive. But in this sphere, too, the enterprises concerned are naturally to be left to make their own decisions, and the Commission is not to be forced into the position of expressing its views on particular projects.

The disputes with the oil-producing countries at the beginning of 1971 also led the Commission to adopt a more active policy. In July it proposed three measures to carry out its 'First Guidelines for the common energy policy': a directive from the Council was to require oil companies to raise their stocks to ninety days' supply;

223

this was an old proposal. Industrial collaboration in prospecting, development, transport, and stocking of hydro-carbons was to be encouraged by the possibility of acquiring 'European Company' status, which as in atomic matters would offer the advantages of Community finance, tax concessions, possibly loan guarantees, rent concessions, on unrepayable loans. A loan of 100 million units of account was to be offered to facilitate the construction of large nuclear power plants. Finally, it is essential that the Community should evolve a common body of law on energy and its supply, the more so since there are numerous national and regional monopolies for the distribution of energy. A common market in energy needs common rules to regulate its proper functioning, as do common markets in other products and goods. Of course, such a common market in energy must include nuclear energy. For that reason no part or particle of the European Atomic Energy Community must be sacrificed, unless it be proved beyond doubt that Euratom is useless in promoting European integration. There have been signs of some destructive tendencies. These have to be closely watched and tenaciously fought, particularly at a moment when we are beginning to surmount the greatest obstacles in the way of evolving a common energy policy. The structure under which such a policy had to be worked out was against us until recently, for it imposed – by its very nature – only policies of partial integration, that is to say, a policy for each source of energy by itself.

To establish a common market for energy will prove no easier than the other aspects of a comprehensive Common Market. There are sectors which exercise great power, and there is a considerable mass of conflicting interests. One sector in the energy industry, coal, is plainly weak for special structural reasons. On the other hand, the long-accepted practice of intervening in the energy industry for reasons of broad economic policy makes the solution of some problems a good deal easier. The State has made its presence strongly felt in both semi-public enterprises and fully nationalized undertakings. In this sector of the economy, as in others, the Community therefore does not have to introduce new methods of *dirigisme*. It merely has to rationalize and harmonize existing methods. In tackling this task, it will examine and prune the forest of existing interventions by public authorities, and, once that job is done, there is likely to be more freedom than there was before. Certainly the way in which the energy industry and energy supply are likely to work will never reflect the Platonic ideal of an 'economy based on free competition'; but equally the suggestion that it is possible to organize the power industry without taking prices into account is as wrong as in the case of agriculture. Intervention so far has been on separate national levels, completely unco-ordinated, and as a result the last remaining elements of competition have frequently been distorted to a quite unnecessary degree. In any case, the consumer has no reason to feel uneasy about the way Europe's energy policy has recently evolved.

This process of rationalization in Europe will brook no delay. The price of energy has in recent years become increasingly important in determining where enterprises are set up within the Community. The evolution and growth of the Common Market has turned the spotlight on the distortion of competition. It is much clearer now than ever before that this obstructs the proper functioning of the market and prevents its production-potential from being used and distributed in the most sensible way. At the same time, competition between the continents of the world has become more intense, and all the indications are that this competition will not lessen.

A common energy policy is therefore essential. Europe's economy to a large extent depends on such a policy if it is to reap the full benefit of its potential resources.

10. *Transport Policy*
Every issue in politics has its ironical side. In the case of the integration of Europe, it is transport that provides the irony. Of all recent technological changes, one of the greatest has been in men's ability to move bodies or objects over distances, i.e. in transport. It is only as the means of transport have improved that our horizons have become wider and our sense of being free to move over ever-greater distances has increased to the point where we could think of building one large modern Europe. Just as the integration of nation-states in the nineteenth century would probably not have taken place without the development of the railways, so today we owe that very real feeling of being 'at home' in one continent to our ever-increasing ability to move about freely over ever greater distances.

225

And yet European transport policy has remained in what one can describe only as a state of old-fashioned pastoral seclusion. It is stationary. What has been done to turn the 'common transport policy', demanded by the Treaty, into fact does not make a glorious tale in the history of the European Economic Community. What progress there has been is modest, not to say meagre. There are beginnings, but it depends on whether one is optimistic or pessimistic whether one chooses to call them hopeful. Chronology alone shows how far the development of a transport policy lags behind, in comparison with what has been achieved in other spheres of Community activity.

It was in 1958 that the Community began its work in Brussels. The Commission presented its first memorandum on transport policy in 1961; it contained a comprehensive draft for fusing the different transport markets and for ensuring competition in these markets. After lengthy deliberations in the European Parliament there followed, as a beginning, in May 1962, an 'action programme'. It essentially consisted of a plan for introducing harmonized measures for a common transport policy according to a time-table. Again, however, the European Parliament took a long time in its deliberations on this plan. As a result, it was not until May 1963 – five-and-a-half years after work had begun in Brussels – that the Commission could submit its first formal proposals.

These lost years were never made up. They were the best, most favourable years the Community had so far experienced in its development. Those who were eager to build Europe were working towards their goal with enthusiasm and drive, and the opponents of the European idea had not yet completely understood what was really happening. By the end of those years, however, we had come up against our first serious political crisis. When the discussions on transport began in the Council of Ministers in the autumn, the points were already switched to move the Community train in the direction of a common agricultural market, and the completion of the accelerated customs union was in sight. In that autumn of 1964 the Dutch Government presented a memorandum on transport policy which made it quite clear that the Dutch were not willing to contemplate any measure which might in any way diminish their prevailing position as 'the carriers of Europe'. The Dutch were particularly opposed to any suggestion that might replace the complete freedom of arriving at freight rates on the Rhine by a system designed to strike a balance of freight rates in Europe, a system which would have served as the basis of a common European policy. By December 1964 the Transport Ministers had to admit that there was not likely to be any agreement on the system of marginal tariff freight rates, proposed by the Commission, at least as far as shipping on the Rhine was concerned. We had to wait until March 1965 before the Council of Ministers reached its first concrete decision on transport policy. It contained a regulation on so-called harmonization which, in its implementation, depended basically on strict adherence to a time-table. That time-table was not adhered to; in fact, fiscal provisions, public subsidies – particularly for railways – and regulations on social security still remain to be harmonized. Moreover, the kernel of any transport policy – the scale of freight rates – was not even touched on. In the meantime, the Community had long ago agreed on the price of cereals, and, against a background of general progress towards unification in Europe, it was not unreasonable to hope that Europe's Ministers of Transport would stop failing to carry out their duties.

In June 1965 it did indeed look as though there was going to be a breakthrough. Once again, 'a binding time-table' was accepted. According to this plan, a common transport policy was to be realized on certain agreed basic principles. Public opinion praised the session at which this decision was taken as 'historic', and saw it as the beginning of a common transport policy. For the Federal German Republic this plan would virtually have meant a complete break with its traditional system of firmly-fixed freight rates. Fixed rates were to be replaced by a system of marginal rates, and as far as water transport was concerned, there was to be no restriction on freight rates, as well as complete freedom of competition between different enterprises. To be sure, there was talk even then of the need for additional regulations on tonnage and operating permits.

The hopes raised by this decision were soon dashed. France left the Council of Ministers a week after the crucial decision taken by the Community's Transport Ministers. By the summer of 1966 all members of the Council of Ministers had resumed their work and everyone assumed that agreement could be reached on the basis of the decisions reached in 1965, especially since the dates for setting up the customs union and the agricultural common market had been fixed in the meantime for 1 July 1968. At that stage, it still seemed possible to overcome the not inconsiderable differences of view on freight rates, especially with the Netherlands. By October 1966 it had, however, become obvious that the ministers could not agree.

In place of a common freight-rate policy, conditions of competition were, as a start, to be harmonized, and there were to be common regulations on tonnage and on operating permits. In its memorandum of February 1967, the Commission already used different language. The basic first principles of a common transport policy were abandoned; instead, the Commission's memorandum concentrated on what transport specialists call 'ruinous competition' – a subject close to their hearts – and on ways of fighting it. It was at this point that new life was injected into the concept of a common European Transport policy from an unexpected and different quarter, namely from proposals by the Federal German Government. They became known as the 'Leber Plan' – Leber was then Federal German Minister of Transport and they were published in the autumn of 1967. They jolted the Transport Ministers and the Commission out of their lethargy. Since it had up to then proved impossible to launch a transport policy on a European basis, Leber, the German Minister, was compelled to tackle the problem of competition between road and rail transport and the crisis of road transport on a national basis. In any case, however one may judge the technical details of Leber's Plan, it forced his European colleagues to think again and make a fresh attempt.

Subsequently, as President of the Council of Ministers, Leber found himself in the fortunate position in December 1967 of being able to press for a formal resolution to be passed that decisions should be reached by 1 July 1968 on transport as well as on other questions. The effective moment for action eventually came on 19 July 1968. After four years of procrastination, the Council of Transport Ministers at last reached its first agreement, in the early hours of a Friday morning at about half-past three. One promise at least had been fulfilled. It was decided to set up a system of marginal freight rates for goods crossing frontiers, and to permit in this context special agreements which establish an element of competition. What effect these decisions will have remains to be seen. It is in the same spirit that the Community system of quotas for goods traffic crossing frontiers by road has been settled, although, admittedly, there are for the time being no more than 1,200 licences authorizing the transport of freight between all the member-states. Furthermore, it has been decided to allow the duty-free import of fifty litres of fuel in the tanks of transport vehicles crossing frontiers, a decision which contributes at least partially to the removal of distortions in competition; it may be a compromise solution, but it at least helps to some extent towards harmonizing different rates of tax on oil. As for the rest, the provisions against agreements restricting competition apply to transport as much as to other matters. True, it remains to be seen whether the provisions on the limitations of tonnage, which have yet to be decided on, do not make competition illusory. In March 1969 the Council took further decisions to harmonize conditions of competition and organize the transport market, whereby in the Commission's opinion, in its Third General Report for 1969, the programme laid down in December 1967 was 'largely' realized. Particularly significant was the regulation, issued at the session in June 1970, which defined what subsidies for transport were permissible. A decision by the Council at the end of 1970, taken at the suggestion of France and the Netherlands, provides for systematic technical, commercial, and managerial co-operation between railway companies.

Despite these first achievements obtained by negotiation, the over-all result in evolving a transport policy is hardly satisfactory. Sea and air transport are still not included in the common transport policy, although this could have been effected by a unanimous decision of the Council (Article 84). On the agenda there are still subjects such as the right of establishment for firms in road and inland-water transport; quantitative capacity rules for inland waterways; the reimbursement of the cost of highways (a proposal was made by the Commission in March 1971), the co-ordination of infrastructure expenditure; traffic safety; the size and weight of goods trucks (in July 1971 the Commission made a proposal on the permitted axle weight of such vehicles); the harmonization of tax rules; insurance provisions; labour laws; the 'social responsibilities' of haulage contractors (on which there are already three ordinances that may become the first stage of a general regulation).

It would be quite wrong to console oneself with the thought that transport has not suffered in consequence. True, the trains travel faster. The formalities at the frontiers – though they are a nuisance – are not prohibitive. New techniques of transport are being applied. The volume of air freight is increasing, despite the failure to establish a European Air-Union. Europe's seaports are making progress in gigantic, though uncontrolled competition – uncontrolled because there is no common policy on seaports: the mammoth developments at Hamburg, Le Havre, Dunkirk, Marseille, Zeebrugge, and not least Rotterdam, take one's breath away. But beneath the surface of these apparent advantages there also lie hidden undesirable trends in the development of national economies, losses as a result of friction, and the waste of productive resources. All these are due to the fact that there is no common policy for transport.

It is therefore useful to attempt to analyse the reasons for this failure to work out a common transport policy, if only to get a clearer picture of the decisions which will come one day:

1. The Treaty is confined in essence to general prescriptions about procedure. It is only a slight simplification to say that it merely empowers the Council to lay down 'any other appropriate provisions' (Article 75). This explains the unanimity principle, which in this field applies *sine die* to Council decisions; what the Council's task is – in reality, although not formally – is supplementary Treaty negotiation.

2. The Treaty contains virtually no time-limits for devising a common transport policy, and in so far as it does so, these are only partly in the transition period. It had already become apparent during the negotiations leading up to the signing of the Treaty that the specialist authorities, in comparison with others involved, lacked a sufficiently comprehensive understanding of what European integration demanded. Transport policy belonged to the 'hard core' of the topics under negotiation, which could only be disposed of during the last weeks of the Conference at Val Duchesse in Brussels. I had personally taken over the leadership of the German delegation for this final phase of the negotiations. When I left the Conference, I had the impression that I had taken

230

part in a pseudo-ecclesiastical council rather than in negotiations concerned with economic policy. With what one can only describe as religious fervour the argument revolved around dogmatic positions, such as whether transport is a form of economic activity or a public service.

3. A further great drawback was the fact that it took far too long to get matters moving. While the first proposals on implementing a common agricultural policy were submitted as early as the end of 1959, proposals on a common transport policy were not put forward until May 1963. Admittedly, it took a long time to take stock of even one aspect of the complex of problems involved – the official controls affecting transport in the different member-countries. It took a long time because there was not sufficient staff at the centres in the member-countries to provide the necessary information. But the attempt to work out a common transport policy in friendly discussions with all the parties likely to be affected before the Commission drew up formal proposals consumed an enormous amount of time. Worse still, no matter how praiseworthy the idea behind this approach to the problem may have been, it was condemned to failure.

4. Quite apart from all this, the prospects of working out a common transport policy were bad because one essential element was lacking: there was virtually no basic political concept to give some shape and form to the discussions of Europe's Transport Ministers until Leber, the German Transport Minister, put forward his plan in 1967. Transport policy was largely left to the specialists, and specialists in this field included Ministers responsible for special spheres of activity. Nobody quarrels with the suggestion that the specialists were faced with great difficulties, difficulties inherent in trying to evolve a common transport policy. But had they, as a result, lost the ability to break the habit of thinking only in narrow national and traditional terms of running their transport industries?

5. Why – in the light of these circumstances – did public opinion allow the Transport Ministers to meet only twice or three times a year? Why was there no political pressure on the Council of Ministers to take action in the sphere of transport policy, as there was in other spheres of Community activity? The answer is that no member-country, or to put it more precisely, none of the

231

national bureaucracies, felt the need to change the existing order. Agricultural policy, for example, can be seen to involve the price of commodities which everyone requires daily. It deals with the level of prices for meat and butter, factors which affect the fate of millions of people and their families – in fact the fortunes of whole provinces. By contrast, the problems of transport appear in a curious way to be removed from the day-to-day issues of political conflict – unless of course such problems as the construction of new motorways, questions of traffic safety or the rates which railways are justified in charging in the light of social considerations come up for debate. The great economic questions raised by a common transport policy have never been tackled in the context of their political implications – as the common agricultural policy has been. They have always remained, and remain to this day, the concern of specialists.

6. Why is this so? Because transport, in the widest meaning of that term, is in nearly all countries regarded, not as an element of the economy which ought to be potentially efficient and pay its way, but as a 'public service', for reasons which largely depend on the fact that most modern transport undertakings are public enterprises of one sort or another. This concept makes it difficult to view transport policy in an unprejudiced way. There is a tradition in many countries, including the Federal German Republic, that the state alone is responsible for the infrastructure of the transport system, and that methods of allowing economic factors, such as competition, which have proved their worth in other sectors of the economy, to play their part do not apply when it comes to transport. Naturally nobody would dream of denying that decisions on transport deeply affect the well-being of a country. Whether a region prospers or stagnates frequently depends on the existence of a railway line or a motorway. Thus transport policy is the servant of many, not to say too many, masters, a fact which makes it inflexible. The level of railway fares is influenced by considerations of social policy, the level of freight rates by plans for regional development; decisions on whether to favour rail or road traffic by the interest attached to sustaining small and medium-sized enterprises; and financial policy plays a part in determining the rates for motor-vehicle licences and petrol taxes. Indeed, transport policy often has a direct effect on foreign policy. Yet transport ministers

232

are ministers with responsibility for a specialist field, and as specialist ministers too many demands are made on them. Only a broad political vision can lift us above specialist considerations and provide the dynamism needed to launch a European transport policy.

7. In addition, there are great differences, and not only between countries. Even more significant is the problem of the inequality in size and power of the different types of carriers in the transport industry: on the one hand, there are the mammoth systems of railways, all of them in deficit – though for different reasons; on the other, there are the partly large and partly small and medium-sized inland waterways and road-haulage enterprises. In the last resort these inequalities turn every attempt to reach a decision on transport policy into a long drawn-out battle, in the course of which long-term political considerations are soon forgotten. In the meantime, the established order of the administrative apparatus remains as before. The structure of the transport system, based largely on public law, and the inequalities within the industry, have continued to turn transport policy into an area where state or private controls predominate: there are fixed rates, limitations on the supply of services offered, quotas, controls over investments, and cartels. One of the few exceptions in this area is the freedom to agree on Rhine freight rates. It was entirely logical on the part of the Commission to try to build on this precedent. Admittedly, its attempt has had only limited success, above all because the Netherlands were not prepared to compromise in any way on the complete freedom of freight rates on the Rhine. There is no justification for blaming the Commission now for having supported the wrong principle in advocating the adoption of a system of marginal rates for Rhine transport. Its initiative was sensible, moderate, and European in concept; it made a positive contribution to competition which was welcome and free of risks. Subsequently, the Commission was most effectively prevented from pursuing this course further.

The great venture of launching and realizing a common transport policy has therefore not yet succeeded. If one is kindly disposed, one can call what had been achieved so far an opening. The road which we have now taken is long and stony. For the time being, the uncertainty about the form a common transport policy

233

is likely to take is bound to continue, with the consequent danger that considerable resources may be wrongly invested within the Community. These are so imminent that people are tempted to see them as inevitable. Since there is no effective competition in some important sectors of the market – while competition works perfectly well in other sectors – it is hardly easy to avoid uneconomic and injustified investments.

But even transport will not be able to withstand the floodtide of European integration. It cannot remain an island on its own. Once the establishment of an economic union is completed, transport will at last have to be organized on a European basis.

11. *Regional Policy*

General economic policy sees man as part of the economic process. It sees him as subject and object of an economy based on the division of labour, which in a free society is guided by the way in which the price mechanism and competition work. It sees him as subject and object of the creation and distribution of income; and finally also as subject and object of the process of economic expansion, a topic of particular concern to those involved in trying to combat economic cycles. Social policy sees man in an organized society as member of a group, and seeks to deal with the social conditions which influence his life. Regional policy sees man in his geographical surroundings. Indeed, the most basic factors determining a man's life are his surroundings and the period of history into which he is born. These factors impose a certain framework on a man's life, and they mark the point at which regional policy begins. Regional policy is therefore not a 'specific form of economic policy' in the sense that monetary, fiscal, transport, agricultural, trade, and other policies are. It does not constitute a particular 'branch' of the economy, but it affects and touches all branches. It is an element, an attribute of every aspect of economic activity. Wherever we take any action in the economic sphere, its effects are felt in our surroundings. As a result, the state, in implementing regional policy, employs means derived from all the other branches of politics: from transport to education policy; from agricultural to fiscal and budgetary policy; from energy to social policy, etc. The decision of the European Conference in Bonn on 11 September 1970 gives a lucid picture of this.

In its first few sentences, in fact in its preamble, the Treaty of Rome stresses that one of the methods by which the harmonious development of the six separate national economies is to be promoted is by diminishing the disparities between the various regions and the backwardness of the less-favoured regions. Article 2 of the Treaty explicitly declared this development to be one of the tasks of the Community.

These few words define the central problem of regional policy: the disparities between the economic regions in the Community. These disparities are due only partially to natural circumstances. There are stretches of land which are fertile and those which are not; there are regions which have rich subterranean resources, and those which have not; there are regions which are more easily accessible than others because they lie close to navigable waters; and there are many other similar examples. But whatever the situation, policy decisions – particularly on economic matters – constantly play their part; it is as a result of policy decisions that streets, canals, railways, airports, and schools are built; policies affect the cultivation of the soil and the construction of houses and living quarters. In deciding between different policy options, those who make the decisions pursue diverse aims. They can aim at improving the attractions of a region and thereby increasing the advantages of setting up enterprises there. Such a course is desirable because it cuts production costs and stimulates expansion and prosperity. But there are limits to this kind of policy. At a certain point additional investment in what is called infrastructure, that is money spent on roads, water supply and the like, no longer pays: it becomes uneconomical. The gain obtained from every penny spent on, for example, roads diminishes. Furthermore, disproportionately high growth in one region creates an unhealthy balance between it and other regions at whose expense it is flourishing – for example, because workers move away from a less-favoured region to seek employment in a more-favoured region. On the one hand, there are areas of industrial concentration, like the Ruhr, Northern Italy, Northern France, and the Paris region; on the other, there are areas of stagnation, like Southern Italy, Southern France, the Hunsrück mountain range in Germany, the Eifel region, etc. Where such a situation exists, regional policy pursues the opposite course and provides aid for the region which finds

235

itself at a disadvantage, by improving its infrastructure, by making subsidies available, or by similar measures.

Plainly, if regional policy is to be devised and executed on sound lines, it must keep in close touch with the regions concerned. The drive for improvement comes from the regions themselves. It is also true that the remedial measures necessary will be better applied to local requirements if the competent authorities are close at hand. It follows, therefore, that the greater the degree of decentralization in a country the better that country is prepared to organize regional policies. It is no accident that if one examines a map of the Community as a whole, the country whose economic and social structure is most balanced geographically is Germany. Take the average level of economic activity for the country as a whole, and you discover that regional variations above and below that level are much smaller than in the other member-states of the Community. This fact Germany owes to its centuries-old federal – or otherwise decentralized – structure. Countries with centralized constitutions and administrations are more likely to produce areas of economic concentration; one has only to think of the Paris region. It is entirely consistent with these facts that one notices strong tendencies towards regionalization in France. True, these tendencies are meeting with opposition which is rooted in France's strong Jacobin tradition, a tradition that arouses fears that the state may be weakened and centrifugal forces encouraged.

More than any other form of economic activity in the Community, regional policy is therefore primarily a matter for the member-states and the smaller entities which form part of the constitution and administration of the member-states, like the *Länder* of the Federal German Republic, municipal associations, and local administrative authorities. The Community itself does not draw up plans for regional policies. It assists the authorities in the regions; it also helps with their planning – for example, by providing facts and figures which locally can be obtained only with some difficulty. For that purpose the Commission has also undertaken systematic investigations. Admittedly, this suggests that the regions might be turned into more than just the scene of regional policy measures, and become members of a federal entity, either European or national. This idea – and it is a bold one – has been advanced in one or two quarters, sometimes with apprehension,

236

sometimes with hope. But for the time being its chances of becoming political reality are limited. One still prefers to leave the church in the confines of the village square.

All the same, the men who drew up the European Treaties were right to give the Community a measure of competence in matters of regional policy. Article 56 of the Treaty establishing the Coal and Steel Community already provides that the Community, together with the member-states, should pay out grants in cases where technical innovations in certain areas caused workers to lose their jobs and to have difficulty in finding others. Article 80, paragraph 2, of the Treaty of Rome permits the introduction of special transport rates for economically under-developed regions, and Article 92, paragraph 3, aid to promote the economic development of backward areas. Furthermore, Article 226, the so-called 'protective clause', allows protective measures to be taken in the case of regions which are suffering hardship as a result of integration. True, these provisions have only rarely been used. In addition, there are the general financial devices at the disposal of the Community – the European Social Fund and the European Investment Bank. But all these are only the specific provisions. There are also the general opportunities for action contained in the Treaty, which can be made to serve a common regional policy. And this holds true for the Community as it does for the states.

The reasons why the Community has been brought into the sphere of regional policy become evident when we examine these broad, general provisions.

To begin with, the Community itself may, in pursuing its general aims, create regional policy problems. It seeks to merge the six national economies of the member-states. It does so with the express aim of changing and improving the existing economic situation. One can virtually, therefore, say that the Community is a huge, continent-sized effort in regional policy. From the beginning it must act in such a way as to avoid, for example, excessive concentration of economic activity in some regions and stagnation in others; and where there is a threat of that happening it must seek to balance out distortions as soon as possible. For example, remote regions can be forcibly industrialized by rigorously applying a system of subsidies, thus creating difficulties even for economically healthy competitors elsewhere; to adopt such a course would be to jump from the frying-pan into the fire. For such a lack of balance means that a brake is put on economic growth and that the over-all volume of production is reduced. It means, in general political terms, less prosperity, less contentedness, and less human happiness. Fortunately the history of integration shows that action on the part of the Community does not have to lead to such negative results. On the contrary, it produces the opposite and positive result, in the majority of cases, of eliminating undesirable backwardness.

Moreover, quite independently of any action which the Community takes in the sphere of regional policy proper, it creates new conditions of which regional policy, in turn, has to take account on the European as well as the national level. The Community provides modern techniques with the large area they require for their proper exploitation. One has to think only of the revolutionary developments which have taken place in the sphere of the means of transport – developments such as containers, pipelines, and air traffic – all of which have virtually made distance a negligible factor. The removal of economic frontiers means that measures taken originally on a local or national basis affect the whole geographical area of the Community. The port policies pursued in Rotterdam and Antwerp make themselves felt in Hamburg and Bremen. The construction of a new canal in France can have a profound effect on the basis on which cereal prices are fixed. If new areas of industrial concentration grow up in Western Germany, the pollution this may cause in the Rhine can hardly remain a matter of indifference to the Netherlands. And, in referring to all these examples, we have not even mentioned the agricultural reforms which are already well under way and visibly altering the aspect of whole agricultural regions. Naturally, in all cases where the Community causes such problems by its actions, it also helps to find solutions to them.

At the same time it is only appropriate to point to the apparent paradox that the changes which cause difficulties often make it easier to overcome these difficulties. It was through the removal of economic barriers that regions, which in the political and economic sense were until recently peripheral areas, are now brought together as parts of a large European Community. As a result, they are gradually beginning to work together in a neighbourly fashion

238

with the aid of the Community's institutions and the common procedures the Community is evolving. An example of this is the way the traffic and communications are being planned in the Liège, Aachen and Maastricht areas. By the same token, regions which have now ceased to be merely national frontier areas and become frontier areas of the Community must be able to count on the fact that the Community as a whole is jointly responsible for them. This holds true particularly for agricultural regions which lie far away from the markets for their produce. They not only face the danger that their countryside may become desolate and their economy be run down; they are also threatened by human, cultural, and political stagnation.

Finally, the Community is under a duty, a duty which can be compared to that of a policeman, of keeping an eye on regional policy. What must be avoided is that member-states use needs of a regional, political nature as a pretext to aid branches of their own economy – by subsidies, for example – and thus bring about objectionable distortions in the conditions of fair competition. Equally, care must be taken that national regional policies do not outbid one another in the objectives they pursue; that member-states do not use regional policies in their own territories to consolidate economic situations which, in the interests of the Community as a whole, should be altered. There should not be a race between the Ministers of Finance to persuade industries to site enterprises in their territories – as has happened in the Federal German Republic, thereby putting a strain on the good neighbourly relations between the *Länder*. After all, the fact that the Community has come into existence has by itself altered the yardstick by which we ought to measure whether the expenditure involved in pursuing a particular regional project is reasonable or a waste of resources.

In the final analysis we are in all spheres of activity concerned with problems of adaptation, and as a rule they are problems of adaptation of considerable dimensions. Regional policy is development policy. It is therefore entirely legitimate for the Community to intervene, and such intervention is likely to continue. We are here concerned not with a problem of transition from a pre-Community to a Community period. For the dramatic change in fact and circumstances, which is what the second Industrial Revolution indeed means, is not a short-term, passing phenomenon, comparable to a trade cycle. Nowhere is this more evident than in agriculture. It took a time before it was recognized how deep the problem went and how irresistible forces of economic evolution were affecting the very existence of the people, their relationship to the land, their occupations, their farms, and their villages. This process of irresistible change has long since made itself felt in all the branches of the economy. Everywhere the first difficulty is to recognize the true nature and magnitude of the 'New World' we have to face. Only then does appropriate technical, administrative and political action become possible.

From the start of its activities, the European Commission has devoted considerable attention to this problem. It has worked out a fundamental theory for a regional policy on a Community basis. The *dossier* of regional policy is in an excellent state, thanks not least to the tireless efforts of the Member of the Commission responsible for this subject, Hans von der Groeben. Towards the end of 1961 the Commission organized a conference on questions of regional economy, but only after extensive preparatory work which included discussions with the national administrations. Soon after the conference, the working parties submitted reports which dealt with the aims and methods of regional policy and structural improvements in all industrial regions. Towards the end of 1963 the Commission and the European Parliament first exchanged their views on these reports. It was accepted 'that the European Communities must assume an essential central element of responsibility for laying down guidelines for a common regional policy'. Furthermore, it was demanded that information on a comprehensive scale should be made available and that collaboration between the national administrations should be improved.

In May 1965, shortly before the great crisis in the Community, the Commission laid its 'First Communication on Regional Policy within the European Economic Community' before the Council of Ministers. The first nexus of basic concepts was established. The Commission pressed for action. The regional aspect of the restructuring of agriculture and energy policy were defined more precisely. A method of ensuring better co-ordination was proposed. It was announced that the draft proposal of the Commission, outlining the first stage of a programme for medium-term economic policy, would contain a chapter on 'Regional Policy'. This programme was made public in the spring of 1966, and, despite the 1965 crisis, the European Parliament proceeded to exploit the initiative opened up by the Commission's programme. Regional policy was divided into five spheres: first, the large frontier regions of the Community, such as Western and South-Western France and Southern Italy; secondly the rural areas not too far away from the great industrial centres; thirdly, the old traditional industrial areas; fourthly, the regions close to the common frontiers of the member-states; and lastly, the zones next to the frontiers of the Federal German Republic as well as Venezia Giulia (Trieste). The programme also encouraged the authorities of the Community competent to deal with these matters, in pursuing the aims they had been set.

There was, however, an enforced pause, the result of the crisis in which the Community found itself, of the slowing-down in work which the crisis caused, and of the fusion of the three European executives. But in the meantime a fresh wind had sprung up to fill the sails of the programme for regional policy on a European basis, and this had happened before the Summit Conference at The Hague. There is no longer any difference of opinion on the proposition that regional policy must be pursued in the perspective of new, European dimensions and that the Community has tasks in this sphere. The Commission has emphatically pointed out how far the problems of regional development, as viewed in a European context, have come to a head. There have already been considerable transformations. All factors of production have become more mobile. The relations between town and country reveal disquieting trends, and three types of regions are clearly emerging: there are the industrial regions which, while comprising only 16 per cent of the geographical area of the Community, are inhabited by 42 per cent of the Community's population; there are the semi-industrialized regions which cover a third of the Community's geographical area and are also inhabited by about a third of the Community's population; and, finally, there are the rural regions which cover more than half the Community's area but are inhabited by hardly a quarter of its population. Between these different regions and within them there are considerable divergences which are bound to give rise to great anxiety. There are cases where whole areas are in danger of social and economic erosion and where it is

241

necessary rapidly to take measures to revitalize social and economic life.

In October 1969 the Commission proposed to the Council of Ministers a plan for an institutional framework for co-ordinating regional policy in the Community. According to this plan, the member-states were to discuss the situation in the critical regions, particularly in the frontier regions, with the Commission at regular intervals. A common standing committee was to be formed to consult on regional plans and especially on the question of how far such plans were compatible with the concepts and aims of the Common Market – for example, as far as the restructuring of agriculture, and measures to create the right kind of infrastructure were concerned, such as roads, communications, oil pipelines, the construction of aerodromes and ports, and the protection of the countryside. Budgets were to provide means for creating a compensation fund for interest payments, and this fund was to be administered by the Commission. An opportunity was to be provided for loans by the European Investment Bank or other financial institutions to be duly guaranteed.

In connection with the reform of the structure of agriculture, the Commission supplemented its proposals in May 1971. Between 1972 and 1976, some 300,000 new jobs will have to be created in previously agricultural regions, where hitherto industry and services have not sufficiently developed.

The Agricultural Fund would put up 150 units of account for every job taken by a farm-worker. To put an end to competitive bidding up of regional aids, the Commission proposed in June 1971 that from 1972 onwards co-ordinating rules should gradually be adopted, first in the central areas of the Community, where bidding up is continually observed. The first rule would be an upper limit of 20 per cent of investments. For this, there must be a common method for calculating aids. At the same time, rules are to be developed for more deserving regions and for peripheral areas in particular straits.

It is in the nature of all work connected with regional policy that it is not reflected in dramatic negotiations and spectacular decisions. It is work that deals with the everyday aspects of human life. Thus there is little talk of the regional plans and projects in which the European Commission is participating: for example, the new important industrial centres in Southern Italy, in Bari and Taranto; the collaboration between the northern frontier areas of the Belgian province of Luxembourg and Lorraine; the project for economic development in the Eifel-Hunrueck region; or the new important tourist centre in Calabria. Still less is public opinion aware of the continuous stream of material and intellectual help that the Community provides for regional development. But this in no way diminishes the significance of regional policy. In fact, policies on a grand scale are bearable only if they are corrected, softened – one is tempted to say humanized – by regional policy which works on a smaller local scale.

At the first conference on regional policy in 1961, when we were at the beginning of our work, I said: 'The whole wealth of Europe, the wealth of its culture, consists of the diversity and the individuality of its regions, as they have been shaped in the course of the great, eventful, history of this Continent. We have thus been entrusted with a precious heritage. It is not only our duty to preserve that heritage. It is also our duty to allow Europe's manifold economic, social, and cultural resources to develop. What an immense field of progress this prospect opens up for us!'

I believe that this is as true today as it was then.

Chapter Six

The Community and the World

I. EXTERNAL ECONOMIC POLICY

1. *Basic Principles*

Internal and external unity are two sides of the same coin. This is true also of the large-scale economic policy made possible by the European Community. Such a policy makes no sense without a Community external economic policy; without one, indeed, its existence is under threat.

Accordingly, the Treaties contain provisions on a common trade policy, on the association of overseas countries and territories, and on the external relations of Euratom, and there are different protocols and declarations of intent of an external economic nature. Furthermore, the Treaty of Rome contains provisions on the conduct of negotiations on international treaties and on the relations of the Community to international organizations.

The intention that emerges from the sum total of these particular provisions, and the way in which the authority for implementing them has been allocated, is quite clear: as regards the outside world, the Community is in future to speak with but one voice in matters of economic policy. This intention is not materially limited by either the letter or the spirit of the Treaty. Just as there is inside the Common Market no sphere of economic and social policy which lies outside the competence of the Community – a fact which emerged clearly from the discussions held to decide on the interpretation of Article 145 of the Treaty of Rome and which was confirmed by the communiqué of The Hague Summit Conference held in December 1969 – so there can be no restrictive interpretation as regards the outside world. In any case, such obscurities as may crop up could be clarified by means of the procedure for minor revisions as laid down in Article 235, a procedure which does not require parliamentary ratification.

In presenting itself as one entity Europe is declaring itself ready

244

and willing to share in shouldering world-wide responsibilities. This will and purpose find expression in broad terms in the preamble to the Treaty of Rome. There the Community commits itself to safeguarding peace and liberty throughout the world and, as early as 1957, to pursuing policies of aid to the developing countries in accordance with the principles of the United Nations. Europe's determination to come to grips with world problems as a unified entity also forms the basis of the treaty obligations by which the Community explicitly bound itself to contribute to the harmonious development of world trade. Such obligations are not to be found in anything like a similar form in any purely national constitution. Equally, Europe's world-wide approach is reflected in the provisions laying down the objectives of European development policy in the associated African states and in Madagascar.

There have been several attempts, on the part of member-states, to use Gaullist opposition to the growing importance of the Community's institutions in order to re-invest national diplomatic services with authority in spheres in which the Community was to act on behalf of all, and to substitute some form of loosely-organized co-operation for Community action. Such attempts have been contrary to the spirit as well as the letter of the Treaty. The Treaty is naturally based on the principle that it is within and through the institutions of the Community that its external policy is formed. The formation of a Community policy towards the outside world is no different from that concerned with the internal problems of the Common Market. There is no change in the scale of values. What is involved is a limitation of national sovereignty, but by way of compensation each member-state is endowed with an extensive right to determine what shape the external relations of the Community should have. Even here there are no insuperable conflicts of national interest between the member-states. On the contrary, it is reasonable to expect, on the basis of the experience of the last ten years, that every legitimate regional economic interest will be taken into account in defining the interest of the Community as a whole – a process that has become ever more effective as a result of the growing evolution of what is known as the *solidarité de fait*. In addition, every regional interest will gain in importance as regards the outside world by being raised to the level of forming a part of the Community's interests as a whole, and it will consequently be possible to give it more effective support.

Seen in this light, the external economic policy of the Community represents the first stage in bringing about, at least partially, a comprehensive Community foreign policy – a process which is in harmony with the ultimate political aims of integration. The most important matters with which foreign policy is concerned nowadays – after those relating to national security – are those dealing with external economic policy. In effectively asserting its competence in coping with external economic policy, the European Community has taken the first concrete steps in exorcising Europe's powerlessness in the world. The Community has already in its own right become a decision-making and therefore a power centre in international affairs, though its influence naturally depends on the treaties actually in force, and on the extent to which the Community develops as an integrated unit. It has won and proved its identity and compactness as an entity in international tariff negotiations, such as the so-called Dillon and Kennedy Rounds, and in other negotiations in which it has presented itself as one unit. Even though the external economic policy of the Community (which is, after all, a customs union) had necessarily to start off by tackling foreign-trade policy, we must never lose sight of the fact that economic policy covers and affects many matters apart from trade. I wish to mention only external monetary policy; external transport policy – particularly as far as maritime and air transport are concerned; the supply of raw materials and of materials necessary for generating power; relations with the outside world in all sorts of technological questions, and problems in connection with international competition.

The world has also accorded the Community diplomatic recognition. The Community has diplomatic relations with most states – excepting only the smaller ones and the members of the Eastern Bloc. Ambassadors from more than eighty states are accredited to the Community. The associated states are represented by permanent delegations. Even the member-countries of the Warsaw Pact keep in touch with the Community, although as far as possible they confine their relations for the time being to arrangements on specific topics and to contacts within multilateral organizations, such as ECE and GATT. And the Community itself

246

maintains a Delegation in London which will be withdrawn only when Britain becomes a full member of the Community.

The most important part at present of external economic policy is foreign-trade policy. The core of trade policy is an external tariff policy. This the Community definitely established on 1 July 1968, when it completed the establishment of its common external tariff. Previously the Community, already speaking with one voice, had successfully carried on world-wide negotiations on the setting-up of its common tariff and in the course of the Kennedy Round. In addition, there are the efforts to put quotas on a common Community basis and to find solutions for trading in agricultural products with non-Common Market countries – a problem that forms part of the common agricultural policy.

Unifying the commercial policies of the member-states had to be accomplished piece by piece and took years of effort. At first Paris blocked progress, then, at times, Bonn's attitude raised complications. Nevertheless, from the date laid down in the Treaty – the end of the transition period, 1 January 1970 – it was possible to conduct 'the common commercial policy based on uniformly established principles' as provided for in Article 113 of the Treaty. True, some transitional provisions still remain in force; in particular, a few special areas of activity, such as commercial policy with the East and export-promotion policy, are somewhat behind the general Community time-table: not until October 1970 did the Council first issue a directive on Community export-credits policy.

At the same time, the Community has become more active in its policy on trade agreements. For example, in pursuing the objective of giving substance to the policy of association with non-member countries, agreements have been concluded or are being prepared or negotiated with Ceylon, Formosa, Hong Kong, India, Indonesia, Iran, Japan, Korea, Austria, Pakistan, the Philippines, Switzerland, Thailand, and Uruguay.

The material interests of the Community are dictated by the elementary facts of its economic structure and geography. Poor in raw materials, it is essentially a processing and manufacturing area which depends on an intensive export trade. Consequently, it is only natural that the Community should, compared to the United States and to the Soviet Union, have a higher volume of foreign trade in proportion to its gross national product and to its population, as well as in absolute figures. Consequently, too, the Community has a vital objective interest – an interest far greater than that of the super-powers – in stimulating and promoting liberal trading conditions throughout the world and in seeing to it that all the other markets in the world are opened up, and free access to them assured without discrimination. It is therefore imperative to the concept underlying the Community's foreign-trade policy that the most-favoured-nation principle, confirmed by GATT, should be maintained.

For some member-states this Community interest represents a radical break with protectionist tradition. Critics of the Community outside Europe do not always take sufficiently into account the significance of these developments. It was only the opening-up of national markets into a large-scale Community economy that made nationally-oriented industries truly competitive, and so made it possible to give up deep-rooted protectionist attitudes. For generally speaking – with a few hard-core exceptions – competitiveness in the large Community area means competitiveness on world markets.

It is only natural that such huge upheavals in external economic conditions should meet difficulties and opposition.

In its first years, in particular, the Community was frequently attacked as 'inward-looking', concerned only with its own interests, isolationist and egoistical. It was of course unavoidable that the method of integration adopted by the Community – the customs union and its consequences – although in conformity with GATT rules, involved different treatment for members and non-members. If that can be called 'discrimination' then it is the kind of discrimination that a man and a woman practise against the rest of the society when they get married. More recent criticism of the Community's commercial policy is of the same nature. It is in part violent and it is voiced particularly in GATT. The main critics are especially the United States of America, Canada, Japan, Australia, and a number of South American states. They base their criticism on Article 24 of the GATT Convention which permits infringements of the general principle of most-favoured-nation treatment only in favour of customs unions and free trade areas. The reproach by the critics is directed against the association agreements between the

248

Community and non-member countries – in this respect the reproach is not new – and against trade treaties which contain preferential clauses.

The controversy touches on fundamental questions affecting the whole system of world trade, and efforts to find a settlement have only just begun. In April 1970 the European Commission issued a memorandum which develops its views on the enlargement of the Community from 1967 to 1969. The memorandum recognizes that the actions of the Community in matters of association and commercial policy, which have come and are under attack, are influenced by a variety of different factors which can hardly ever be separated one from another in any particular case. Some of the factors are historical and are connected with past colonial policies. Such is the case with the association agreements with seventeen African states and Madagascar, and with agreements, either concluded or envisaged, with the countries of the Maghreb, with Algeria and Libya. Similar reasons apply in the case of association with Nigeria and the East African Union and they also apply, now that the negotiations for Great Britain's entry are completed, to some of Britain's former colonies in Africa, the Indian Ocean, and the Caribbean. Some of the factors which shape the Community's attitude in matters of association and commercial policy arise from the need for finding transitional solutions. Such is the case with the agreements concluded with Greece and Turkey, which are eventually to lead to full membership, and with the arrangements made with the developing countries which are eventually to broaden out into a generalized preferential development policy. Other factors affecting the Community attitude arise from a situation where a country's neutrality makes it unable to share the political actions and objectives of the Community. Its status must then be reconciled with the mutual need to find suitable structural links. Finally, foreign policy plays its part. There are overriding reasons for the Community to want to be able to defend its external political interests. The Community's need for a coherent policy in the Mediterranean area is a case in point.

All this has to be brought into harmony with the rules of GATT, whose authors can in no way be reproached with having been unable to take all these facts and factors – and the consequences arising from them – into account. On the other hand, one must

249

give credit to the advocates of the Community's policy for the fact that it was at all events their purpose to serve and work towards the ultimate aim of the GATT system: that is, to secure and strengthen the scope of free trade in the world. It is for that reason and in that context that the Commission has proposed that the geographical limits of the preferential policy should be laid down, that the policy of the Community with regard to Latin America and the Far East should be defined precisely; and that the Community's devices for implementing its external economic policy should be extended beyond the implementation of customs policy to include technical, financial, and labour-market aid. It is regrettable that the new and welcome American initiative to launch a round of negotiations on GATT, which are to be concerned primarily with obstacles to world trade other than those imposed by customs barriers, should as yet have led to no concrete results.

In conclusion, it is hardly fair to charge the Community with some of the consequences of its agricultural trade policy. That agricultural policy was *de facto* lifted out of the GATT system of world trade for the simple reason that in this field the innumerable exception and waiver clauses, agreed to at the Havana Conference, had by then virtually made the GATT system meaningless. Furthermore, it cannot be proved that third countries, interested in importing their agricultural products into the Community, would – taken together – have had better opportunities for selling their goods if the Community had never come into existence and if, as a result, each member-country had continued to pursue its own agricultural policy. People seem only too eager to remain silent on the extent to which the volume of imports of agricultural produce into the Community has increased. In addition, one can hardly blame the fathers of the Treaty if their already gigantic task of fusing six different, officially controlled and regulated agricultural systems into one Community system guided by one Community policy was further complicated by the fact that the same decade saw Europe's techniques of agricultural production revolutionized.

This is the broad principle underlying the Community's external economic policy. Besides, there are important factors which make for differences in formulating and executing policy. This is true particularly of the Community's relations with the other great industrial powers and with the Third World.

250

2. The United States of America

The supreme necessity facing the Economic Community is to cultivate economic relations across the Atlantic, in particular with the United States of America. For every responsible European and American politician this is a permanent task of the highest significance. If it is true to say that the industrial nations of the Northern Hemisphere determine the economic development of our planet, then it is equally true that in the Northern Hemisphere trans-Atlantic relations to this day still occupy first place. These relations involve problems which go far beyond those of trade policy – although problems of trade policy will, next to monetary relations, require special attention for the foreseeable future. The two partners on the two sides of the Atlantic are the two greatest trading powers in the world: the European Community accounts for 17 per cent of the world's trade; the United States 15 per cent. Since 1958 the volume of goods exchanged between the two has multiplied three times (today it runs at 13,000 million dollars). American exports to the Community have risen by 182 per cent – as against 118 per cent for America's remaining exports elsewhere.

True, the fact that growth in both economic areas – in the Community and in the United States – is proceeding in parallel at headlong speed, while economic policies in the two areas differ, inevitably leads to tensions. For this reason means must be found above all for a permanent dialogue to reconcile conflicting interests and smooth out disagreements. The OECD is a suitable forum for this purpose. The first topic, linked to the 'Grand Design' of the Kennedy Administration and the 'Trade Expansion Act' which was part of it, was the lowering of tariff protection. In the meantime, discussion has shifted to problems of agricultural protection; to non-tariff or para-tariff barriers to trade; to the adjustment of indirect frontier taxes; and to the trade preferences which the Community is increasingly extending to the developing countries, particularly in the Mediterranean. Further difficulties may arise as a result of the enlargement of the Community, including the future of the remaining EFTA countries. On the part of the Community there is concern about the continuing deficit in the American balance of payments; and, since 16 per cent of the Community's exports go to the United States, there is also special concern about the protectionist tendencies which are noticeable

251

both in Congress and in American industry and which, quite understandably, the American Government and administration cannot afford to disregard. Furthermore, since American investment in the Community has increased fivefold, problems of investment are becoming increasingly important on both sides. European investments to America amount to 8,000 million dollars. Such questions have already been discussed directly with the Americans and in the GATT. The Community has shown its willingness to compromise by making unilateral concessions on a series of agricultural goods (citrus fruits, tobacco, and poultry). But thought has rightly been given to the suggestion that the dialogue should be taken beyond the framework of one-way diplomatic relations and be in some way institutionalized. The strengthening of the Community's Washington office, and its upward change of status, is a step in this direction. But beyond that it has been suggested that the dialogue should be institutionalized at the level of those responsible for decisions – but so far without success.

Measures of this kind are useful, and indeed important, for every dispute has material effects on the basis of relations between the United States and the Community. In such circumstances it is salutary for the situation to be discussed frankly and openly. But it is even more important that the problem should be seen from the right points of view. The real question is what is to be understood and accepted as a good partnership. Naturally every partnership has its inward, 'bilateral' side, and it would be lifeless if there were no conflicts. But still more important is the common task, imposed from outside, which each partner knows can be better discharged together than alone. This is the situation of America and Europe, in all realms of human co-operation, and especially in politics – economically, militarily, socially, culturally – and in face of the enormous changes and challenges of our time. Mediterranean policy alone gives a mass of proof that commercial conflicts take second place to the need so to share and organize the common task that it brings the greatest benefit to both sides.

Unfortunately, the task of finding and implementing solutions is made more difficult by the fact that the executives on both sides are in a somewhat weak position and sometimes scarcely able to take effective action.

Europe takes too little account of the American government's

252

great difficulties in its relations with Congress. Congress interprets its competence in the process of concluding treaties so widely that the American government frequently finds it difficult to enter into binding agreements on matters of economic policy which require legislative action on the part of Congress. This is proved by the inability of the Kennedy and Nixon administrations to secure Congressional approval of the agreements reached during the Kennedy Round on the abolition of the 'American Selling Price System', an antiquated and completely anachronistic system for protecting the American chemical industry. It is also proved by the desire on the part of the Nixon administration that conversations on non-tariff barriers to trade should not be conducted formally at a negotiating table, on the grounds that the American administration was for the foreseeable future not in a position to carry on meaningful negotiations. I suppose that the same reasons in the last resort led the Johnson administration to refuse the offer of the Community to enter into global negotiations, within the Kennedy Round, on agricultural protectionism on the basis of comparing the various national 'cost supports'.

Naturally, it does not follow that the United States can on this account expect Europe to make special concessions on specific matters. The difficulties that exist are exclusively of an internal political nature, concerning America alone. It is up to Congress to furnish the American government with powers enabling it to carry on effective negotiations.

The state of affairs in the European Community is not very different: the petty, punctilious way in which the Council of Ministers has up to now laid down the lines on which negotiations are to be conducted has considerably reduced the Commission's ability to negotiate effectively, and has thereby diminished the weight the Community has carried in international negotiations. As in the case of America, however, the Community cannot expect its negotiating partners to reward it with concessions on matters of substance merely because of its difficulties with the Council of Ministers.

3. *Japan*

Japan will become increasingly important in future as a partner of the European Community. In the autumn of 1970 negotiations began for a comprehensive trade agreement with this economic power, which is developing at such a furious pace that by the end of the nineteen-seventies it promises to have as high an income per head of population as the countries of EEC, and which is again becoming not only the centre of the East Asian economic area but indeed is extending its influence beyond that area.

This trade agreement will be the first that the Community has concluded with an industrial power. So far, the volume of trade between the two has been disappointing: 2 per cent of the Community's total trade, 5 per cent of that of Japan, 30 per cent of whose trade is done with the United States. But it is growing rapidly: in 1969 the Community's exports to Japan rose by 16 per cent, and Japan's sales to the Community by 36 per cent. Japanese protection is high: in addition to the highest tariff of all industrialized countries, it has strict quotas on imports and administrative and tax rules affecting not only the import of goods but also capital movements and investments. But large-scale liberalization is in progress: already in 1970 it was announced that Japan hoped to halve quota restrictions by the end of 1971; in January 1971 this move was followed up; and in March 1971, after long and difficult negotiations, the Japanese textile industry declared its willingness voluntarily to limit its exports of wool, cotton, and synthetic textiles to the United States. Thereby not only was a major point of dispute with America removed, but also, by means of a skilful link between these measures and those expected from other textile exporting countries, the impulse may have been given for a multilateral solution of the textile problem. One of the Community's main negotiating aims is to remove trade restrictions. Since these include Community quota regulations – almost the last that it still maintains – it would also have the side effect of bringing closer together the member-states' differing levels of liberalization *vis-à-vis* Japan. Another aim is to secure a protective clause, like that already enjoyed by France and the Benelux countries, for use in the case of disturbance to the market: this will be a difficult point. The Commission has also proposed, quite rightly, that iron and steel products should be included within the terms of the agreement; in this field some 'self-limitation' agreements are already in force.

4. *Eastern Europe*

In its relations with the Eastern Bloc, the Community has also inherited the problems of all the member-states. The core of the economic difficulty is the fact that East European industries are still not fully competitive; consequently their chances of selling their products in the Community's markets are limited. This also presents the Community and its members with its gravest problem as far as the granting of export credits is concerned – a point that was clearly illustrated by what happened in the deal on tubing between German industry and the Soviet Union at the beginning of 1970. Although the Eastern countries, on their own estimate, account for a third of world production, their share in world trade is only 10 per cent, two-thirds of which is with each other. On top of that, there are political problems: in the present state of East-West relations there would plainly be a danger in becoming too dependent on raw materials from the East. Moreover, it is disturbing how slow and unwieldy negotiations are with state monopolies for foreign trade, bound by rigid plans. As far as Germany is concerned, the *Ostpolitik* pursued since 1969 has made an essential difference to all this; and the hope of renewing the negotiations broken off in 1966 for a new trade or economic agreement based on the trade and shipping agreement of 1956 has been blocked by the Russian refusal to recognize West Berlin's being represented by the Federal Republic. As against these factors, this is the place to correct an error that has from time to time been carefully nourished: namely, the fact that the Eastern States have not yet accorded the Community diplomatic recognition has not hindered the development of a Community trade policy. The Eastern states cannot be accorded the right to retard the evolution towards unification in Europe by refusing to recognize the Community. For years, the Community has had *de facto* contacts with almost all the East European countries, and not only in GATT, to which some of them belong. This proves that the two sides know how to arrange things and have no wish to see the two-way flow of goods and services impaired. Some of the Community's agricultural regulations, which make things easier for Eastern European countries, are the result of these talks and correspondence. There is also contact between enterprises on both sides (for example, with Hungary). Jugoslavia is the first Communist country to accredit a Delegation to the European Community and, in March 1970, to conclude a trade agreement with it. It is also the first Communist country to express the desire, as have Finland and Greece, to take part in the technological co-operation on computers, metallurgy, meteorology, maritime research, and anti-pollution, to which the Community has invited nine Western European countries.

The COMECON investment bank, established at the beginning of 1971 to 'promote the development and deepening of the integration of the Socialist economy', is also to facilitate operations with non-Socialist countries: that part of its capital which consists of convertible currencies is for 'the acquisition of capital goods and licences on the capitalist market', and there are also expected to be credit operations (loans, in which Hungary has already led the way). These facts make it all the more necessary to stress that the Community cannot be compared with COMECON. It is not correct to speak of two opposing trade blocs facing one another. The organization of COMECON is conceived on an entirely different economic and political basis: in particular, its institutions have no competence whatever in matters of foreign trade, nor even limited standing in international law. As a result we shall always have to deal with the Eastern states separately, with the Soviet Union, with Poland, Hungary, etc., and not with the institutions of COMECON. It also seems inconceivable to me that the Soviet Union, a superpower, would ever submit to the discipline of COMECON, and surrender to that extent even only a part of its sovereignty in the sphere of external trade in favour of the smaller East bloc states. COMECON is nothing but an instrument of economic policy with the limited objective of controlling and bolstering the supremacy of an imperialist union. For this reason, even the word 'integration' there carries an overtone of compulsion. The weaknesses of the system have been experienced for decades, and are continually discussed. Since 1967, in particular, in order to compensate for the lack of currency convertibility within the bloc, there have been plans for a 'transfer' rouble. Recently, the twenty-fifth meeting of COMECON at the beginning of August 1971, in Bucharest, decided on a comprehensive long-term 'Complex-Programme', a kind of Basic Law for the co-ordination of the participating Communist-planned economies.

Since the beginning of 1970 there has been an indispensable minimum of a common trade policy towards the Eastern bloc states which do not recognize the competence of the Community in matters of trade policy. This was achieved only after overcoming some opposition, including German opposition. Up to the end of 1972 the member-states remain able to negotiate bilateral agreements, but they must beforehand consult a committee, chaired by the Commission, on all important matters (such as import and export arrangements; the duration of the envisaged agreement; notice to be given for terminating it; revision; stipulations on price; protection clauses). On a proposal by the Commission, the Council of Ministers will authorize the member-states to open negotiations. Before these are concluded the Commission is informed of their results. If no member-state raises with the Commission objections to the terms of the proposed agreement, and if the Commission itself approves, then the agreement can be concluded. But if there are objections, then the agreement can be concluded only after the Council of Ministers, on a proposal by the Commission, has given its approval by a qualified majority.

5. *The Third World*

In formulating its policies towards the less-developed countries, the Community has to face world-wide political issues which are of the greatest significance. What are involved are the Community's relations with the developing countries outside Europe and with the Mediterranean area.

Its greatest achievements in this sphere have been the agreements which have been repeatedly renewed and improved – and the extension of association to the three English-speaking East African states (the Arusha Convention of July 1968 with Kenya, Uganda, and Tanzania). To begin with, association was an inheritance left by history, which was taken on with reluctance rather than enthusiasm, and only because France had since the 1956 Conference in Venice made this a condition of its signing the Treaty. Out of these unpromising beginnings there have in over ten years grown momentous and successful links between Europe and Africa. The over-all economic success of these links is one of the most durable achievements of aid to the developing countries in general. It is real, concrete and convincing, and it is due to three things: the application of purely economic criteria in the choice and execution of projects, the absence of any direct or indirect political pre-conditions and the fact that these relations never

257

contained a bilateral element. As a result, Euro-African relations have been spared the reproach of being called a form of neo-imperialism or neo-colonialism by even the most critical observers. Our policy towards the developing countries will continue to be successful so long as we continue to observe these fundamental principles.

The association agreements contain a small number of reciprocal preferential clauses, with an innate tendency to disappear, and effective capital aid through the European Development Fund. In its first five years this Fund was endowed with 581·25 million dollars, subsequently for the next five years with 730 million dollars, and subsequently with a sum of 918 million dollars for the following five years. It has mainly supplied outright grants, but also some loans; there is a reserve fund of sixty-five million units of account for emergencies (a collapse of world-market prices, famine, flood, etc.). The projects covered have so far chiefly concerned infrastructure (especially road building) and the modernization of agriculture, followed at some distance by training and health measures; particular attention has also been paid to investments and the diversification of production. The third five-year programme seems to be placing more emphasis on industrialization. As far as the provision of medium-term aid is concerned, the European Investment Bank has also played an increasingly important part, to the extent that it has been possible to finance projects by means of loans.

These methods of implementing financial policy could be still improved further, on the basis of the example set by the World Bank, and thus help to meet all legitimate requests for aid in accordance with appropriate banking practices. In particular, one might think of extending the facilities provided by the European Investment Bank for so-called 'soft loans'; also of co-ordinating still more closely the work of the Investment Bank and the Development Fund, without thereby detracting from the independent decision-making authority of the Development Fund and its responsibility towards the Commission.

Admittedly, the success of the Community's Africa policy has found both political and economic opponents.

Its political opponents, China and the Soviet Union, have nothing comparable to set against what the Community is doing;

258

on the contrary, their initiatives in Africa have on several occasions in the past met with failure, and they are at present concentrating on supplying arms. By contrast, the Community and its members should regard it as an obligation – above all others – to keep Africa free of such political disturbances, which can only prevent or at the very least retard the peaceful and difficult task of helping to develop what is at present the most needy continent in the world.

The answer to our economic opponents is less simple. The opposition stems from those who feel themselves especially bound to GATT; it comes particularly from the United States. They fear a preference zone that might become a precedent and harm the development of the world economy. One answer to that objection is that the position of French Africa – which for decades had belonged to the protectionist and autarkic French-franc zone – left no other choice. It would have been impossible for the Community to begin its career by clinging to a group of states which had just become, or were on the point of becoming, independent States which were also less-developed countries who had previously enjoyed, as dependent territories, privileged access to the markets of various member-countries. The dismantling of preferences can proceed only on a long-term basis and must keep pace with the increase in competitive capacity of the African economies, which are linked to the Community. Precipitate measures are not only bound to have uncontrollable political consequences; they would also lead to further demands for capital by our African friends. Nobody, however, is prepared to meet these additional requests for capital aid. Apart from that, the preferential treatment given to the import of African goods in Europe is slowly to be replaced to a substantial extent by the world-wide preferences which the industrial nations belonging to the world Trade Conference (UNCTAD) have declared themselves ready to accord to all developing countries. The preferences offered by the African states in return are of a more symbolic nature. They are intended to demonstrate what should be the sound basis of all economic political agreements, that is, to strive for a balance of economic give and take. Seen in this light, our association agreements provide a way of introducing the African associated states to a world economy which is based on GATT. Our motives appear to have won some sympathy in GATT, as was shown by the atmosphere

259

in the GATT Council in December 1970, despite continued American criticism of the Second (1969) Yaoundé Convention. If GATT be regarded – as has been done by its Director-General, Olivier Long – as a most-favoured-nation system with a provisional superstructure of non-discriminatory preferences granted by the developed to the less-developed countries, and by the latter to each other, this is in fact a realistic, because a dynamic, interpretation which may well help to take dogma out of the dispute. The preferences that less-developed countries grant each other, moreover, cover a small group – thirty-four less-developed countries, twenty-four of whom are members of GATT, i.e., fewer than half of the less-developed countries in GATT – which came together in October 1970 as the 'Committee for Trade Talks Among Less-Developed Countries'. They are seeking to achieve tariff reductions to be extended to all less-developed countries, but not to the industrialized members of GATT. Trade between less-developed countries in 1969 amounted to 9,760 million dollars, or 3·6 per cent of world trade.

There has also been criticism on economic grounds from Latin America. It is based on the argument that there is a danger that African products are given preferential treatment in comparison with South American export goods of equal quality; the products involved are few in number, like cocoa, coffee, bananas, and vegetable fats. But so far these fears cannot be statistically substantiated. On the contrary, since the Community came into existence, trade with Latin America has, despite the preferential treatment accorded to the African states, on average developed much more favourably than that with the eighteen associated states – and there is every reason to believe that this tendency will continue in future. There is also no question of the export of capital to Latin America being impaired in any way by the Community's African policy. For its part, however, Europe cannot avoid questioning her Latin-American friends about their own view of world affairs. What kind of Africa would they like to see? What political advantages could they expect from Africa (which, despite its distance, nevertheless has transatlantic links with them) if it were a prey to economic chaos and political instability?

True, every European statesman ought to be aware that our thinking with regard to Latin America has in the past not always been as constructive as might have been wished. Considerable attention is being given to this question by the European Parliament and the Commission, which in July 1969, at the suggestion of Italy, submitted a memorandum on relations with Latin America to the Council of Ministers, who in turn set up an *ad hoc* group. As a result, the Council made effective on 1 January 1971, a year ahead of schedule, tariff cuts agreed during the Kennedy Round, affecting some of Latin America's leading exports. The Community was thus also prepared for the talks which Latin America now sought. In July 1970 twenty-two Central and South American countries, this time without the United States, came together in CECLA, the 'Special Conference for Latin-American Co-ordination'. After sometimes violent disputes between the Atlantic states more closely related to Europe and the Pacific group, they agreed on the 'Declaration of Buenos Aires', proposing to the European countries, and especially to the European Community, talks 'at the appropriate and high political level' about mutual relations, especially in the economic field. These relations were to be strengthened, and exchanges of all kinds were to be increased. CECLA described itself as 'the proper forum for the co-ordination and unification of its member-countries in their relations with Europe, notwithstanding bilateral or sub-regional negotiations'. Their long catalogue of concrete requests was headed by that for general, non-reciprocal, and non-discriminatory preferences for finished and semi-finished products, and by the removal of discrimination *vis-à-vis* the associated African states. On 14 December the Council of the Community gave an encouraging answer. In June 1971 the first conference of representatives of the Community countries and of the members of CECLA concluded its work in Luxembourg with a joint declaration about the organization and procedure for co-operation: there were to be annual conferences of representatives at ambassadorial level; more frequent meetings at expert level; and possibly meetings of Ministers. Their first task would be to discuss trade relations, if possible seeking non-preferential solutions, and without prejudice to the generalized preferences, which are open to all CECLA members. The exclusion of preferential solutions answered to the Commission's desire to set geographical limits to the Community's preference policy.

In the meantime, trade negotiations had begun with Argentina,

261

which had played a leading role in the CECLA Conference. Next to shipbuilding, the main problem was Argentinian beef exports, which account for about a fifth of the Common Market's agricultural import levies. In June 1971, these negotiations were successfully concluded. The next South American country seeking to negotiate is Uruguay.

Similar motives, similar solutions, and similar difficulties arise in the Community's external economic policy *vis-à-vis* Mediterranean countries. This area especially was clouded by conflictng interests and controversy over trade policy, which for a time threatened to unleash a trade war in the West. Since then, the skies have not completely cleared, but energetic and also successful efforts have been made to lessen the tensions and to bring the causes of tension under joint control. The large multi-national organizations, UNCTAD, GATT, and OECD, have played their part in this 'peace strategy'; but more than just temporary improvements have been achieved also by bilateral talks – between the United States and the European Community, and between both of them and Japan. Finally, there have also been one-sided acts of good-neighbourliness. On a summary judgement, two points stand out: the fact that all these problems are riddled with politics, including of course internal politics, which in turn now includes intra-Community politics; and the present lack of a favourable climate for any further drive to liberalize world trade. The former situation will last a long time; the second leaves room for hope that the efforts already undertaken (for example, the work done in GATT on non-tariff barriers) are not abandoned, but merely interrupted, and that in the not too distant future they will be resumed.

A new slant for the Community's policy on aid to less-developed countries was opened up by its participation in the food aid system agreed on in the Kennedy Round, under which it is supplying no less than a million tons of wheat per year. This is partly Community action, partly national. In the longer term, food-aid may cause problems for its beneficiaries; but as long as it is considered advisable, the Community should always show itself ready, especially in view of its surpluses, to play a leading part in world-wide action of this kind. The need is still very great.

A word should be said, finally, about the role of the Community in the negotiations at the United Nations Conference on Trade and Development (UNCTAD) on the subject of preferences for the industrial products of the less-developed countries. In this, the biggest international organization dealing with the economic problems of the less-developed countries, the European Community gave a good example. In the autumn 1970 session of the UNCTAD Council, the negotiations (which had been going on since 1964) produced a first successful result, which for the benefit of the less-developed countries made an important breach in the most-favoured-nation principle that had hitherto governed world-trade policy as organized in GATT. The stabilization of markets for raw materials and agricultural products, which matters far more to the less-developed countries, since it concerns some 80 per cent of their trade, remains essentially to be settled in the future. But for their finished and semi-finished industrial products, world-wide unilateral tariff concessions are now to be made by the industrialized countries such as the United States; the Commission opted for a rapid and generous solution, and this was accepted by the Council of Ministers. From July 1971, therefore, nil tariffs became the rule, up to a certain level of imports: the result is duty-free imports into the Community of goods worth 1,000 million dollars, more than twice as much as were imported over the tariff in 1968. There are special rules for cotton textiles, for goods made from jute and coconut, and for processed agricultural products. The beneficiaries are countries of the so-called 'Group of 77', which includes in particular the South Americans and most of the Africans, but not Taiwan, Cuba, Israel, Turkey, Greece, Spain, and Portugal.

In the meantime conversations have begun with Argentina and Uruguay. Should consideration not also be given to the European Community participating in the equity capital of the successful Inter-American Investment Bank through the European Investment Bank? The aim would be not only to provide the Inter-American Investment Bank with a broader financial basis for its operations but also at the same time to procure for the Inter-American Investment Bank, by means of appropriate agreements, better access to the European capital market – access which could perhaps be guaranteed by the European governments.

To sum up, we can point to a substantial number of actions in the sphere of development policy. No wonder the Community has become an incomparable pole of attraction for the less-developed countries. If this attitude has nevertheless – even in Europe – not yet attracted general political attention, then the cause surely lies in the fact that there is as yet no general European doctrine on development policy. It is a matter for satisfaction that the Commission has taken up this challenge, and in the summer of 1971 published a first Memorandum on the subject.

6. *Institutions and Procedures*

The Community's capacity to negotiate with the outside world is still a sorry sight. The obstruction comes mainly from the traditional advocates of national sovereignty, senior officials, and diplomatic services. The Council of Ministers has interpeted the Treaty provisions for the transition period, which basically gave the Commission, even then, responsibility for external economic matters, so restrictively as to be scarcely defensible. As a result, it has retained – or, in its efforts to 'rediplomatize' the Community, it has assumed – powers of decision and function to which it has no claim. The protocol dispute during the crisis of 1955–6 is in this respect a symptom of French efforts to reverse the Community's institutional development. Unfortunately, the other member-states put up only a limited fight for the right order of things. Diplomatically, the Community is gravely handicapped by not having made general use of its right to appoint its own ambassadors. It has only one diplomatic mission, in London, and small liaison offices in Geneva (GATT, UNCTAD), Santiago de Chile, and Paris (OECD); in 1971, however, it upgraded its representation in Washington. The establishment of a full diplomatic mission in Washington was at one point accepted even by France, but the agreement was not kept. Yet the experiences before, during, and after the Kennedy Round negotiations have shown how useful, indeed how basically indispensable, it is that the Community's interests should be represented and its weight in negotiations asserted by speaking in foreign capitals with one voice. The system initiated by the Council of Ministers, whereby the commercial attachés of the national embassies pass reports through their respective foreign ministries and the Secretariat-General of the Council of Ministers to the Commission, is an anachronism. Similar timidity on the part of the Community governs information policy. We have not advanced beyond the point of having a meagre network of Press and Information offices, mainly in Europe; but we are naturally glad to have at least these reliable spokesmen in the outside world.

The situation is little better where economic policy relations between states have been institutionalized – in the great international organizations. Again and again there has to be a struggle before the Community can speak with one clear voice, through the Commission, and the struggle is not always won. Yet this method has proved brilliantly successful, for example in tariff negotiations in GATT. It is of the greatest importance that the Community should play a responsible part in these international organizations. The parallel growth of the great industrial economies must be steered so that they benefit rather than harm each other. Other topics for discussion in the international organizations are the external problems of industrial policy, and orientation of investment in order to control reactions to what is regarded as the danger of too much foreign influence, or to settle whether – and, if so, how – an eye is to be kept on multi-national corporations. For Europe, the most important means for promoting understanding is the OECD, where the Americans, Canadians, Japanese, and the European industrial nations are organized to deal with their external economic problems. It is there, especially, that the Commission's scope for action should be improved. The fact that outstanding officials manage to do good work in ill-defined or even contradictorily-defined jobs is a matter of good luck rather than good organization.

In May 1970 in the first year of the Community's definitive phase, the Community at last armed itself with some of the weapons required for the common policy on foreign trade, which the Treaty calls upon it to pursue; and it made express provision for their improvement. It now has Community rules for protection against dumping; a Community procedure for the administration of quotas; and Community regulations for imports from non-member countries and state-trading countries. These are steps in the right direction.

II. NEW RECRUITS

Article 237, paragraph 1, sentence 1 of the Treaty of Rome says: 'Any European state may apply to become a member of the Community.'

The fate of the programme contained in that sentence is essentially the history of Great Britain's relationships with the Community. Twice the British refused our invitation: to join the Coal and Steel Community and to sign the Treaties of Rome. Then in 1961 Harold Macmillan made the first application for membership, and Harold Wilson in 1967 the second. The eventual results will determine what will constitute the core of European union. Other countries – Ireland, Norway, and Denmark – have followed Britain's example. But Britain occupies a key position, which arises from its economic, political, military, and historical importance and from its democratic tradition.

The applications are the most significant aspect of British postwar policy towards Europe. At the end of the war Great Britain at first went through a period which can be described as an attempt to continue, under changed conditions, its pre-war role as a world power. When there was talk of Europe, what was meant was the Continent, without Great Britain. Winston Churchill's Zurich speech in 1946 is a classic example of that attitude. Great Britain admittedly made efforts to create a political balance in Europe, but it did not regard itself as a part of Europe which should contribute to its integration, as did the countries on the Continent. On the one hand, Germany had dropped out and France had been greatly weakened; on the other, the power of the Soviet Union had grown to an unimaginable degree. In these circumstances Britain's diplomatic stance seemed to offer special opportunities, even – for a time – the chance of playing a leading role. The Treaties of Dunkirk and Brussels were attempts to redress and stabilize the badly-upset balance in the face of Soviet power. As a result of this attitude, Great Britain rejected every attempt to allow the Marshall Plan organization, OEEC, created to distribute American money, to develop into a European economic organization. To the limits of her powers Britain fought and suppressed the plans for federation put forward in the Council of Europe in 1949 and 1950 – although Churchill, Leader of the Opposition at the time, had put forward

266

the idea of a European Army. Subsequently, Britain – by then led by Churchill himself – obstinately opposed the European Defence Community and the European Political Community. And there was no contradiction in Anthony Eden's policy when he rejected British participation in the European Defence Community, but gave what he had repeatedly refused when it came to the Western European Union, because this was looser and more easily reversible. The method was still to seek a balance, albeit unstable, but directed by Britain in conjunction with others. Until the middle of the 1950s London saw itself as the centre of three circles: of the Commonwealth, of free Europe, and of the Atlantic area. In this perspective there was no place for a united Europe, organized on a federal pattern.

Britain still did not recognize its inability to play a world role in view of its declining military and economic strength. Before that could happen, she had to experience the world-wide process of decolonization and the failure of the Suez expedition. Consequently, Great Britain's attitude towards the economic Communities was sceptical, dismissive, indeed hostile. True, she had allowed a few English officials to take part in the early stages of the preparatory work leading up to the Spaak report; but they had already left by Christmas 1955. The prevailing British view was that the whole business was a 'waste of time'. The first counter-move took the form of an initiative to create a free trade area consisting of all the member-states of OEEC. The ups and downs involved in this project clearly followed the success graph which marked the internal development of the Community. December 1958 saw the collapse of the negotiations led by Reginald Maudling. The monetary reforms which France introduced at Christmas 1958 opened the way to the establishment of a European internal market. The dismantling of customs tariffs began on 1 January 1959.

For the time being, British diplomacy continued on its set course. Its response was the foundation of EFTA. For reasons of trade policy, EFTA brought together in an industrial free trade area those European states who felt themselves economically prejudiced by, or were at least uneasy about, the Community's integration. Looking back, I shall always remember the creation of EFTA as a great diplomatic miscalculation, in so far as it was conceived as a

267

kind of fighting association. It failed as a means of counter-attack – a point that became evident when, after 1960, the Community decided to accelerate its development. But if EFTA was of benefit to its participants, then it could serve to lighten our political responsibilities. The second round of entry negotiations with the Community in 1970–1 was to show, moreover, that EFTA had been – for those about to enter, as for the others – a good preparation and a useful starting-point for the definitive solution to the problem of relations with the Community.

Plainly, the time had come for Britain to adopt a new policy. Furthermore, Britain's leaders could no longer ignore the fact that in their post-war efforts to restore the classic European balance of power, and especially in their consequent opposition to a European federation, they had never had American support. Since the end of the war, Washington has had no illusions about the weakness of Britain's position and has therefore actively and decisively worked to promote the unification of Europe and to persuade Britain to join in and to give up its role as a world power. America's influence on the process of decolonization and its reserved attitude towards the Suez adventure must be viewed in this context. Equally it is not without significance what discretion, not to say what reservation, the United States showed in the face of all attempts on the part of Britain to maintain a world-wide role by its own efforts in the field of armaments, aviation, space travel, and the build-up of its own nuclear potential.

Consequently, once J. F. Kennedy had taken office, and after he had announced his 'Grand Design' in the spring of 1961, Harold Macmillan gradually came to the decision to apply for admission to the Community in accordance with the saying that 'if you can't lick them, join them'. He made his decision public in July 1961. It was a decision in which the American President greatly encouraged him. The choice of a chief negotiator proved a happy one: it was Edward Heath, a member of Mr Macmillan's Cabinet.

Much of what happened during the negotiations, of which I gave the European Parliament an account and an appreciation in February 1963, remains of interest even now that the 1970–1 negotiations are successfully completed. Of the difficult complex of problems raised by the existence of the Commonwealth, questions affecting the less-developed countries and the import of industrial products from Canada, Australia, and New Zealand, were essentially resolved; by contrast, solutions for agricultural imports from the temperate zones were only partially worked out. No agreement was then reached on the position of British agriculture in the Common Market. Relations with the other EFTA countries had still not come up for discussion. Several questions on customs tariffs remained open, and there were still reservations on the part of Britain towards economic union. On the whole, in the Commission's judgement, neither success nor failure was certain in the negotiations, but the chance of success was sufficiently great to justify going on.

From the political point of view, Britain's deep-rooted tendency to assume a leading role was still very much in evidence – particularly in any dialogue with the United States – a new version of the 'special relationship'. At the same time Britain wished to lose as little freedom of action as possible, and also therefore to continue the old 'balance of power' system in a more modernized form of a 'balance of voting-power'. From the economic point of view, Britain plainly had an interest in becoming Europe's chief armaments supplier. On all these points it may well have been able to count on the approval of Kennedy, who was in any case concerned with guaranteeing Europe's ties with the United States.

In view of all this, the conflict with de Gaulle was inevitable. The General claimed a leading role in world affairs for himself and his country, a role to which he felt France was entitled for many reasons: its permanent seat on the Security Council; its status as an atomic power won by its own efforts, and not as a result of American help; its place among the victors in the last war; its colonial empire and the world-wide responsibilities which followed the dismantling of its empire; and the special cohesion and mission of the French nation. Such an attitude could not be reconciled with the ambitions of competitors. True, de Gaulle's hands were at first tied by the Algerian conflict, and from that point of view the timing of the British application seemed well chosen. But as soon as the Algerian conflict was over and the General had his freedom of action in external affairs restored to him by the referendum held in November 1962, he decided the question of the British application on his own at his Press conference in January 1963.

It is probably unavoidable that traces of Harold Macmillan's application can be recognized in the motives and objectives of Harold Wilson's application in 1967. Admittedly, it is not exactly easy to analyse reliably and precisely the explanations which accompanied the second application. They were partly contradictory or ambiguous, and they partly harked back openly to an older school of thought, for example, in connection with the problem of predominance. One still sensed a wish to avoid becoming involved in tightly-knit Community institutions, in fact to lean towards and support the unsatisfactory state in which the Community's institutions in effect found themselves, rather than to subscribe to the stricter rules which ought to prevail. Furthermore, it was obviously not easy to recognize, as was necessary, the dynamic nature of Europe's integration and still less to accept it without any reservation, and acknowledge that the Community could not allow its development to be blocked by the admission of the new members.

Many official and semi-official sources of information, in fact, reveal how much behind events both Britain's leaders and British public opinion have been in their assessment of the evolution and cohesion of the unification of Europe. Nothing could reflect this attitude more than the British 'White Paper' of February 1970.

The second British application for membership also ran into French opposition; the Council of Ministers noted on 19 December 1967 that 'no agreement had been reached on the procedure to be pursued, but the applications for membership . . . remain on the agenda of the Council'. There followed fruitless discussions on half-measures such as a 'trade arrangement'. Only the retirement of de Gaulle opened up the road. One of the most important results of The Hague Summit Conference was the decision to set out on that road. The Hague communiqué (Point 4, paragraph 2), stated:

The European Communities remain the original nucleus from which European unity has been developed and intensified. The entry of other countries of this Continent to the Communities – in accordance with the provisions of the Treaty of Rome – would undoubtedly help the Communities to grow to dimensions more in conformity with the present state of world's economy and technology . . .

And in Point 13 the heads of state or government of the Six stated:

> They reaffirmed their agreement on the principle of the enlargement of the Community, as provided by Article 237 of the Treaty of Rome.
>
> In so far as the applicant states accept the treaties and their political finality, the decisions taken since the entry into force of the treaties and the options taken in the sphere of development, the heads of state or government have indicated their agreement to the opening of negotiations between the Community and the applicant states.

The applicant states accepted the principle set out in the communiqué as a condition of admission. Accordingly, full membership is incompatible with any reservations a country may have on the grounds of neutrality. When negotiations were re-opened on 30 June 1970, in Luxembourg, the then President of the Council of Ministers, Pierre Harmel, Belgian Foreign Minister, further elaborated on the negotiating position of the Community, defining particularly the following points:

> The solution of any problems of adjustment must be sought in the establishment of transitional measures and not in changes in the existing rules; the transitional measures must be of fixed duration and conceived in such a way as to ensure an over-all balance of reciprocal advantages; in the sphere of the exchange of goods the duration of the transitional period should be the same for all the applicants, although in other spheres the period can vary.
>
> The various accession treaties should come into force on the same date.
>
> The enlarged Community must continue its policy of association with the developing countries of Africa, and it must do so without weakening the existing ties of association; the question of the other Commonwealth countries should be discussed at a later stage.
>
> Negotiations with EFTA countries which have not applied for membership should take place at a later stage, and the treaties with them should come into force at the same time as the treaties

271

of accession of the applicant states; attention is drawn once again to the basic principle that the enlarged Community can consist only of members with equal rights and obligations.

The negotiations are to be conducted by the Community and in accordance with a uniform negotiating procedure; they will in principle but not invariably be conducted jointly with all the applicants.

The applicant countries, for their part, replied to Mr Harmel's exposition by stating the points which were causing them concern: agriculture and fisheries; the existing free-trade arrangements; questions of finance and the Commonwealth (Great Britain); existing social policy and labour laws (the Scandinavian countries); the movement of capital and the right of establishment; regional policy (Norway).

In fact, the economic problems raised by the entry of the four applicant countries are great. Admittedly, the problems facing Denmark, Norway, and Ireland are not essentially different from those facing the six present member-states. The British economy, however, has for years struggled with the difficulty of reconciling the necessary rise in its growth rate with lasting equilibrium in its balance of payments. Balance-of-payments crises have repeatedly forced Britain to adopt deflationary policies. As a result, there were signs of stagnation inside Britain and a restriction of trade and payments with other countries. Strenuous efforts on the part of the British Government, and active international monetary solidarity, were mobilized to overcome this handicap. Plainly the reasons are not merely conjunctural, but structural, in so far as they are not connected with the burdens Britain has inherited from the past – including those left by the Second World War – and with her international position in the post-war period. In these conditions, joining the large Common Market with its extraordinary growth undoubtedly offers greater benefits than merely continuing with the present system of economic relations with the Commonwealth. Joining will not only bring trade advantages, it will also serve as a lever for improving, that is to say modernizing, the structure of Britain's economy. True, this demands energetic measures of adaptation which again will be made easier by co-operation in the Community.

Within this process of change, currency presents particular and important problems so great that they affect the position of sterling as a reserve currency. Next in importance is the problem of agriculture. Here, the situation of the Community as a whole will be changed only quantitatively as a result of the admission of the four candidate countries, although admittedly also in the sense that the recruits include rationally-organized and very productive agricultures – and not only in Denmark. As against that, in view of the advanced state which the Community's agricultural policy has reached, Great Britain can hardly continue to import its agricultural supplies at low world-market prices while subsidizing its domestic agriculture by means of 'deficiency payments'.

Of quite another nature is the problem posed by the so-called 'high-technology' industries. British achievements in this field are among the most significant in the world and are probably superior to those of any of the present member-states of the Community, as regards both the amount of money spent and the number of people involved in research – criteria which by themselves of course offer no guarantee of inventiveness and dynamic business drive. In this context Britain's nuclear industry deserves particular mention. It rests on a broad, extensive basis, is assured of adequate supplies of uranium and is served by a surplus of specialists. As far as other aspects of technology are concerned, British participation is regarded as particularly desirable in electronics, aeroplane construction, and space exploration, among others. But even when Britain's potential is combined with that of the Community, Europe will still remain very far behind the United States, with no prospect of catching up; but it will offer the opportunity of stopping a further widening of the 'technological gap'. The conditions which would make this possible are the same as those which prevail in the Community as it exists at present; unified common objectives and programmes; division of labour; the opening-up of a truly common market for products (including non-discrimination in the awarding of public contracts) – in other words a common policy for research and development. For this reason, British membership of Euratom will be very important indeed. For it will remain no more than a pious wish to expect the enlargement of the Community 'naturally and by itself' – as it were – to lead enterprises to act in accordance with the terms of a common policy for research and development. Further, such a common policy could

273

have the beneficial effect of speeding up many Community projects which have been delayed, such as patent law, company law, fiscal harmonization, and technical standardization. But none of the obligations of membership has greater significance or higher priority than that which arises from the dynamics of the Community and what could be called the incompleteness of its constitution. The first declarations of the British Government after the opening of the negotiations show that it is not only the Community which is aware of this problem: it is worth noting that European defence was mentioned in this context. Viewed objectively, the moment at which the Community takes on new members is always a matter of chance. That means that for the candidate countries merely to accept the rules for the unification of Europe that have already been decided (those of the Treaty and the subsequent Community regulations, etc.) does not suffice to guarantee that integration will continue on its present lines and at its present pace. There is also, rooted in the nature of the Community, an obligation to go further. The enlargement of the Community makes this especially important. For the increase in the number of member-states naturally involves a 'burden', as the Commission is pointing out, because it is more difficult to accommodate ten partners under the same roof than six. The new members are unfamiliar with the procedures of the Community and will unconsciously continue thinking and acting along the diplomatic lines to which they have become accustomed. And, finally, they carry in their political baggage legitimate interests – just like the founder members – which must find recognition and a home within the wider context of the Community. To say all this should not be considered as a reproach or lack of friendship. Joining the Community means entering a moving train, and the fact that the train is moving is not a tactical gambit: it lies in the Community's nature: it is an integral part of its evolutionary process.

In the second round of negotiations it took exactly a year to reach agreement on the essential points. The negotiation was difficult, but no more so than was inevitable, given the magnitude of the task. The British Prime Minister, Edward Heath, who took office on 20 June 1970, put into them all his perseverance and decisiveness. Agreement among the founder-members of the Community raised many problems, and often took time; at the

274

end, they were aided by a crisis within the Community over monetary matters. The Commission, participating as in the first round, made an essential contribution right up to the last moments of negotiation, notably in the person of the French Commissioner who was chiefly responsible, Jean-François Denaiu, who as a senior official of the Commission in the first round had already shown himself an outstanding master of the subject.

Agreement was reached on the morning of 23 June 1971. The final decision on British entry then depended on the British Parliament.

What had been agreed was as follows:

Britain is to enter the European Community on 1 January 1973. From that time onwards, Britain – and, if they agree to enter, the other applicant states – will participate in the Community's institutions, throughout which the British will take part on the same footing as the three largest founder-members: the Federal German Republic, France, and Italy. The principles of the voting rules are unaltered. Where weighted voting is required in the Council, i.e. where a qualified majority applies, Germany, France, Italy, and Britain will have ten votes each; Belgium and the Netherlands five each; Denmark, Ireland, and Norway three each; and Luxembourg two – sixty-one votes in all. A qualified majority requires forty-three votes. The consequence is that the four new member-states together can block a decision; the same is true of two 'big' member-states. The European Commission will have fourteen members (two German, two French, two Italian, and two British, and one national of each of the other member-states). In the European Parliament, the four big countries will supply thirty-six members each; Belgium and the Netherlands fourteen each; Denmark, Ireland, and Norway ten each; and Luxembourg six. The Economic and Social Committee will be increased to 153 members, of whom twenty-four will come from each of the four big countries; twelve each from Belgium and the Netherlands, nine each from Denmark, Ireland, and Norway, and six from Luxembourg.

The dismantling of internal customs duties will begin on 1 April 1973, and be completed, in five steps of 20 per cent each, by 1 July 1977. Moves towards the common external tariff will not begin until 1 January 1974, although with a first move of 40 per cent, in

275

order to leave time for the solution of EFTA problems, and also because the British need a further year to adapt this tariff structure. Except for a few products, the new external tariff will be lower than the present British m.f.n. tariff. (The opposite applies where British preferential tariffs *vis-à-vis* some Mediterranean countries are still lower than the Community's preferential tariffs; against this disadvantage of the move to the common external tariff those concerned have registered objections.) Exceptions have been made in the case of tea (which will be important for India and Ceylon) and for a dozen industrial raw materals, in order to safeguard existing trade relations; some are negligible and temporary, others subject to quotas. The Channel Islands and the Isle of Man, which for centuries have had their own legislation, tax systems, and tariff regulations, are not to become full members, but may be associated. Gibraltar, which in any case does not form part of British customs territory, will not join under Article 237 of the Treaty.

The Community's agricultural price, intervention, and levy system will be adopted in six equal steps, between April 1973 and the end of 1977 – six months after the last cut in internal industrial customs duties. The over-all effect on consumer prices is estimated at an annual rise of 2·5 per cent, representing an annual rise of 0·5 per cent in the cost-of-living index; the effect on British production is estimated to be an 8 per cent increase. This applies to most European produce; it is not expected that traditional supplies (Argentina, Australia, Canada, and the United States) will be unnecessarily harmed. Special exceptions have been made to the Community's fisheries policy to enable Britain and other countries to adapt themselves; and the interests of British hill-farmers in Scotland, Wales, and Northern Ireland (who account for 7 per cent of Britain's production in 30 per cent of her territory) are to be safeguarded in the context of the Community's regional policy.

Changing circumstances have made Commonwealth problems less difficult to solve than in the first round of the British negotiations. Of the industrialized Commonwealth countries, Australia (a far bigger supplier of the United States and Canada) and Canada (far more turned towards the United States) have scarcely called for any special treatment; but they are beneficiaries of tariff

quotas for the twelve products referred to earlier, and their agricultural trade is also to be taken care of. India, Pakistan, Ceylon,
and Malaysia are to conclude trade agreements with the enlarged
Community, quite apart from the advantages of the UNCTAD
generalized preferences for less-developed countries, from which
Hong Kong will also benefit. The advantage is shared also by the
less-developed Commonwealth countries in Africa and the
Caribbean, and by Mauritius, Fiji, Tonga, and West Samoa; in
addition, they have the choice of adhering to the Yaoundé Convention or concluding more limited association or trade agreements;
and they need not make the choice until between 1973 and 1975.
This group includes the Commonwealth sugar producers (apart
from Australia), whose problems for a time weighed heavily on the
negotiations. These problems are to be dealt with after British
entry, and Britain has formally interpreted the agreement on this
subject to mean that sugar imports from the countries concerned
will be maintained on at least their present level. For the second
delicate agricultural problem, that of New Zealand, an 'open and
semi-permanent exception' has been made to the common agricultural policy: guaranteed butter imports are to be cut in five
equal annual steps to 80 per cent of their present level, and cheese
imports to 20 per cent – making 71 per cent in 'milk equivalent'
for both products together, and this at the average prices prevailing between 1969 and 1972. From 1977 onwards there is
to be no further exception for cheese. Two years previously,
the Community is to look at 'appropriate measures for the maintenance' of the agreement, in the light of progress towards a world
agreement on milk products and of New Zealand's progress in
diversifying her economy. This pleased even the New Zealand
Prime Minister.

The monetary problems, which at a certain point became
dramatic, although they were not strictly part of the negotiations
as such, were eased by Britain's unprejudiced attitude. Britain is
prepared to run down her official sterling balances after entry. Mr
Heath has also expressed British willingness to work towards
economic and monetary union. The remaining controls on capital
movements are to be reduced to the EEC norm within five years,
first as regards direct investments, then for personal capital transactions, finally as regards the acquisition of securities. Tax prob-

277

lems have not arisen, because Britain already plans to introduce
the tax on value-added by 1973. But as regards the free movement
of labour she has renounced any claim to a transition period.

The finance regulation, which for a time was the third headache
in the negotiations, is a quantitative compromise. The British
contribution to the Community budget begins at 8·64 per cent, then
rises slowly at first, then more quickly, until in 1977 it attains a
level corresponding to the gross national product (18·92 per cent).
Two years later, in 1980, Britain plays her full part in the self-
financing of the Community. If the Community budget in 1973 is
3,300 million units of account, Britain will then pay 119 million
pounds, of which she will get back 15 million. If in 1977 the
budget is 4,000 million units of account, she will then pay 315
million pounds and get 135 million back.

At the same time as she joins the general Common Market,
Britain will join the European Coal and Steel Community. For the
steel industry, a five-year transition period is provided. Controls
on imports of scrap within the Community can be maintained for
two years more. Imports and exports of coal are to be freed
immediately; trade in steel will be subject to the general dismantling of internal customs duties. Entry to the European
Atomic Energy Community (Euratom) is to take place at the same
time; there will only be a one-year transition period for changes in
the tariff.

With one essential exception – fisheries policy – the negotiations
with Denmark and Ireland can be said to have been concluded on
the same terms as with Britain. The case of Denmark raised only
minor difficulties from the beginning; she was even willing to do
without a transition period. Only the taxation of capital returns and
capital movements seems possibly likely to prolong matters. As
regards Ireland, small and only recently industrialized, there was
the important problem of her automobile-assembly plants, which
are protected by a prohibition tariff. It was agreed that these should
not face Community competition until 1985 – the only exception
to the basic principle that the transition period should be the same
for all countries and all products. Meanwhile, however, provisions
discriminating against Continental in favour of British products
must be gradually abolished before 1985, and the share of imported
vehicles must be increased from the beginning. The political

climate, especially in the Irish Parliament, is more favourable than elsewhere. With Norway, on the other hand, the negotiations were difficult from the beginning. Norwegian agriculture suffers from uniquely unfavourable conditions, and as a result has higher prices than the Community. Politically, too, the Government has little room for manœuvre. In this situation the Community had to make a great effort on Norway's behalf.

For all three countries – and also for Britain (with 12,000 coastal fishermen in England and Wales and 8,000 in Scotland) although she at first seemed to leave the running to the others – fisheries policy was a serious problem. The enlargement of the Community will turn it from a net fish-importer into a net fish-exporter. In addition, the new member-states feared that the opening of their waters to all Community fishermen would endanger their own fishing industries; and there was also no agreement on fishing limits. The previous normal limit was six miles; but Norway, followed by Ireland, demanded a twelve-mile limit, and although the British Isles' problems and those of Ireland were quite soon solved, solutions for Norway and Iceland proved more difficult. The Community at length succeeded in finding them, but disputes over fishing limits are not yet a thing of the past.

There remained the other EFTA countries. There was a general inclination to maintain free trade with them. This is understandable, although it may be expected to cause difficulties with the Americans. But those concerned hoped for more: influence on the economic, monetary, and industrial policies that in this case would affect them more deeply; and Sweden even wanted to join the Community's customs union. Most especially affected were the three neutrals, Austria, Sweden, and Switzerland, all highly industrialized, fully competitive, and with close economic links to the Community. With good reason, the Commission opposed the institutionalization of co-operation with them, and this applied particularly to agriculture: the Community of ten will in any case be in danger of becoming unwieldy, and the neutrals do not share the Community's whole complex of aims and principles. For this reason, the Commission proposed two alternative solutions: either an industrial free trade area – the solution ultimately adopted, or the *status quo* in the tariff field during 1973 and 1974, with negotiations after that. The second solution was

279

finally dropped, for its effect would have been to accord different treatment to different members of the enlarged Community.

The other EFTA countries, Portugal, Finland, and Iceland, had only two points in common. First, they did not seek Community membership, for political reasons (neutrality in the case of Finland, and constitutional law in the case of Portugal, whose overseas territories are legally part of her national territory), or for economic reasons (their state of development). Secondly, they wished to preserve the free trade they enjoyed as members or, in the case of Finland, as an associate member, of EFTA – although the real level of liberalization was certainly very various, being 40 per cent in the case of Portugal and 20–30 per cent in that of Iceland.

Of the three, Portugal showed the clearest and most comprehensive willingness to accept integration. For her European territory she sought an intensive form of association, that is to say, free trade, and acceptance of the Community's economic system, including agricultural policy; the right of establishment; rules for the supply of services and for the movement of capital; competition rules; transport policy and technological co-operation – all of this naturally made easier by transitional rules and measures of adaptation. Portugal, indeed, which is a member of NATO, was anxious to prepare the way for still closer co-operation.

The attitude of Finland was wholly conditioned by the infinite difficulty of her position and the extreme caution that this imposes on her foreign policy. She was anxious to preserve her freedom in trade policy and other matters. Within these limits, she sought solutions to her economic problems, that is to increase the rate of her economic growth and her foreign trade, especially with the founder-members of the EEC and EFTA, of whom Britain, Sweden, and the Federal German Republic was already her main trading partners. For industrial products, therefore, Finland wanted trade barriers removed, although she did not seek a customs union, especially as she had almost fully free trade with the Soviet Union. and this was to be maintained. Further complications were Finland's quantitative restrictions on petroleum products, which were similarly linked with obligations *vis-à-vis* the Soviet Union; the free movement of labour; and her desire to remove all import restrictions on the Community's market for paper. There was no question of institutionalized co-operation.

For Iceland, which is also a member of NATO, the problem of fisheries, which make up 80 per cent of her exports, was well to the fore. In this respect she faced the same problems as the new members of the Community, although in her case they were especially crucial. Trade is very important to her: she spends 45 per cent of her gross national product on the import of goods and services. For some goods, especially petroleum products, she was anxious to maintain import controls; 80 to 90 per cent of her fish sales to the Soviet Union are paid for in oil. Furthermore, her customs revenues play an important fiscal role, since they finance some 30 per cent of her public expenditure.

A final problem was that of timing. Even before the instruments of ratification are deposited, it will finally be certain that the enlargement of the Community is assured: indeed, this was already certain even before the texts of the agreements were formalized and signed. In the meantime the Community cannot stand still; yet she cannot any longer treat the prospective new members as non-member countries. For the interval between signature of the Treaty and its entry into force (the so-called 'Interim Period') it was therefore agreed that consultations would take place. Indeed, by the terms of a Statement from the Council on 27 July 1971, this applied as soon as the negotiations were concluded.

The entry of Britain and other countries into the European Community is perhaps the greatest and most constructive task to face Europe since World War II. From now on, there will no longer be any antithesis between 'Little Europe' and Western Europe as a whole. The potential of the Community is being strengthened – how much it is hard to say, but harder still to exaggerate: it is acquiring greater material substance, more technical ability in the broadest sense of the word, more authority, greater world stature and experience, broader responsibilities, and – irresistibly – more power, as time goes on, to defend itself. All this will be a great test for the political potential of our so-called economic integration. Europe will have the opportunity of acquiring the form in which it can realize its potential with the minimum of frictional loss. All members of the Community can benefit thereby. But the better balance of forces that this can bring goes far wider than the nations directly concerned. In the sight of history, the greatest value of the whole endeavour is this: not only

281

does it offer the participants greater well-being and more lasting peace among themselves, but it also equips them better to meet their responsibilities in the world around them. The good faith in which, both in form and in substance, the new member-states have helped to reconcile our viewpoints and theirs gives all of us reason for confidence.

The enlargement of the Community is bound to have an effect on other countries outside the Common Market. It will in fact make the effect produced by the foundation of the 'Community of the Six' more marked: economic expansion within the Community will compensate third countries for not participating in the advantages derived from internal Community preferences and will secure them a place in world trade. The EFTA countries which did not apply for admission, as well as the developing countries, have needed special attention. The non-applicant EFTA countries have had to face the weighty problem of whether or not to allow the customs barriers, which were dismantled under the EFTA agreements, to stay dismantled. As regards the countries of the Commonwealth, it was possible to follow up the results achieved in the earlier negotiations on admission. Those apart, it will be easier to find solutions because closer relations with certain Commonwealth countries have been forged in the meantime. The Kennedy Round has also brought about a general lowering of customs duties and there have been particular cases of eliminating customs duties between Commonwealth countries and the Community in agreement with Great Britain. This raises the prospect of an extension of the African Association Agreement to include all the African Commonwealth countries, that is to say, to include a further ten countries. If that happens, the greater part of Africa – with the exception of South Africa and the Portuguese possessions – will, together with the European Community, form one unified group.

III ASSOCIATION

Article 238, paragraph 1, of the Treaty of Rome declares:

The Community may conclude with a third country, a union of States or an international organization, agreements creating an association embodying reciprocal rights and obligations, joint actions and appropriate forms of procedure.

Such agreements involve less than full membership but more than a treaty based merely on reciprocal obligations, as in the case of the traditional trade treaty. They create lasting and institutional ties, which are a kind of constitution: a common purpose is crystallized, the members of the association present themselves as a body, and all this is made possible by common procedures and institutions (Council and parliamentary representation). But it is not the Treaty setting up the Community which determines once and for all the content and extent of the ties with every associated partner; these are determined by the treaty of association, in every case in accordance with the needs and wishes of the negotiating partner. Association, therefore, is a flexible form of union: the degree of 'integration' is adjusted to the requirements of each particular case. Or – seen from a different point of view – association can be regarded as a form of 'partial' or 'relative' membership: to take a concrete case, it can theoretically fit into a range of full membership stretching from 0 plus 1 per cent to 100 minus 1 per cent. The reason for preferring association to full membership may be political (for example, neutrality), or economic (for example, the degree of development). Association does not mean 'lower status' by comparison with full membership, a superficial suggestion that is occasionally made; association at least means that an associated state retains a greater degree of 'sovereignty'. The variety of forms which association can take makes it particularly suitable for transitional solutions – and in two senses: on the one hand, a trade treaty can be concluded in the expectation, held by one party to it or shared by both, that it will eventually lead to association (examples of this are Israel and Spain, where this idea is very popular). Even the traditional type of trade treaty is institutionalized in so far as committees usually meet periodically. On the other hand, a treaty of association can be concluded with the express purpose of turning into full membership at a later stage (as in the case of Greece and Turkey).

A special form of association is the 'African' type established by the Yaoundé Convention. Its characteristic is that it is an organization concerned purely with development policy, created for a group of new, independent states all in much the same situation. The impending enlargement of the European Community has increased the value of both forms of association, in that they have been considered as possible solutions for some of the problems involved: the 'Africa' type of association for similarly placed countries for whom Great Britain historically has a special responsibility, and Association under Article 238 in other cases. If both prove their worth in this new context, some sceptics may be silenced.

For views in the Community have so far differed on whether the idea of association was a fortunate one or not. The associations set next to the Community system a second one, composed of different elements, which can easily collide with the first. The Community's obligation to take the interests of the associated states into consideration, and the duty to engage in mutual consultation, can at least from a procedural point of view place a perceptible burden on the Community's decision-making process.

In practice, Article 238 has been applied – or its application considered – in three sets of situations connected with the enlargement of the Community: in the Mediterranean region; in the Alpine republics; and in some of the Scandinavian countries.

1. *The Mediterranean*

Since the spontaneous Greek and Turkish initiatives of 1959 and 1960, the Community has been faced with the problems of extending its market towards the south.

Treaties were concluded with Turkey and Greece, both of which seek to become members of the Community. These treaties give the two countries about two decades to enable them to bring their economic development into line with the Common Market by determined improvement of their competitive capacity in the industrial and agricultural field, and by improving their trade relations. The initial phase for Turkey came to an end at the end of 1970, and her transition period began. Further association agreements have been concluded with Morocco, Tunisia, and Malta. Cyprus is considering association, as has Portugal, in connection with the enlargement of the Community. The initial declaration of intent on association for Libya has not yet been made effective; and Algeria appears to be in no hurry to recommence the soundings that it began in 1963 to see if association might be possible, since now it is more interested in a 'global agreement' for wine, oil, and migrant workers. Preferential trade agreements under Article 113 of the Treaty have been concluded

284

with Spain, Israel, the Lebanon, and Jugoslavia (the first agreement of this kind with a Communist, although not 'satellite', state). Negotiations are pending with the United Arab Republic. But all these agreements differ, not only as regards their general subject-matter (e.g. technical and financial aid), but also as regards their detailed contents, including such essential points as the level of preferences for the same product. In this respect they bear traces of undue casuistry. Already the Community's network of trade links in the Mediterranean is nearing completion, and this raises the question of our relationship with the Mediterranean area as a whole.

The area, quite apart from the fact that it can geographically count as part of Europe or Africa, constitutes a unit from the geo-economic and the geopolitical point of view. For many reasons – historical, economic, and political – one can hardly deny it the chance to play a part in the great European market. To provide the economy with reliable data, particularly for its investment projects, it is equally essential that the links between the Mediterranean and the Community be given some lasting legal form. That does not exclude agreements to proceed along these lines by several stages, even long-term stages – indeed, such elastic agreements are necessary because of the development gap between some of the Mediterranean areas and Central Europe. In this connection, the Community should insist on a permanent balance of transactions in respect of goods and services. To show its solidarity, a highly-developed area like the Community must be ready to supply goods and services before there is any comparable return from the other side, especially if it is to appear credible to the less-developed countries. The return that will eventually accrue to the Community must rest on the hope – a hope which is more or less justified – that the Mediterranean region will in the long run develop from a market divided by trade barriers into one unified market embracing more than a hundred million people.

This presents the Community now and in the future with a political difficulty and a political task – expressed in suspicious slogans like 'neo-imperialism' and 'neo-colonialism', and in reproachful conjectures that Europe wants to establish a Commonwealth in the Mediterranean. With regard to Africa, the way our relations with the associated states have developed over the last ten years has deprived reproaches of this kind of all substance; similarly I have no doubt that they will in due course be silenced when there is talk of our relations with our South European neighbours and those on the southern shore of the Mediterranean. Where these states have not – like Greece and Turkey – expressly declared their ultimate aim to be full membership, the Community must naturally avoid anything which could feed the suspicion that political conditions were being imposed. Only in cases involving membership is the ultimate political aim, the *finalité politique*, essential.

This is not the only political problem. In this area, some of the clouds that threaten us with the storm of a trade war have made the skies especially overcast. Lately, it is true, weather conditions have been improved by the multilateral and bilateral efforts already mentioned; but in the Mediterranean, even more than elsewhere, it seems evident that trade-policy questions are closely bound up with political questions in general.

The extension of the Common Market, by means of association, into the Mediterranean area presents economic difficulties which arise out of the structure of trade relations in the Mediterranean and out of the state of development of industry and agriculture in the area. The most striking feature of trade in the Mediterranean is that more than 80 per cent of it is carried on in only fifteen, predominantly agricultural, products. But each of these products raises a problem so far as Italy is concerned. By the very nature of the European Economic Community, of course, Italy enjoys continuing preferences for its agricultural products in the Common Market as against those coming from non-member countries. But that does not in the long term exclude increasing agricultural imports into the Community from other countries in the Mediterranean area. Italy will not be able on its own to satisfy the growing demands of the European market for such products as citrus and other fruits, vegetables, wine, tobacco, and olive oil. It cannot produce enough quantitatively, even if it wanted to intensify its production still further. Furthermore, Italy's economy is going through a period of change, in which the accent is increasingly on industry rather than on agriculture. In order to find wider markets for its industrial products, Italy should therefore seek to open its markets to the agricultural products of our Mediterranean partners as widely and as soon as possible. To coin a catch-phrase, Italy's future lies not in being the vegetable garden and granary of the Mediterranean area but in becoming its workshop, its Ruhr. The successes that are beginning to emerge as a result of the opening up of the *Mezzogiorno*, promise not only another Italian economic miracle in the seventies, which Europe can only welcome, but at the same time the end of that period in Italy's economic history in which agriculture predominated. I believe therefore that the opening up of Europe's markets to the products from the South will be only a question of time and of correctly spacing out the stages by which it should be brought about.

These peaceful achievements in the Mediterranean lie under the dark shadow of two unhappy developments.

The first is the expansionist attempt of the Soviet Union to exploit the Israel conflict to bring the whole of the Near East under its military and political control. By playing on Arab emotions evoked by the foundation of the State of Israel, the Soviet Union has tried for nearly two decades to continue the imperialist strategy of the Czars and to prevent the stabilization of the Near East. This global Soviet strategy, which avails itself of all conceivable operational and tactical means, has so far not met with the firm unified response from Europe which on grounds of security alone it would have deserved. In particular, Europe should not sit back and allow the Soviet Union to drive a wedge between public opinion in the Eastern Arab states and Europe. There is a long tradition of friendly French-Arab, Italian-Arab, and German-Arab relations. The foundation of the European Community has not interrupted these. It should not have remained a secret to the many clear-headed Arab politicians that their area is assured of a peaceful future only if they extricate it from the disputes, rivalries and tensions which divide the super-powers, and direct their policies towards the calmer, more peaceful zone of Europe. Who can calculate how much hunger, backwardness and neglected development is the result of exorbitant expenditure on armaments, preparations for war or on the consequences of war? Will the impoverished masses living between the Euphrates and the Nile have to continue to accept this situation in future only because the political leadership has allowed itself – perhaps contrary to its original purpose – to be turned into a tool of Soviet power politics? Why should it prove impossible, patiently and systematically, to prepare a summit conference of Arab and European heads of state and government in order to find a solution to the Israel conflict? Might not such a solution prove more effective and more lasting than one the United Nations may perhaps achieve? Might not such a solution also extend the peaceful atmosphere, at present prevailing in other parts of the Mediterranean area, to the Near East and thus establish the basis for an economic evolution – perhaps on the lines of the Marshall Plan? These problems are not insoluble. None of the nations involved has a basic interest in seeing the burden of armaments increase to incalculable proportions, and in seeing a lighted match permanently held to a powder keg.

The second shadow looming over the Community's work in the Mediterranean is the situation that has arisen in Greece. The circumstances which led to the establishment of a military dictatorship there are well known. After what I have said on the subject of the European Convention on Human Rights, it stands to reason that a Greek military dictatorship cannot qualify for full membership of the Community. To this extent, then, the *finalité politique* of the Greek treaty of association has for the time being been suspended. It is a regrettable development, but it should not cause us to become hysterical or to refuse to look ahead into the future and to do so on a rational basis.

The Greek people belong to Europe just as much today as they did before the military dictatorship was set up. Greece's economic development continues to be treated as a matter of European solidarity. The argument that this solidarity also benefits the military dictatorship strikes me as curious. Should the Germans by the same token refrain from doing all that is possible to help those of their compatriots who are ruled by Herr Ulbricht's successors to lead a better life, simply in order to add material suffering to all the other reasons that make their rulers unpopular? That is the question with which we are faced in the case of Greece. No: the sooner and the closer the interpenetration of markets becomes (which means the interpenetration of industry and of agriculture and also of opinions) the more rapidly shall we put an end to isolation of the country and to the protectionism of all kinds that a dictator needs to retain his grip on power. The Greeks are not made up of eight million gullible people who are likely to allow themselves to be deceived indefinitely about the true state of affairs by the propaganda poured out by a censored press and controlled mass media.

2. *Austria and Switzerland*

Since the creation of EFTA, we have been faced with the question of how its members could be fitted into the Common Market.

Switzerland and Austria present two special cases which are somewhat alike. Both countries are neutral; but while Swiss neutrality is the result of its traditional political attitude, Austrian neutrality was a pre-condition of its regaining its sovereignty by means of the State Treaty of 1955. Geo-economically, and as regards their economic structure, both countries belong to Central Europe; but Switzerland's economy is considerably more competitive than Austria's, which is hardly surprising in view of the erratic course taken by the Austrian ship of state during the last fifty years.

While Switzerland, therefore, is mistress of her own decisions as to how far she wishes to participate in the process of integration, Austria has to take special considerations into account. In view of these, a closer relationship with the European Community involves a particular problem which is comparable to no other kind of link with the Common Market. Furthermore, the degree of Austria's dependence on the Community – particularly if Great Britain joins it – demands particular sympathy. It is in this spirit that negotiations were undertaken for several years, culminating in a draft Treaty. No lucky star watched over it. The first interruption occurred when the question of the South Tyrol, or Alto Adige, entered a critical phase. Then one of the member-states allowed itself to be impressed by warnings from the Soviet Union. Then, finally, when the Austrian Government was considering a provisional agreement to make partial tariff cuts, in anticipation of a comprehensive solution, there was strong pressure to seek a solution together with the other EFTA countries. The draft treaty provided for an 'interim agreement' whereby the Community and Austria will grant each other 30 per cent tariff reductions for industrial products; and the definitive solution. This amounted to an arrangement avoiding all 'politicization' of the problems, in that it provided for no participation in the Community's common policies, and reduced the institutional provisions to a joint 'Mixed Committee', such as has long been a normal feature of modern trade agreements. This Committee was to 'administer the agreement', and deal with differences of interpretation, safeguard clauses, and requests for amendments. A fairly simple trade-policy solution was envisaged, in the form of a free trade area (with rules of origin), although there were a few special problems (paper, and the transfer to the pricing and transport policy of the Coal and Steel Community). On grounds of neutrality, Austria demanded the right to suspend the Treaty, wholly or partially, in the case of war or the threat of war. These general arrangements have now been adapted to fit in with the general solution of the EFTA problem.

The case of Switzerland is unique, in integration as in other matters. Geographically, historically, culturally (and also linguistically) she belongs to the heart of Europe. In foreign policy, thanks to an impressive ability to stand aloof from European affairs, she enjoys vigorous neutality; 'the everlasting armed neutrality of Switzerland has become a well-known institution of international law', proudly declared the masterly opening statement by the Swiss Government at the beginning of negotiations with the Community. Internally, the country is sound, owing to an original and century-long system of direct democracy, deeply rooted in the consciousness of its people. Economically, Switzerland is very highly developed, and closely interrelated with the countries of the Community. No wonder that she has had more difficulty than any other country in adjusting to the new and very different reality brought about by the unification of Europe. The basic solution that Switzerland proposed for her relationship with the European Community reflected her dilemma, torn between holding fast to the tried and trusted past, and responding to the needs of the present: beyond free trade, no thought of joining the Community's institutions, but 'systematic co-operation' in its development, especially in economic and monetary union, industrial policy, technology, and protection of the environment, by means of special institutional measures. This, it seems to me, was an attempt to square the circle. To achieve a 'systematic co-operation', I see no other solution than to secure top-quality diplomatic (and journalistic) representation with the Community.

Fortunately, these problems too have now been solved in the general context of the EFTA problem.

3. *Scandinavia*

Scandinavia is more than a geographical expression. Despite their different foreign policies – Denmark and Norway are members of NATO; Sweden and Finland are neutral – the four countries that since 1952 have been linked in the Nordic Council all have a high degree of social (a free labour market; co-operation on transport, on health services and on culture; a passport union; and amalgamated postal charges) and hence political unity.

Since all four belong to EFTA, there no longer exist any internal customs barriers in Scandinavia. As a free trade area EFTA has no common external tariff, and each country continues to maintain its own customs tariff *vis-à-vis* the rest of the world. But that has not prevented the Scandinavians from presenting a united front during the Kennedy Round and as a result obtaining considerable successes at the negotiating table.

Encouraged by this experience and spurred on by the poor prospects for direct negotiations with the European Community, the Scandinavians began in 1968 to consider transforming the old Nordic Council into a Nordic customs union. The efforts made in this direction became known as the NORDEK Project. It failed. More even than the attractive force exerted on undivided Nordic States by the European Community, it was Finnish opposition that led to the failure of NORDEK, as to that of a new Danish initiative at the beginning of 1971, where the entry negotiations were already in progress. The question now is whether the Nordic countries' new positions *vis-à-vis* the European Community will make it possible to preserve the unity of the Scandinavian economic area. Formally this is possible. And neither the inclination nor the interest of the Community calls for that unity to come to an end. Quite the reverse.

Chapter Seven

Political Union

The concept of full European political union is as old as that of 'economic' integration. Ever since the draft for a 'European Political Community' was shelved, together with the project for a European Defence Community, the problem of integrating Europe in all political fields has therefore continued to be topical. Today one speaks of 'Political Union'.

The expression 'Political Union' is ambiguous. This was intentional. Its choice was an attempt to reconcile – or to appear to reconcile – Gaullist policy with the policy of integration. Anyone using the expression, therefore, should always make it clear in what sense he is using it.

In the broadest sense, even the so-called 'economic' Communities are political unions in that their main purpose (the self-preservation of the European Continent), their subject matter (economic law and policy), and hence their institutions, are political.

In a narrower sense – and that in which it is most often used – 'Political Union' means those questions that are 'strictly' political (or that have political as well as economic aspects). To avoid the term 'power politics', which acquired unpleasant overtones, it means economic policy. It means security (defence) and foreign policy; if cultural policy is to be integrated then it, too, belongs to this sphere. Hand in hand with all this must go the strengthening of the institutions in a federal direction.

In a third sense the expression 'Political Union' means the same as federation: a union of states, with a constitution which preserves their national character. As regards the European Community, this involves two things: the fusion of all economic and other policies, and the transformation of the institutions, which are already partially federal, into truly federal organs. In this last sense, therefore, 'Political Union' is identical in meaning with the 'political unity of Europe' which the existing Community is designed to bring about and which its founders had in view as their ultimate goal.

Political union accordingly presents the same problems as those that we faced in drawing up the constitution of the Community. Some of the solutions – naturally the fundamental ones – are also the same: the supreme guiding principles are legitimacy and democracy. The basic values are the same: peace, unity, equality, liberty, solidarity, prosperity, and security. Indeed, it is only when these values become criteria in the formulation of foreign and defence policy that they attain their true significance and have their greatest impact; for they are then concerned with the fate and future of nations and not only of citizens. They give unified Europe its own individuality in the family of nations. The rights of man determine what is to be represented and defended.

But when it comes to questions of structure (composition, subject-matter, and formal type) there are differences as compared with the 'economic' Community.

As regards composition, the most important question is the relation between membership of the economic Community and of the political union. Are the members to be the same in both cases? Are all members of the economic Community also to be members of the political union? Or can one of the two grouping be bigger than the other, with only some members of the political union also members of the economic Community; or, the other way around, with only some members of the political union also members of the economic Community? Unfortunately no clear answer is given to this fundamental question; indeed there is perhaps even disagreement. After all that has been said here in explaining the policy of European integration, there can be only one answer; it is essential that members of both should be identical.

Of the three possibilities just mentioned, one can be eliminated at once on purely theoretical grounds. Plainly the political grouping cannot have more members than the economic one. That would be conceivable only if political collaboration restricted the willingness of members to act together less than did economic collaboration. But that is not the point at issue. What is in question is a union entirely different from the Council of Europe, because

293

its aim is unified political action, particularly in foreign and defence policy. But that presupposes fundamental agreement in determining political objectives – which, in particular, excludes systematic neutrality.

Equally, it is simply not possible to have more members in the economic Community than in the political union. The sacrifices which the members have bound themselves under the Treaty to make will be fully balanced out only within the many-sided, complex Community; indeed the reason for these sacrifices will be realized only when the Community reaches its political goal. This expectation, the belief that the Community has a European vocation, must remain credible. Furthermore, the options facing the economic union, and the conclusions reached, are inevitably determined more and more by 'purely' political considerations and preparatory decisions. To mention only a few examples, that is particularly true of trade, development and monetary policy, the over-all control of economic trends, major technological projects, industrial policy – at least as far as the armaments industry is concerned – and also social policy.

A state which did not take part in the primary political decisions, but was subsequently bound by the 'consequential decisions', in matters of economic policy, would find itself in an intolerable position, amounting to discrimination. The resulting conflict would not only affect the domestic affairs of the state concerned: it would also undeniably set off unfortunate and perhaps destructive tensions in the economic Community as a whole. On the other hand, a political union which was not identical with an economic union, but left economic policy to be dealt with by an organization consisting of different members, would be weaker than need be. For these reasons Western European Union is not the proper place for political union or even for its preparatory phases.

All these reflections bring to the fore a more profound difficulty than merely limited disadvantages or the practical danger of friction. It is simply not possible to put together associations exercizing authority, with functions equal or similar to those usually entrusted to a state, according to arbitrary formulae of ingredients to be mixed in some kind of receptacle – one association composed in one way to perform one particular function, and another in a different way to perform another function. This is confirmed by the European Community's powerful tendency to bring together again in a full federation the scattered partial elements of state authority. Does it then follow that a state which is not prepared or not in a position to enter into the required political obligation is as a result to be excluded from the Common Market? By no means. Association has been created for this eventuality as much as for others. As we have seen, association is a special kind of membership of the economic Community: a form of participation which is less complete and related to the circumstances of the case, a form which relieves the associated state of obligations it regards as imposing too heavy a burden on it. It must also not be overlooked that there are looser and hence less exacting associations which candidates can join if they consider excessive the demands which political integration would make on them: there is the Council of Europe for collaboration in the political field, and in the economic field there is the OECD (which at the same time provides links across the Atlantic). Nothing could be further from the truth than to accuse the founders of the European Community of wishing to crowd out the larger associations. On the contrary, they have always seen them as a necessary complement to our more strictly-conceived construction, and that is in fact how they work.

In considering political union, the question of its subject is as important as that of its composition. It cannot be separated from the question of organization, which in turn cannot be separated from the time-table for the various solutions. Once the final stage, full and complete federation, is reached, the question of who deals with what depends on the division of authority and competence between the federation and the members, a division which is the centrepiece of all federal constitutions. It is probably only then that the Community will be able to assume competence over other questions of internal policy apart from economic and social questions (for example, over fundamental questions of internal security), and take over from the particular national authorities, where such competence at present rests. And it is only then that the political forces and groupings and public powers will be able to break out of their narrow national confines and operate at the level of the European Community, a process which, once completed, will make Europe truly one.

But how are we to reach this final stage? Since the weight of what has already been achieved provides the best momentum for further progress, the most sensible solution in my view is still the one put forward by the Commission in the introduction to its 'Action Programme' in 1962. It is based on the existence of three Communities. Subject to their fusion in one Community, they are to be kept in being until the final phase is reached. This provides the best way of countering the danger that competence will be claimed for the political union to define its own area of competence, that is to say, the authority to usurp the responsibility of the existing Community and supplant it with its own machinery – machinery which will probably be subject to the rule of unanimity for longer than the Economic Community. This question played a decisive role in the attempts to draw up a treaty for political union following the Bonn resolution of the heads of state and government on 18 July 1961. The French desire for economic policy to be included among the subject-matter of the projected political treaty revealed de Gaulle's intention to subordinate the Community to an inter-governmental political organization and thus to change its very nature.

There is no unanimity on whether the new subject-matter of integration, such as the so-called 'political' subjects, should be entrusted to the old Communities or to one or several new Communities. I consider the second to be the better solution.

But what is the subject-matter of political union? Defence and foreign policy appear to be accepted by everyone who agrees with the basic concept of political unity. Whether cultural policy should also be included is a delicate question – as the history of all existing federations proves. This will have to be approached with caution. But there ought to be an agency to see to it that national cultures are not shut off from, but cross-fertilize, each other, and that cultural policies are sensibly pursued. In addition, the European University, envisaged by the Euratom Treaty, should at last see the light of day.

There remains one last question: is the political union to be given the task of dealing with all other matters which – economic and social policy apart – are to be tackled on a Community basis, or are further particular Communities to be set up? This is above all a question of practical organization. Seen from the political point of view, and on grounds of efficiency, new matters that have to be dealt with should as far as possible be brought together within one single organization. Only the future can teach us whether an exception ought to be made in the case of defence. In any case, special organs are indispensable for performing certain particular functions, for example, planning and armaments.

Finally, even if the existing Community does not offer a framework for organizing the new areas of political activity, it at least provides a model. Particular attention must be devoted to ensuring that any organization charged with looking after matters of common European interest should be independent. In this respect a wealth of suggestions emerged from the discussions which followed the Bonn Resolution of the heads of state and government in July 1961, on creating a 'Union of the Peoples of Europe'. Again, useful suggestions can be extracted from the various Treaty drafts.

The skeleton of a constitution, which is also a model for thinking about what might be the bare minimum of a Community system, emerged from the report of the political committee of the European Parliament on 12 December 1961, presented by René Pleven. The report was on the first Fouchet Plan of 2 November 1961. The Pleven report proposed in particular the appointment of a Secretary-General who was to be 'independent of the governments'. He was to report to the European Parliament and to be subject to dismissal on a parliamentary vote of no confidence. He was to carry out the decisions of the Council of Ministers, but was to be free to choose his collaborators, and he was to be given the right of taking initiatives on his own. Should the Council of Ministers be prevented from making a decision by the rule of unanimity, Parliament was to be asked to give its views. Parliament was to have the duty of ratifying international treaties. The executive of the existing Community was to be represented at top level at the sessions of the Council of Ministers.

In the first Fouchet Plan, France had shown itself accommodating. Admittedly, it had not satisfied all European wishes but – as the subsequent Pleven Plan demonstrated – it had given encouragement and hope. All this took place during the tough discussions on the irrevocable introduction of a common agricultural policy, a step which France had made a condition of its agreement to the beginning of the second phase of the Rome

Treaty's transition period. That condition was met on 14 January 1962. On 16 January the French Cabinet decided to withdraw the first Fouchet Plan. On 18 January the second Fouchet Plan was submitted. It contained none of the clauses of the first Plan which had shown a spirit of accommodation. A particular point in the second Plan was that economic policy was to be included. The purpose was clear: to reverse the evolution of the Community.

The last plan of the other five member-states, by contrast, drew on the essential points of the Pleven Plan. It also showed evidence of their having been influenced by aspects of the structure of the Community, aspects which the smaller countries in particular felt they could not forgo: the inviolability of the existing Communities; an independent Secretary-General; the jurisdiction of the European Court of Justice; and a revision clause providing for progress by obligatory stages (for example, for the progressive introduction of majority voting in the Council of Ministers).

These negotiations provide several lessons. One of them is that the practical way to make political union a reality is to proceed by stages. But it is essential to lay down the obligations and objectives of each stage as precisely as the relevant dates.

The Foreign Ministers of the Six had decided in Strasbourg on 23 November 1959 to meet once every three months to consult on foreign-policy questions. The first concrete attempt to bring about a political union had failed in the summer of 1962. In the meantime, on de Gaulle's initiative, conversations had begun which were eventually to lead to the conclusion of the Franco-German Treaty.

At The Hague Summit Conference in 1969, economic integration entered its final phase as a result of a number of important decisions; the Community was provided with its own income; economic union was activated; and binding decisions were taken on negotiations on enlarging the Community. What could be more appropriate, therefore, than to seize this moment to give 'political integration' a definite nudge? It did not happen. The French and German governments, both of which were primarily responsible for the way events developed at The Hague, held back – each for its own reasons.

The communiqué issued by the heads of state and government certainly gave the optimists some ground for hope. Point 15 stated:

> They agreed to instruct the Ministers for Foreign Affairs to study the best way of achieving progress in the matter of political unification, with the prospect of enlargement.

But the discussions of the foreign ministers in Viterbo in May and in Brussels in July 1970 – discussions which had been prepared by the political directors of the respective foreign ministries – resulted in deep disappointment. Joseph Luns, the Netherlands Foreign Minister, was right when he said: 'The mountain laboured and brought forth a mouse.'

True, the objectives to be aimed at were ambitiously defined: to improve understanding of the great problems of international politics by a steady flow of information and regular consultation; to strengthen solidarity by harmonizing different points of view; to bring differing attitudes into line, and, where opportunity offered, to take common action.

The means by which these objectives are to be achieved, however, in no way justify the hope that the Community will be able within the foreseeable future 'to speak with one voice'. The Foreign Ministers are to meet twice a year, apart from special sessions. A 'political Committee' consisting of the political directors of the respective foreign ministries is to prepare these sessions; this committee is to meet four times a year. The chair is to be taken by the country whose turn it is for the time being to provide the President of the Council of Ministers. There is to be consultation on all important questions: every member-state is to be entitled to submit subjects for discussion. The Commission is to participate whenever matters concerning the Community are to be discussed. Once a year the President of the Council of Ministers is to report to the European Parliament; twice a year the Ministers are to exchange views with the political committee of the European Parliament in sessions that are not open to the public. This, in addition to anything else, is undemocratic.

The Ministers express their wish to continue their efforts at political unification in order to bring about closer co-operation in foreign policy and to make progress in various other fields (subject, admittedly, to the different areas of competence within the Community). A general report on progress is to be presented at the latest after two years. Countries prepared to join the Community are to be kept regularly informed; there are also to be meetings of the Ten.

Even in the form in which it is presented, this whole scheme gives the impression of being a late product of Gaullist thinking. To begin with, there is this demonstrative insistence on mystery-mongering in arriving at decisions, which is obviously designed to point up the diplomatic character of the whole scheme. Then there is the terminology that is used (the expression 'common policy' is avoided like the plague). And finally there is the strictly 'international', that is to say diplomatic, form of organization, a form that differs sharply from any kind of integration; there is no organizational embodiment of Europe's common interests.

The substance is equally meagre. Two days a year are supposed to be enough to bring together the foreign policies of the member-states. There is no mention of defence (one hopes that it is understood to form a part of foreign policy). There is no obligation on member-states to consult each other. Consequently no treaty is being concluded; what is involved is merely diplomatic custom. The links with the Community are extremely tenuous, although the Community's organization contains all that is needed to help bring about a European foreign policy. Above all, there is no provision for what we know – at least since the Kennedy Round – to be the most important: that the Community should speak with one voice. One can only be uneasy when one thinks of the 'European Security Conference' proposed by the East European countries. That on that occasion, if no common representation is organized, the various democratic governments will say the same thing is either a chimera, or at least an illusion.

If we look for any concrete results from all this, we must be content with procedural innovations. The only material subject-matter of this modest co-operation which has so far been made public is the Israeli question, a painful matter for all concerned. If only from a European point of view, it was very inept to begin with this question – of all European foreign-policy questions – since it is extremely delicate for one of the Community's member-states. This is certainly no way to give the rest of the world the

300

necessary confidence in the new foreign-policy dimension we are hoping to add to the European Community.

Matters stand even worse (if that is possible) as far as the second chapter of political union, the development of the institutions, is concerned. The governments are still not prepared to decide on the overdue step of introducing direct elections to the European Parliament. A number of member-states have therefore rightly taken the initiative to prepare legislation on this point. True, the budgetary powers of the European Parliament have been strengthened. But more is at stake: for example, the extension of its legislative powers and its participation in the appointment of members of the Commission. There is the question of reforming the Council of Ministers, which by laggardliness in the use of majority voting has greatly weakened its power of decision and hence its authority in recent years: 160 Commission proposals at present await the Council's decision, 20 of them more than a year old, 40 of them more than three years old. There are even signs of minority rule that are undemocratic as well as contrary to the Treaty. It has been seriously proposed that, by raising the status of the Permanent Representatives, the Council should abdicate some of its powers in favour of its own subordinates. Even the authority of the Commission is frivolously weakened, often on minor details; this has a very bad effect on public opinion.

The decisions that have been taken lag far behind public opinion in Europe. To the question put by public-opinion polls, whether the European Community should develop into the Political Community of a United Europe, 69 per cent in Germany and 67 per cent in France have recently answered yes. In June 1970, one of the French Government parties, the 'Independent Republicans', led by Valéry Giscard d'Estaing, put forward an outline plan for a European confederation to be established by 1980. With impressive consistency, the outline takes the constitutional elements of the European Community as its basis, builds on them (it refers, among other topics, to the dialogue between the Council of Ministers and the Commission whose right of making proposals is to be strengthened, to majority voting in the Council and to an armaments Community), and it develops these themes with considerable originality.

In addition, what the governments have neglected to do has

301

dangerous consequences abroad. Delaying political unification irritates the Americans, encourages the Russians, and bewilders the candidates applying to join. The Americans have not spent years supporting European unification in order to have their world economic concept thrown into confusion and to raise a powerful economic competitor for themselves; they gave their support because they expected political unity to lead to greater stability in Europe. Soviet Russia must feel encouraged in its efforts to win supremacy in Europe when it sees no sign of a West European centre of political decision-making – which would be a thorn in its flesh. And, finally, the candidate countries must be confused (and are already confused) as they wonder whether accepting 'political objectives' also includes the willingness to undertake Community obligations in the field of European foreign policy.

The task of building political union therefore essentially still lies before us. Have at least the beginnings of progress been made? There are statements of principle; there are procedural commitments; there are requests for proposals. There are also governmental declarations forming part of political programmes.

The Hague Conference laid down the 'political aims' of the Community, and the new members are committed to them. Furthermore, the Foreign Ministers have pledged themselves to consider fresh steps, and after two years' voluntary consultations to propose them in a Report.

Finally, at the time when the European Parliament was given budgetary powers, the Commission announced that within two years it would make proposals for strengthening the Parliament's powers, and the Council agreed to consider them.

The President of the French Republic has put forward some ideas about the final form of Europe's political unity which have led to discussion; and that is a service, irrespective of their content. He bases them on the existing Community system, in happy contrast to the 'qualified co-operation on foreign policy'. He speaks of a European Government and of a European administration which would be responsible only to it; he speaks of a 'real European Parliament'. This confirms the notion that full political union in Europe will take the form of a state, for only states have governments and real parliaments (which must be interpreted as meaning a representative body with powers to legislate and to

302

control the government; in a similar connection the Federal German Chancellor, Willy Brandt, has spoken of a European Government subject to parliamentary control). If all this is nevertheless described as a 'confederation' rather than a 'federation', that can be passed over as a mere supposition or a *falsa demonstratio*, as a quite common French imprecision in the use of both terms – provided that the use of the word 'confederation' does not have material consequences (such as the rule of unanimity in the decision-making institution!). Less conclusive – and hence the occasion for as many questions as fanciful interpretations – are other hypotheses in the President's deliberately discursive reflections: notably, that 'special "European Ministers"' should deal with European questions in the Council, instead of Foreign and other departmental Ministers. Later, only those 'European Ministers' would have strictly European powers, and would no longer belong to the national governments (surely a position which the present Commission holds, but with more power?). From this would grow a European government. The thesis, finally, that the decisions of the Council must be unanimous, because it is comparable to a coalition government, is not valid; it would expose the Community – especially the enlarged Community – to the danger of paralysis.

The leader of the opposition in the German Bundestag, Rainer Barzel, has countered these proposals with a political 'plan-by-stages' for the Community, which carries the debate further in both form and content. He has outlined not only some, but almost all the essential elements of a definitive solution and the steps towards it, as well as the relationships between them. In particular, he seeks to guard against the shift of weight from the Commission to the Council, which might occur in the transitional phase between national and European 'Ministers for Europe'; his proposal is for a confirmation of the Commission's right of initiation and a strengthening of the European Parliament's powers. Finally, there should be a European Federal Assembly, which just before the completion of economic and monetary union should draw up a federal constitution.

Most important is the fact that this plan is a true 'plan-by-stages', whose parts are clearly defined, articulated, and interrelated. It ought to be given statute form. To all constitutional

303

questions, in fact, there are relatively few solutions which apply in all circumstances, whatever the other rules may be: there are the basic principles, such as legitimacy and democracy. For the rest there are only global answers. Even the constitutional system of the continually evolving Community is no place for aphorisms, no playground for idle thoughts.

I. FOREIGN POLICY

1. *Why?*

If it is generally regarded as difficult to evolve a Community foreign policy, then that is probably due mainly to an emotional obstacle which cannot easily be overcome: the fondly-cherished view that foreign policy is a matter of 'national' concern. Once one shakes off that view, one can recognize that there is a large measure of harmony in the foreign policies pursued by the countries of our Community. The reason for this is that our traditions, our values, and our interests are the same or closely related. Furthermore, this harmony goes back far enough to provide a basis on which to bring together the various policies. I venture to suggest that this is no more difficult to organize than economic integration which, as the extensive legislation of the Community reveals, involves a vast mass of complicated particular questions, because of the network of dramatic current problems and the enormous amount of detail entailed in running our economic system. Indeed, I believe that it is easier to bring about the fusion of foreign policies – provided only that the will to do so exists. It is hard to imagine that any reasonably conceived aspect of member-states' foreign policy cannot be appropriately fitted into a Community foreign policy. This is true, for example, even of France's Mediterranean policy, including her policy on Algeria, and it is surely true of her East European policy – including atomic supplies – as it is true of the German *Ostpolitik*, which are presumably both already the subject of 'qualified foreign-policy co-operation'. Moreover, there are regions of the world where the external interests of the Community do not go beyond economic and cultural relations. In such cases, it should be possible soon to evolve Community procedures for conducting common foreign policies on non-economic operations. The problems will become greater when it comes to harmonizing foreign policy in relation to areas of political tension where the views and attitudes of member-states are conditioned more by tradition and emotion than by rational considerations.

Even in this respect, however, we share one wish above all others, which is to overcome the division of Europe between East and West. It is the second division which Europe has to bear, the first being its division into separate nation-states. The second division is of an entirely different kind from the first. It reflects the contrast between Communists and Democrats, and is a part of the division of the world. All countries taking part in Europe's unification belong to the West. But not one of them wants to see the 'Iron Curtain' maintained – an 'Iron Curtain' which directly affects the very existence of one European country, Germany. Germany's division is a part of the division of Europe.

There is a legend about how East and West came to be divided which has been solicitously nourished by Gaullist propaganda: the legend has it that the division goes back to the Yalta Conference (at which only the Americans, the Russians and the British took part). It is a legend that is open to criticism, as the case of Germany shows. It was after Yalta, at Potsdam in the summer of 1945, that the three Great Powers decided to preserve German unity under the collective authority of the occupation powers and to set up a central administration. A number of factors, among them the refusal of France to participate in this project, prevented this organization for the whole of Germany from being set up. As a result the occupation powers created their own political organizations wherever their troops were stationed; Stalin was the first to do so. Europe thus became the main theatre of the duel between the only two world powers which were left after the Second World War: the United States and the Soviet Union. Since then, it is they who have determined the political conditions affecting Europe's fate in the world. Cold wars, *détentes*, and the many variations between these two extremes, are not political conditions which have been or are being chosen by Europe itself. Two national attempts by Europeans to influence the basis of their relations with the East on their own initiative, to evolve their own *Ostpolitik* – by France and by Germany – have so far met with little success. Consequently, Europe is not only divided; it is also a dependency.

Thus the relationship between the 'super-Powers' is plainly the

305

most important factor in determining Europe's place in the world. Not in the sense that the two combine in exercising a kind of joint guardianship over Europe's position, but rather in the sense that their relationship is a search for a sort of equilibrium between themselves – and an unstable equilibrium at best – since (or so long as) neither can count on deciding world policy on its own. Now European history has always been viewed – and rightly so – as a continuous succession of periods in which struggles for supremacy have been followed by attempts to establish some kind of power balance. What is new in our day is that the search for balance is on a world-wide scale, between powers of whom one is, geographically at least, not at all European and the other only partially European. What is also new in our day is that Europe – in its present form – is virtually powerless when it comes to exerting any influence on the world balance of power. Consequently, there is no guarantee whatever that sufficient account is always taken of Europe's interests. This is not meant as a reproach against one or the other; it merely reflects the state of affairs which lies in the nature of the situation as it exists. The Nuclear Non-Proliferation Treaty provides merely one example. It contains no 'European option'. The right to decide whether Europe wishes to defend itself against atomic attack (a defence which is at present possible only if one possesses nuclear weapons) is not to be reserved for a body responsible for Europe's future common defence policy. This decision, on which Europe's survival could depend at some time in the future, has already been taken in advance – and, from Europe's point of view, in the negative sense. We are put off with a legalistic interpretation, according to which this state of affairs is to be remedied in case Europe's defence becomes highly centralized in a fully federalized state – a highly unlikely event, and not only in the short term. Once such a fully federal state exists, it is to be made possible to transfer France's atomic armoury (and Britain's, as it should by then have joined) to this state. This attitude on the part of the authors of the Non-Proliferation Treaty – and this is a risk not to be ignored – could act as a brake on the integration of Europe's defence and as a guarantee for the continued existence of separate national defence policies.

If one wants to escape being a pawn in other people's balance-of-

306

power struggles, one can do so only by acquiring weight and importance on one's own account. But that is possible only by combining the separate European states, each of which by itself no longer carries sufficient weight. One must fuse the economic, military and political potential of the states in the Community. The level of civilization these states have reached provides opportunities for development which are as great as those of the world powers. One must place this part of Europe, the Community, in a position to speak with one voice in foreign affairs as well. Then a new entity will have been created, capable of shouldering worldwide political responsibilities because, although not equal, it will be comparable in weight and importance to the world powers. These are hopes and expectations which are justified by our experiences in beginning to evolve a common European external policy – in trade as well as in monetary policy.

This objective of ours does not spring from a European chauvinism different only in scale from the nationalism of the past. It derives from a fundamental assessment of our own interests and – no less important – from a sense of responsibility towards the world as a whole.

The first reason is the fact that Europe's political standing in the world depends in effect on the relationship of the world powers. If Europe wins the right to share the decision-making process with them, then it really wins back its autonomy. It has not only an interest in achieving this; it also has a right: the right to decide its own fate. No permanent peace arrangements, no agreements on disarmament or divisions of zones of interest which affect Europe, are acceptable unless these have been approved by all Europeans. Such approval, however, is not feasible unless Europe first takes stock of its interests and security problems and states its conclusions with one voice.

Another reason is the fact that the world as a whole has an interest in Europe's playing a part in the decision-making process. There is today more than ever before one all-embracing, overriding political aim which is universally recognized – peace. We know that the world is hardly likely to survive a third great conflict, at least in a fit state for human habitation. A Europe gradually approaching the level of political effectiveness of the world powers will fill an essential role in shouldering its share of responsibility for world

307

peace. That is how we have always understood Europe's role: not only to keep the peace inside a united Europe, nor only between a united Europe and the rest of the world, but also to strive for peace wherever our influence gives us the opportunity to do so. The character of Europe's thinking and Europe's aspirations has always been universal; that is how we have always seen ourselves. Isolationism is not a European characteristic. Our task today is to establish a system to safeguard world peace. This applies also – and not least – to an integrated, organized Europe.

Consequently, in practical concrete terms, the two main themes of Europe's common foreign policy will be its policy towards Russia and its policy towards America; for only speculation is so far possible about China's future role in Europe's fate. What are the conditions with which these policies will have to cope?

2. *The Soviet Union*

The Soviet Union is certainly no longer what it was twenty years ago. It has rapidly transformed itself into an industrial society, the result of unprecedented efforts in cultural and educational development. Its leading universities, schools, academies and institutes are of a standard that equals those in the rest of the world. The same is true of the best that Soviet industry and technology have achieved. It would be unrealistic and dangerous to close one's eyes to these facts, which will have a long-term effect. At the same time the Soviet Union has become a consumer society, and one can observe in that society the development of what political scientists call the 'revolution of rising expectations'. All this is accompanied by a growing awareness of problems involving the relationship of the individual to the state, an awareness which is stimulated by modern, progressive Russian literature. One already senses that there exists a wish here and there that there should be minimal constitutional safeguards. Undoubtedly this whole development is exacerbated by the problem of the generation gap, which is particularly marked in the Soviet Union.

But it would be crude self-deception if, in noting all this, one were to lose sight of the permanent principles of Russian foreign policy. The expansionist tendency of Soviet European policy remains unmistakably opposed to the decisive objectives of our

308

own European policy. Soviet Russia's medium-term aims continue unchanged: it wishes to consolidate what it regards as the *status quo* in Europe and particularly in Germany today, and what it will regard as the *status quo* tomorrow, and this includes the recognition of all present *de facto* frontiers; it wants an end put to all forms of integration in Western Europe – military, economic, and especially political, in so far as there are signs of this developing; and it welcomes all the consequences that would follow, particularly the withdrawal of American troops from the Continent and of the US Sixth Fleet from the Mediterranean; it seeks to have Germany permanently down-graded from the military, and particularly from the nuclear, point of view. These are not aims one has to decipher by careful study: they are openly expressed. In short, the over-all objective in the medium term is nothing less than exclusive Soviet supremacy in Europe, embracing both the Baltic Sea and the Mediterranean. And after the events in Czechoslovakia we cannot help worrying whether all this is not merely the minimum aim.

To be sure, this set of aims has not prevented Europe's policy of integration from affecting Soviet policy towards Europe and *vice versa*. At the beginning, the Soviet attitude towards the European Economic Community was completely negative. It was first defined in 1957 in a kind of political grammar and in a form which was plainly to be accepted as the authoritative and obligatory pronouncement on the subject by Communists throughout the world. It was issued by the Moscow 'Institute for World Economy and International Relations' and it dealt with economic integration in seventeen theses. In the traditional language of Communism, the creation of the European Economic Community was described as the work of American imperialism, an enterprise which is of course condemned to failure according to the laws of history.

This attitude, however, changed with astonishing rapidity – in 1962 to be exact – once the European Economic Community had achieved its first successes at the end of the fifties and the beginning of the sixties, for all to see. An article by Khrushchev published in *Kommunist* in that year reflected the change. The article was written after an ideological congress held in Moscow in the summer of 1962. The work of that congress and the conclusions it reached were influenced especially by the Italian Communists.

Khrushchev's article recognized the positive results of Western economic integration and conceded its 'objective' character. It envisaged a state of affairs where economic collaboration would be possible not only between states with different social and economic systems but also between associations of such states; the point could hardly have been made more explicitly. The article also held the Franco-German Treaty to be the backbone of the Community. Moreover, the article did not gloss over the success which integration had achieved. It pointed out that economic development was proceeding more rapidly in the area of integration of the Community than in the United States; that the Community was increasing its share of what was produced in the capitalist world; that the same held true as far as international trade was concerned; and the article mentioned – among other things – that the Community's gold reserves had risen. It specifically noted the birth of a 'centre of attraction'.

All this is interesting as well as instructive. It is less pleasing, however, to note that the crises which subsequently bedevilled the development of European integration also affected Soviet Russia's attitude towards and judgement of the Community. This shows that our work is being observed with considerable attention. It also shows that it is an essential element of an effective *Ostpolitik* that European integration should evolve dynamically and free of disruptions.

The present Soviet attitude towards the European Community is therefore merely a pale reflection of the positive stance which Khrushchev adopted in his article. Broadly speaking, it takes the form that Moscow is no longer hostile to seeing West European Communist parties and trade unions participate in the work of European institutions. Naturally, in allowing this to happen, Moscow also hopes to be able to exert some influence on the decisions being taken. The Soviet Union still regards it as in its interest to prevent the formation of a comprehensive and autonomous centre for making decisions in Western Europe. Such a centre would, in Moscow's view, stand in the way of Soviet supremacy or domination, because it would strengthen the defence of Western Europe and make it impossible to pursue policies based on the maxim of 'Divide and rule'. Indeed, a free modern community of peoples, capable of solving the social and economic

310

problems of our age, might seem increasingly attractive to some inside the Eastern bloc – an uncomfortable thought from Moscow's standpoint. The Soviet Union therefore continues to refuse to recognize the Community in international law despite the well-known *de facto* relations that exist between the Community and the East bloc countries, and despite pragmatic adjustment to reality in international organizations (for example, in the UN Committee on Trade and Development, where raw-materials agreements are being negotiated, the Commission is acting as spokesman for the Community countries, with the agreement of the Soviet Union). It continues to use all sorts of means to fight integration in Western Europe, and the choice of means depends entirely on the circumstances: it will encourage efforts to enlarge the Community on one occasion and discourage them on another; it will promote tendencies towards neutrality and anti-Americanism within the Community; it will play on anti-German sentiments which may lead to discrimination against that country and its citizens. Among the aims of the so-called European Security Conference, the attack on Western European integration naturally has pride of place.

Only if the policy of European unification continues to be pursued with tenacity and is neither provocative nor submissive will the Soviet leadership be convinced in the long run that such a policy does not disrupt but that on the contrary it serves its true interest. What greater security can there be against the alleged 'German danger', in particular, than Germany's voluntary and unreserved integration in a union whose strongest interest with regard to Russia is the preservation of peace?

3. *The United States of America*
Quite different conditions determine the relationship of Europe, especially Western Europe, with the United States of America.

The difference is not only a question of fundamental principles. America is Europe's child and is aware of that link. It is part of 'Western Civilization', and carries the imprint of Christianity and humanism and of the ethics of both. It speaks one of the great languages of Western Europe. Geographically, strategically, and politically, it is linked to Europe by the Atlantic, the Mediterranean of our time. Dean Acheson was right: the United States is a European power. Moreover, like Western Europe itself, it has not

311

succumbed to the errors of a modern European futurologist called Karl Marx.

The United States entered world politics in 1917, at the same time as the Soviet Union. After the end of World War II it developed a systematic European policy to replace the world political system, centred on Europe, that two World Wars had destroyed.

The United States were thus faced with three phenomena. In the first place, they did not want to be drawn for a third time into conflicts, and especially not into those which had their origin in Europe. Secondly, they had become the greatest military power in the world; moral logic therefore condemned them to the *pax Americana*. They could not escape the responsibility of also exerting their political influence in other parts of the world. Finally, the Americans found themselves face to face with Soviet expansionism. From all this, they drew the following conclusions: they decided to help Europe to rebuild its economy (with the Marshall Plan and the aid distributed by OEEC); against the threat from the East they decided to guarantee the security of the peoples of Europe who were still free (by means of NATO) – with the unprecedented result that even in times of peace troops were stationed in Europe; and they decided to aid the unification of Europe.

The first two tasks – economic aid and security for Europe – can be said up to now to have been satisfactorily solved. But has the relationship of the United States to the integration of Europe, which is still not complete, remained unchanged? In Europe, doubts are stirring.

In fact, there have been changes, and more than just a natural decline in the original enthusiasm for the new 'United States' on the other side of the Atlantic. For years Europe had priority in the foreign policy of the United States. That came to an end in 1963, when Asia and the Pacific came to the forefront. Some of the reasons for this were connected with developments in Europe itself. De Gaulle bears a good share of the responsibility for this. Doubts arose in America as to whether the Europeans were still capable of achieving full political union and whether, if so, they were willing to be allied with the United States. America's attitude to the geographical enlargement of the Community has become cooler. And day-to-day life has taken its toll. Natural causes of friction have emerged. One example was the tariff negotiations in GATT, which

312

were certainly as tough as all good trade-policy negotiations. Others are such external economic actions of the Community as its agricultural policy and its (preferential) trade policy – which run the risk of causing serious ill-will, and even a recrudescence of protectionism.

More important still, however, is the growth of America's internal problems: the racial problem which has assumed revolutionary proportions; overcrowding and violence in the cities; and poverty in a country immeasurably rich. This situation is dangerous because internal politics are given priority on Capitol Hill (and, it seems, increasingly so as far as foreign policy is concerned): the weakness – if not of the American constitution then of its parliamentary interpretation – is to be found in Congress. The Vietnam war, too, has become so prolonged because it has become a matter of internal politics. As a result, the self-confidence, the self-discipline, the self-reliance of the American people, a people who have never yet lost a war, has suffered. (Perceptive Americans say – without cynicism – that this ordeal has brought them closer to the Europeans!)

For some time, therefore, the question has once more been raised: what does Europe mean to America? Is it to be seen as a power on the opposite shore of the Atlantic and a sphere of political interest; as a future partner in world politics and an ally; as a strategic outpost; as an economic bastion against Bolshevism; or negatively, as a large economic competitor and as a mischief-maker disrupting the long-sought settlement with Moscow? The answers are varied, and also changing. They cover a wide field if one goes all the way back to the last war: to Roosevelt, the Marshall era, Acheson, Dulles; from that period to Kennedy and to Johnson and Nixon.

To maintain, however, that at any time the Americans had abandoned Europe, is not merely untrue. It is nonsense. It would be a grotesque underestimate of American intelligence – a mistake that admittedly is sometimes made in the Old World – to believe that the Americans were not aware of the fact that their country's defences lie either in Central Europe or along their own Eastern coast-line from Maine down to Florida. But they do have the feeling that the time has come for the Europeans to take on their share of the common burden, which means above all that they

313

should unite. It is an iron principle of American-aid policy in the broadest sense of the term to give generously to a difficult enterprise – on condition that one day that enterprise must become self-supporting.

It was none too soon – in February 1971 – that President Nixon helped to calm American irritation in his foreign-policy message to Congress. 'Our relations with Western Europe,' he said, 'must be the cornerstone . . . Western Europe remains central' – among other reasons – 'because her nations are rich in tradition and experience, because she is economically strong and diplomatically and culturally dynamic. Thus she is in a position to undertake an essential role in the building of a peaceful world.' The priority of Europe was thus once more restated.

For Europe, on the other hand, there exists one overwhelming need which placed it firmly at America's side: it is that Europe cannot in the foreseeable future enjoy external security without American aid.

Finally, it holds true both for America and for Europe that, even in the medium term, the burden of their world-wide responsibilities cannot be carried by an isolated America alone – still less by isolated Europe on its own, even if it be united.

There is a school of thought which seeks to give Atlantic interdependence – based as it is on the necessities of our situation – an intellectual, and later perhaps also an organizational, framework. Such, indeed, was and is the basis of President Kennedy's proposal – then rather in advance of American and European opinion – to work towards an 'equal partnership' between the United States of America and the United States of Europe. There is no avoiding this idea. It does not involve a community in the sense of the 'European Community'; the time for giving Atlantic relationships such a federal structure will presumably come only when we are close to setting up a world government. What is involved is rather a community of action in world politics, based on a common sense of values and common interests. It is part of an evolution whose first stage was the domination of Europe (during the last phase of the war) and the second the guardianship of Europe. And the concept of partnership is itself in evolution; it began with the 'Kennedy Round', and has now, in the words of President Nixon, 'matured into a measured, dynamic, and complex postwar policy'.

314

Kennedy was already concerned lest Europe might one day allow itself to be led to accept policies towards the East which would be full of risks, and alienate her Atlantic partners. In his view this danger could be avoided if Britain were to join the Community, and he therefore pressed for British membership. Those responsible for European policy must always be conscious of the fact – especially after the adventurous course of Gaullist policy towards America – that the question of Europe's possible attitude towards the East is present in the mind of our American partners, even if it is not put into words. And occasional appeals to the great values, traditions and ideas we have in common on both sides of the Atlantic will not always suffice to allay suspicions. In politics it is deeds, and deeds alone, that carry conviction.

III. DEFENCE

To assure peace not only within but also for a united Europe has always been one of the decisive aims of the policy of European unification. This already implies that armaments are regarded not so much as a means whereby to win the next war as a means of preventing it. Since the West is not going to start a war, the central theme of defence policy is therefore to deter a potential aggressor. 'Realistic deterrence' is the latest slogan.

The Europeans' desire for security – the subjective aspect of the security problem – has fluctuated greatly over the past twenty-five years. In its first phase, it was very strong; a high point was the Prague *putsch* of 1948. After that, periods of tension alternated with periods of *détente* (real or presumed). The first period of *détente* began on the death of Stalin in 1953. It was in this period that armistices in Korea and Indochina were agreed, the Austrian State Treaty signed, and diplomatic relations established between the Federal German Republic and the Soviet Union. That period ended when Soviet troops entered into Budapest in October 1956. A second period in which there was hope of *détente* began with the end of the Cuba crisis, which was a great military and political success for the United States, and with the fall of Khrushchev. Russian diplomacy became more carefully modulated in its aims and actions; it sought above all to isolate the Federal German Republic in the Western alliance and in Europe. And not without success: the psychology of *détente* tends towards wishful thinking. This happened despite some disquieting developments: the military as well as the political and economic situation of the Soviet Union was not only stabilized but also improved, even after the Czechoslovakian crisis. The defence budgets of the Soviet Union and of the Warsaw Pact Powers were drastically increased. An acutely dangerous situation developed on NATO's southern flank as a result of the crisis in the Near and Middle East, the Israeli conflict, and, above all through the Soviet presence in the Mediterranean, which the American Sixth Fleet cannot neutralize but keeps a constant watch on, and which is aimed at winning control over Europe's vital Near Eastern and Mediterranean oil supplies and securing safe access to Africa, so as to outweigh the Americans and forestall the Chinese; Soviet influence in the Arab countries was growing daily as more weapons and advisers arrived. Western illusions about Russia have been strengthened by more or less reliable speculation about Soviet social evolution. Even the invasion of Czechoslovakia, on 21 August 1968, provided no more than a brief glimpse of reality. Moreover, it added a further question to existing anxieties: under the Brezhnev doctrine, must Soviet policy not tend to make the whole of Germany into an outpost of the Soviet empire, with the German Federal Republic enjoying at best the status accorded to Finland? For the outposts themselves have proved unstable. The problem of security has not ceased to be topical.

What then is the situation as regards Europe's security, its resources, and its guarantees – the objective aspect of the security problem?

The first attempt to organize a common defence was the European Defence Community. The preparations and negotiations for setting up such a Community began even before the Coal and Steel Community came into force. The Treaty was signed in Paris in May 1952 by the same founder-members. Its constitution was based on the same principles as that of the Coal and Steel Community. In particular, there was a 'supranational' executive authority. Armed forces and armaments were to be integrated. The Treaty was ratified by several of the member states' parliaments. It came to grief after the French National Assembly indefinitely postponed a decision on ratification – following a long

316

and excited debate on the subject by the French public; one of the strongest arguments employed by the majority in the Assembly was that the British had refused to participate. This set-back also brought down the first attempt to move towards political integration, which was linked with the establishment of a European Defence Community: the creation of a European Political Community which was to be built up at the same time on the model of the Coal and Steel Community.

This has been to date the only great failure of the policy of European unification. It is idle to speculate today how different Europe might have been if the Defence Community had become reality. It is virtually certain that Europe would soon have become an equal military partner of the United States in NATO, exercising within a realistic system joint responsibility even in nuclear affairs; it is also highly likely that some aspects of the defence doctrine and some attempts to reach a settlement with the Soviet Union (for example, the Nuclear Non-Proliferation Treaty) would have developed along different lines. Admittedly, it is no less likely that de Gaulle would have destroyed the European Defence Community, which he would hardly have viewed with more sympathy that the elements of integration that exist in NATO; and such an attitude could not have failed to affect the other aspects of European integration.

In the absence of a genuine European link, the defence of Western Europe now depends on NATO. The German Federal Republic entered NATO by crossing the emergency bridge of the West European Union, formed by enlarging the Brussels Pact to include Germany and Italy. There is no doubt that we owe all the military security we have to the Atlantic alliance, and even the development of European unity is inconceivable without this shield. Yet this defence system is not European, but Atlantic. Moreover the European members do not belong to it as a group but as individual states. This has contributed to a situation which can hardly be described as one of equilibrium: one world power is linked to many smaller states, of whom only a few can possibly still be regarded as medium-sized powers. On the one hand, this situation came to be looked upon as increasingly unsatisfactory, as Europe's links grew closer in other spheres and a new collective European consciousness developed. On the other hand, it was

317

hardly conducive to a sense of joint responsibility for defence in Europe; inevitably, it led to a protectorate mentality. Europeans indulged in the luxury of major disagreements over the central issues of foreign policy, especially *vis-à-vis* the Soviet Union. There were soon signs, therefore, of a desire for reforms. Above all, the mechanism for consultation in NATO was, and still is, regarded as inadequate; from the sound recommendations of the 'Three Wise Men' (Lange, Gaetano Martino and Pearson) in 1955 to the Harmel report of 1969, there have been efforts to improve the methods of crisis management (a nuclear-planning group; consultation procedures on the use of nuclear weapons; a situation centre; a NATO telecommunications network). Political consultation has also been improved (by means of a political committee, consultation rules, regular assessments of the political situation). Furthermore, the great concept of Atlantic partnership – launched by President Kennedy in the economic sphere, especially in matters of trade policy – inevitably had its effect on military relations. Nevertheless, although American reaction to the idea of an alliance resting on the two pillars of Europe and America was not explicitly negative, it has always been weak and vacillating.

Nor in the purely military sphere itself is there any lack of disturbing symptoms. Estimates as to the relative strength of the conventional forces of the West and the East vary between 1:1 and 1:2·5. In view of Soviet supremacy in fighter-aircraft, tanks, and armoured divisions, one would be well advised to base one's opinion on the less favourable estimate – which is disquieting. NATO strategy, therefore, cannot and does not exclude the need to complement conventional defence with nuclear weapons. The other basic military fact is that an atomic attack can be met only with atomic weapons. This does not exclude the possibility of limited wars. Since the end of World War II either one or the other of the atomic powers has been involved in fourteen disputes in which actual fighting took place, without atomic weapons having been used and without there having been a direct confrontation between the atomic powers. In the future too, we must expect to have to cope with danger zones, with areas of political unrest, with economic instability, and with areas not covered by defence arrangements.

In addition, there has been progress in the Soviet Union in space exploration, and in atomic and missile techniques. Hundreds of medium-range missiles today threaten Europe. But the East's superiority cannot be measured only in quantitative terms. If the East attacks, then it is the East that determines the rules of the game, and when, where and how the attack is launched. The East's closer proximity and its better overland communications to the Iron Curtain enable it to launch an attack from 'a standing position'. And NATO's southern flank has been weakened or endangered by the separation of France's North African possessions and the independence of Malta.

Does NATO's defence strategy meet this situation? It is today based on the calculation that the atomic equilibrium between the world powers has made the threat of 'massive retaliation' no longer credible. The new watchword is 'flexible response'. That means that, at the beginning, defence is to concentrate on the use of conventional weapons, and on their use as far forward as possible. Atomic weapons are not to be used until later and 'selectively', when the loss of territory has become inevitable. It is incomprehensible how this concept of defence can be reconciled with the 'rotation system', i.e. the withdrawal of Allied troops from Europe and the announcement that they will later be replaced by means of a big air-bridge, the so-called 'Big Lift'. This principle does not even produce appreciable savings. Yet it has been laid down. Not that the 'Big Lift' – a bad solution in any case – will ever take place. For once hostilities have broken out, there will be no landing-places for aircraft. And when there is a threat of war breaking out, it is hard to conceive of anyone taking responsibility for moving troops back into Europe, because that would be bound to lead to an 'escalation' of tension; one can take the Czech crisis as an example. The danger of having to give ground is therefore great, and Europe will have to live with it. Wishful thinking, it would seem, plays a part here too, in assuming that there is no reason to fear a surprise attack, instead of basing one's plans on the strength of the potential enemy. The invasion of Czechoslovakia has, it is true, had a sobering effect, and the withdrawal of troops has been postponed. All the same, the Canadians have in the meantime in 1970 reduced the number of troops stationed in Europe – a reduction that they first announced in 1969 – and NATO's European partners have cut back their defence budgets. Moreover, there is still

319

pressure from some parts of the American Senate for a reduction in the number of American troops stationed in Europe. In America the fear of 'over-commitment' – a fear that is not viewed only in quantitative terms – is too great, the desire to reach some military accommodation with Moscow is too strong, and the mass of economic and internal political difficulties play too prominent a role in the shaping of policy. We have good reason, therefore, to be thankful that President Nixon's government has resisted this tendency and halted military withdrawals from Europe. It is fully understandable that Europe should be asked to make a corresponding contribution, in the form of improved 'burden-sharing' (and not merely compensatory payments).

All these events and changes have engendered a determination that efforts be made to stabilize a dangerously fluid situation. These efforts originated from different sources and pursued diverse, even contradictory objectives: the general aim is to assure peace: but what kind of peace? None of the efforts has yet succeeded. In every case, final success remains uncertain. There is, first, the American initiative which led to negotiations with the Soviet Union on the reciprocal reduction of strategic nuclear weapons (the so-called SALT talks), accompanied by proposals by NATO for the reciprocal reduction of conventional forces in Europe (the Reykjavik initiative). There is the Soviet proposal for a 'European Security Conference'. And there is the German *Ostpolitik.*

The initiative to hold the SALT talks arose from the extraordinary Soviet progress in missile development, which gave the Soviets superiority in certain spheres. There is a common interest in seeing a reduction in the enormous costs of an unlimited 'armaments and research race'. Europe has a vital interest in these talks, because the medium-range Soviet rockets are the most dangerous threat to the European Continent. As in all East-West attempts to reach agreement on disarmament, the difficulty lies in finding qualitative, not merely quantitative, symmetry between the respective arms reductions, and in devising effective controls. NATO is facing the same difficulty in seeking the reduction of conventional forces (following the suggestions put forward at the Reykjavik Conference of 1968 and the Brussels Conference of 1969). In persisting in its efforts, nevertheless, NATO is acting in

320

accordance with the maxim it has followed since the Geneva Conference of July 1955 – not only to make certain that it is prepared to defend itself but also to help reduce tension by positive political action. The difficulties already mentioned are further complicated by Soviet expectations that the attitude of the American Senate will help them achieve their objective of a reduction of American troops in Europe without having to give anything in return. President Nixon thus faces a weighty decision which is bound to have important consequences, not least because President Eisenhower publicly promised in March 1955 to leave American troops on the continent of Europe as long as that appeared necessary. Another factor in the situation is that the Soviet Union is becoming increasingly less interested in the reduction of conventional armaments, because it is worried about withdrawing military units which are needed to hold its empire together. Finally, one must not lose sight of the fact that any reduction in conventional forces automatically lowers the threshold at which the use of nuclear weapons by NATO has to be contemplated – which once again brings us back close to the strategic concept of 'massive retaliation', a concept which, it has been thought, lacks credibility.

By contrast, the 'European Security Conference' is a term which the Soviet Union uses to describe a settlement whose elements emerged only gradually with any degree of clarity – beginning with the proposal made by Rapacki, the then Polish Foreign Minister, at the United Nations in 1964, and then in the series of consultations of the Warsaw Pact Powers starting in 1965 and continuing up to the present. The emphasis placed on these elements varies with the tactical requirements of the Soviet Union: there are demands for the dissolution of NATO, for the removal of all foreign military bases, for the withdrawal of all foreign troops, and for the final settlement of the problems arising out of the German question in the way in which the East would like to see them settled; finally, there are calls for treaties jointly renouncing the use of force (although the Charter of the United Nations already imposes such obligations) and for closer technical and economic links between East and West. In the last analysis, all this means legalizing the so-called 'realities' left behind by the Second World War in Europe: it means the neutralization of Europe, the establishment of Soviet supremacy in Europe and a permanent lowering of the status of the Federal German Republic in the military and, particularly, in the nuclear sphere. It is a misuse of language to call this whole package 'European security'. It is therefore understandable that Western reactions are guarded; the West makes it a condition of such a conference that the chances of success be good, that there should be concrete proof of good intentions (especially over the Berlin question), and that the conference should be carefully prepared. As a preliminary, there should be real progress in the co-ordination of European foreign policies. The idea of such a conference is popular in several East European states (in Rumania, Hungary, perhaps even in Poland) because they hope that it might lead to an easing of Soviet pressure; that, as likely as not, is the reason for the repeated hesitation with which the Soviet Union itself has approached the project.

Plainly, all these discussions and exchanges revolve not only around questions of security. What is at stake is power: the struggle for Europe has entered a new and urgent phase since America has appeared less inclined to assert itself in Europe, and the Soviet Union has felt the need rapidly to consolidate its Western frontier. East-West tension is a symptom of this power-politics situation. The stabilization of power is also the reality which dominates the negotiations undertaken by the new Federal German Government towards the end of 1969 in its *Ostpolitik*; it is a reality which cannot be obscured by dressing up the issues under negotiation as questions relating to security (the 'renunciation of the use of force'). The general aim of the policy which on the German side underlies these negotiations is neither new nor controversial. It is to reduce tension, and it is an aim all German Federal Governments have pursued since establishment of diplomatic relations between the Soviet Union and the Federal German Republic in 1955. The same applies to the renunciation of the use of force; that principle is generally accepted. The concrete methods of the new policy, however, are severely criticized inside the Federal German Republic. The substantial political power that the East is seeking to obtain in legally binding form is very great. What is at stake – and has been at stake for some time – is no longer merely a national question, whether one likes it or not, but the future of Europe. It is because of this that the bilateral nature of the negotiations creates a problem.

In this overall situation, democratic Europe theoretically faces three possibilities: Europe can become neutralist; or it can strengthen its national armaments; or it can organize its defence collectively on a permanent basis within the Atlantic framework. Neutralism is no guarantee of security; on the contrary, it means abandoning security; no power vacuum of such attraction could remain unfilled. The national system is both irrational and anachronistic; there exists in the European Community – *pace* General de Gaulle – no need to be secured against dangers 'from all points of the compass'; there is in fact only one danger the Community faces. There remains the third possibility: a common European defence system would contribute to European security in the best possible way and would at the same time enable the alliance with the Americans to be organized as a partnership.

That, then, is the right choice. To implement it, admittedly, is very difficult. Not so much for technical, objective reasons. In that respect it is no less a 'feasible' than economic integration. Experience gained in federations and in NATO provides models for command-structures and decision-making procedure. The problems involved for Canada would have to be thought out; but they would be soluble. And far from creating a rift between Americans and Europeans, this third choice would prevent it; this, after all, was the purpose of the Atlantic dialogue which Kennedy sought through the partnership concept, which in his view had to cover all questions of mutual concern. Furthermore, I do not believe that the Americans will raise difficulties; naturally they must be absolutely convinced of European loyalty to the alliance. Finally, is it not possible that such a change in the alliance would enable France once more to participate in its organization? As far as disarmament is concerned, the third choice can only be of advantage; it is important, therefore, that Europe should join what is at present a Washington-Moscow dialogue on arms limitation. For who has a greater interest in disarmament than Europe?

The main problems, indeed, are psychological, that is, political. It already proved difficult even partly to 'supranationalize', to 'Europeanize' officialdom. To remove the army from the exclusive control of the separate states is not likely to be any easier. The history of integration in NATO proves that point. But at the same

323

time it also provides examples of the stages and methods by which it is possible to advance.

The second difficulty is 'the German problem'. It is important to recall what was said during the discussions in the negotiation and parliamentary ratification of the EEC Treaty. The complex – in both meanings of the word – has, it is true, become less strong since then; Franco-German reconciliation has made a great contribution here. But we shall probably have to wait for the next generation to grow up before the last vestiges of the victor-vanquished mentality completely disappear. Naturally, Soviet propaganda will not miss a single opportunity of stirring up trouble, all the more so since the Federal German Republic has in the meantime become the strongest conventional military power within the alliance in Europe. All this, however, is no reason for delay, especially if we assume that the merger of atomic potential will for a long time to come be restricted to the British and the French.

The problems outlined above will chiefly influence the method, especially the stages of integration. We shall have to proceed cautiously, not least because it is hardly conceivable that the method of definite integration could be separated from the evolution of a Community constitution – in other words, from the second chapter in political union. One can probably envisage a 'Defence Community' only at a later stage, when the fusion of all the Communities has brought us close to the establishment of a full federation.

A start has already been made on a European grouping by means of the NATO 'Euro-group'. Since the autumn of 1967, in discussions of a 'European Defence Nucleus', there have been British soundings with a view to establishing a 'European Caucus'. In December 1968 there was a first informal meeting of European Defence Ministers (with the exception of Portugal, France, and Iceland), with a view to reaching a common European viewpoint on questions of special European interest (the presence of American troops, rationalization measures, and 'burden-sharing' within the Alliance). In the years that followed, this became a regular conference, which gradually came to meet independently from the NATO Council, and which set up its own subordinate machinery (working-parties for various fields of practical co-operation, such

as forces, training, armaments, logistics, communications, etc.),
whose chairmanship and secretariat were shared out among the
participants on a practical basis. Those members of NATO not
taking part were kept informed, as was the NATO Secretariat-
General. A first result of this work, which attracted much attention,
was the so-called European Defence Improvement Programme
(EDIP) of December 1970. The Euro-group is an outstanding
example of the well-established pragmatic method of European
co-operation. It offers the possibility and the hope of gradually
developing into the still more comprehensive psychological and
material pooling of European defence tasks that we need to
achieve. The enlargement of the Community cannot but assist this
evolution.

In the same way, the European countries should encourage
European voting in the nuclear-planning group and similar bodies.
These are the beginnings of the work of a common general staff.

An 'armaments community' could also profit from the experience
the European Economic Community has gained in the sphere of
civil technology. This is a further argument in favour of identical
composition for the economic and the 'political' community. The
more costs rise, the more pressing is the case for standardizing and
mass-producing weapons. If individual states are not prepared to
give up producing their own arms because of the damage to their
own economy and because they fear to lose their political independence, then the only solution is Community arms production.
This development, no doubt, would have to keep in step with the
integration of armed forces. The last stage would be a definitive
decision on atomic defence – although this is made infinitely more
difficult by the Nuclear Non-Proliferation Treaty.

To be an effective deterrent, European defence solutions must
obviously be credible. That requires something more than all
organizations, fusions and procedures that may be devised, something more than the accumulation of men and material: it requires
a convincing will to defend oneself. Without that will, Europe is a
partner in whom no one is interested, and an opponent of no
consequence. For an aggressor cannot be deterred only by the
desire for peace on the part of his victim. But this is a general
problem, not merely one of security.

Without that vitality which is shown in the elementary instinct

325

of self-defence, Europe would be lost in the face of the harsh future that confronts us all. Even with that vitality, it still needs American forces on its soil. It is still impossible to foresee a time when the political, military and psychological need for an American force in Europe will no longer exist.

Conclusion: The Fruit of Experience

We must learn from the failures and the successes of European policy.

It has not been possible to establish unity at one stroke. The tremendous political effort needed to achieve this end could have been generated only by the most overwhelming, immediate and compelling circumstances, such as an immense and imminent danger. The collapse of the Continent after a war that had involved unparalleled efforts was by itself not enough. For that collapse made Europeans concentrate on coping with immediate necessities: on survival, on establishing a minimum degree of order and security, on reconstruction.

But what was lacking was only the power to take a comprehensive decision – not the awareness of the need. It therefore proved right to proceed 'pragmatically', as we have grown used to saying. We had to keep alive our great objective. But at the same time we set ourselves limited, concrete aims, which offered immediate advantages. We were successful in merging first the heavy industries and later the complete national economies of European states; we failed in merging the national armed forces. But even where we succeeded, we met obstacles. They were psychological, and therefore political. It was difficult for public opinion, and partly also for those who held positions of responsibility in the states, to grasp the full extent of the consequences involved in seeking unity. It was not easy to keep up with the various stages by which our great undertaking was carried out. The limitation of sovereignty met with strong resentment in some sections of the nation-states and was fought on emotional grounds. Since some countries – unlike Germany – had no experience and concept of what federation meant – this was where the fear arose that countries might lose their national identity. Furthermore, the willingness to co-operate with defeated Germany only developed gradually, despite some splendid exceptions.

327

In all these difficulties one can perceive the role that time plays in the European problem. Time 'helps' no one, neither us nor our opponents. But it is a decisive element in every political operation. One cannot turn back the clock. Consequently, it is always wrong not to take action when it is possible to do so. But, equally, time is the main factor in another respect, in getting people used to change; they can hardly be forced to accept it in their hearts and minds. When we launched our great enterprise in 1950, it seemed reasonable to assume that we would need about forty years, the space of a generation, to achieve full political union. Today, since everything has moved forward much more rapidly than expected, we are more optimistic: we could reach our goal by 1980. Time also justifies our method of seeking unity not in every sphere but, to begin with, in those spheres which stir up fewer emotions and where the practical reasons for fusion are compelling and obvious. In pursuing matters of common advantage, in fighting common dangers, in working together jointly in the political field, ideas and habits of thought and action become integrated 'in time'.

The Communities set up to deal with the partial and specific matters of economic policy and social policy were a success. That integration can be carried out, even in very complex fields, has been fully proved. No practical problem remains insoluble. There have been no insuperable conflicts of interest. Economic union has therefore not made too heavy demands on the member-states.

To continue and complete the work of unification is therefore a question of making up one's mind, of the 'political will', as it is often put; this, however, means nothing but being prepared to do the numerous small or great things which need to be done, the sum total of which constitutes 'political unification'.

The first task to be tackled is to complete the economic union begun long ago. We must continue to Europeanize the whole of economic policy. This involves a number of specially urgent and important political and economic matters. The climate of confidence in the Community must be strengthened; this applies above all to monetary policy and conjunctural policy. The central driving force for economic union continues to be the single market, i.e. the removal of frontiers. In this sphere there has to be a concentrated effort to harmonize indirect and consumer taxes, for they represent the 'hard core' of the economic barriers that still exist. European technology policy – closely linked with European armaments – lags sadly behind. In this field there has not even been a general discussion of such key problems as the relationship between public authorities and industry; the co-ordination of procurements; the possibility of planning budgets several years ahead. The institutions, moreover, have in the last few years partly stagnated or been weakened. Yet they are the core of Europe's anatomy. Without them there is no policy. Questions in which the European Community has been denied or deprived of the necessary institutional framework do not simply drop into a kind of institutional void where everything is settled of 'its own accord' on a basis of good-will; instead, other institutions – national institutions – grow up and take over. The first task here is to reassert the Treaty's intentions with regard to majority voting in the Council of Ministers and with regard to the status of the Commission, especially as regards the common policy for external trade. A further task is to strengthen the status and competence of the European Parliament. On this depends the democratic legitimacy of the Community's institutional structure, which at present is only improvised. It will be a disappointment if our British friends, with the greatest democratic traditions in the world, are unable to make this their special task. It is a task that is essential if our great enterprise is to take root in the hearts and minds of Europe's citizens. For the Community is to be a community of citizens and not merely of governments and diplomats.

These institutional problems are for several reasons no less urgent than those arising from economic technical matters.

Like all such documents, the Treaties establishing the Community were drafted in terms that were too narrow: there is a limit to human imagination, and a compromise has to be struck between the bold and the timid. Nevertheless, economic policy rapidly won the room it needed in which to operate effectively. We were successful in breathing life and dynamism into the new organism, and as a result even those sections of the Treaty which had been formulated only timidly and incompletely acquired considerable vigour. In the wake of this evolution it admittedly became the practice to create a fair number of special institutions and so provide the necessary institutional framework, but this process could not quite keep pace with developments and largely became bogged down at an early stage. There is therefore a need to redress the balance between what has been achieved in substance and the development of our institutions.

The enlargement of the Community increases this need. Naturally, the increase in the number of member-states, the growth in the differences of interest, and the fact that the new members will not be used to the ways of the Community, are factors which will make the decision-making process more difficult. This has to be offset by tightening up the Community's organization. Only if that is done will enlargement not lead to the weakening or the sterilization of the Community.

All this lies within the framework of the Treaties. But the Treaties are not just self-sufficient collections of detailed provisions, some of which remain to be defined to achieve their ultimate purpose. The Communities are also politically part of a greater whole, an intermediate objective on the road to the ultimate goal. That ultimate goal remains a European federation of states. Since Winston Churchill in 1945 (who spoke of 'a kind of United States of Europe') and Robert Schuman in 1950 (who spoke of 'federation') no one has yet come forward with a different definition. Gaullist policy has shaken this idea, but there can be no doubt about it. It is only when we have reached the final stages of our enterprise that we can be certain that it will be really permanent. Only that will justify the so-called 'sacrifices', the political contributions of the member-states. The *sine qua non* of the admission of new members to the European Community is an unambiguous commitment to the ultimate goal.

The Community was built with this ultimate goal in view. This is apparent in the allocation of matters over which the Community was given competence: it was constructed as a political community (even though its authority was limited to economic and social policy); it is also apparent in its constitutional elements, its federalistic structure. In defending the present Community, therefore, we are safeguarding the fundamental elements of future reality.

If we look into the future in this general way, we cannot afford to ignore the experience which the European Community has taught us. To some questions, that experience provides unambiguous

330

answers, with no alternatives. It shows that we must proceed by stages. Our method must be evolutionary: progress must be made organically on the basis of what has already been achieved. The common European interest must be embodied in a special common institution, independent of governments, in order to make possible a continuous dialogue with the representatives of partial, national interests. As long as there are several Communities, their composition must be identical. For other questions, various options are possible according to circumstances. For example, authority to deal with new problems can either be allocated to the existing Communities, or one or several new Communities can be set up for the purpose.

It has become customary to call the second part of the programme of European evolution 'Political Union'. It embraces two subjects: on the one hand, extension of Europe's as yet underdeveloped constitution into a full federation (which will then evolve as a result of combining economic and political integration); on the other hand, the inclusion of several new specific functions: foreign policy, defence, and perhaps, also, certain fundamental principles of cultural policy. There is a widespread legend that it is more difficult to integrate foreign and defence policy than economic and social policy. Even more difficult? That seems doubtful, especially if past experience is used in deciding how to proceed. Such divergences as may exist in fixing concrete objectives are limited in scope; historical rivalries, in particular, have greatly faded. All the member-states subscribe to the principles of the United Nations Charter. Peace is for all of them the guiding principle. Their geographical situation dictates the similarity of their vital interests. All have a very similar outlook. Within this broad common framework of fundamental principles they also share many individual values – although there are always different degrees of commitment, ranging from spontaneous intervention to letting things drift. There is an identity of views, for example, on security *vis-à-vis* the East; on peace in the Mediterranean and the Near East; on stabilizing conditions in Africa; and on economic aid to less-developed countries.

One of the subjects of European foreign policy is the German question, although for the Germans it is more than a question of foreign policy. Here, too, a common denominator must be found.

331

The integration of the Federal German Republic into a united Europe is in the interest of all Europe. Like the other members of this ever more closely-knit Community, the Federal German Republic joined with all its assets and liabilities, and without any discrimination against it. The prospect of healing the division of the world which has also caused the division of Germany depends entirely on securing peace in Europe and in the world, and in winning back for Europe a share in determining world affairs. These are the political aims of European unification.

A vast potential is invested in our European policy. Our economic success has aroused the greatest interest. (Within the last twelve years, internal trade within the Community has increased by 623 per cent, its external trade by 283 per cent, its gross domestic product by 226 per cent and its industrial production by about 200 per cent). But the political investment in our great European enterprise, in terms both of the tasks undertaken and the solutions found, is more imposing still. The scope for the authorities involved has expanded beyond all expectations. This has not been painlessly achieved. This book recounts many a struggle. But struggling with the member-states is not a symptom of illness; it lies in the nature of a federal structure. A brilliant interpreter of federal constitutions, Heinrich Triepel, has said that the best attainable relationship between central and local authorities is one of 'armistice'. Wounds have been sustained, but the dynamism of the European enterprise has only been curbed, not broken. Externally, it has had world-wide repercussions. A dialogue between the continents has begun across the Atlantic, and its first result has been a world-wide liberalization of trade.

These successes have become 'vested interests' for those concerned. None of the participants could now withdraw without suffering great damage. All other European states which are free to make their own decisions would like to join us in one way or another, whatever reservations they may have had at the start.

But the edifice is not complete. And it will not grow by itself. If it is left as it is, then even the parts that are already finished will deteriorate. Whatever form life might then take in this partial construction, it would never be the full life for which the whole building is designed.

Nor does waiting improve the prospect. Already within the

Community old habits have begun to reassert themselves. Already the situation in the world around has become worse. Never before have we so clearly realized that our European enterprise is of world significance, not only in its immediate effects, through the shift in the world balance of political weight brought about by the emergence of a new political continent, but also in the conditions it creates. It has generated powerful opposition in the East, opposition which stems from an expansionist policy of hegemony. We shall continue, with patience and tenacity, to work for a better understanding of what we are doing: already the integration of democratic Europe, a reliable safeguard for peace, is becoming a reality and one which is also in the interests of the East European nations. In the West we put our faith in European and Atlantic solidarity, which has been forged not merely by an arbitrary decision but by a common destiny, based on a community of spiritual and material circumstances in the present state of the world.

It is therefore high time to go further. For there is no alternative, either to our objective – unity – or to the road we set out on twenty years ago, and of which today we have covered half the distance.

William the Silent, of the House of Orange, an indomitable champion of progress and tolerance in a troubled century of Europe's history, once said: 'One does not need hope to act, or success to persevere.' How much greater, then, is our obligation to act and to persevere; for we have hope, and we have success.

Index

Acheson, Dean 311, 313
Adenauer, Konrad 20
Africa 282, 285–6; association with the Community 257–60, 282
Agricultural Fund 187, 242
agricultural policy 131–2, 178–93, 250, 276–7; marketing of products 25–7, 50–2, 100; prices, 'unit of account' system 131–2, 139, 140; Stresa Conference 182; 'Mansholt Plan' 182, 184; inflation 191
Algeria 284
'American Selling Price System' 253
Amsterdam-Rotterdam Bank 159
applications to join the Common Market 266–82
Arab States 287–8
Argentina, relations with the Community 261–2, 263
Arusha Convention (1968) 257
Association agreements 282–91; 'African' type of association 283, 284; Alpine republics 289–290; Scandinavia 291
Australia 276, 277
Austria 279, 289–90; revaluation of currency 149

Banco de Roma 159
Bank for International Settlements 132–3, 136
Barre, Raymond 138
'Barre Plan' 138, 155, 167
Barzel, Rainer 303
basic values of the Community 42–47

Belgium 89–90
Brandt, Willy 303
Bretton Woods Conference 139–41, 142, 143
Britain: application to join the Community 93–4, 96–7, 134, 183, 212; pound devaluation 131, 134; difficulties of the pound 132–3; relations with the Community 266–79, 281; projected entry into the Community 275–278; contribution to Community budget 278
Brussels Conference (1969) 320
Brussels Pact 317
Budgetary Committee 155

cartels 116–17, 117–18
CECLA 261–2
CEEP 177
CERN 206
certainty as a basic value of the Community 47
CETS 206
Ceylon 276
CFTC 177
CGIL 177
CGT 177
Channel Islands 276
Churchill, Winston 21, 266–7, 330
CIC 177
civil servants, contact with the Community 80–1
coal-mining industry 214–16
COMECON 256
Commerzbank 159
Commission, the 57–63, 98; functions 57–9; members 57, 59;

335

Turkey 284, 286
turnover-tax system 158, 160

Ulbricht, Herr 288
UNCTAD 259, 262, 263, 264
UNICE 177
United Nations Charter 331
United Nations Committee on Trade and Development 311
United States: support of Europe's efforts to integrate 21; siting of enterprises within the Community 123; dollar, target of speculation 135; 1971 balance-of-payments deficit 148; and European agricultural policy 188 scientific achievement 197–8, 199, 200, 201, 202; and negotiating ability of Europeans 205; economic relations with the Community 251–3; American government's difficulties in relations with Congress 252–3; trade with Japan 254; and Britain's efforts to restore classic European balance of power 268, 269; and political union of Europe 302; relations with the Community 311–15; growth of internal problems 313; and European defence 323
United States Atomic Energy Commission 217
United States Supreme Court 35
unity as a basic value of the Community 43
Uruguay 262, 263

value-added tax 158, 278
vested interests 84–92
Vienna Atomic Agency 211

Warsaw Pact 246, 316
Werner Committee 145–7
Western European Union 267, 294, 317
Wilson, Harold 266, 270
World Confederation of Employees 177
world production, Europe's share of 18–19

Yalta Conference 305
Yaoundé Convention 260, 283